Teachers' Narrative Inquiry as
Professional Development

CAMBRIDGE LANGUAGE EDUCATION
Series Editor: Jack C. Richards

This series draws on the best available research, theory, and educational practice to help clarify issues and resolve problems in language teaching, language teacher education, and related areas. Books in the series focus on a wide range of issues and are written in a style that is accessible to classroom teachers, teachers-in-training, and teacher educators.

In this series:

Teachers' Narrative Inquiry as Professional Development

Karen E. Johnson

The Pennsylvania State University

Paula R. Golombek

The Pennsylvania State University

CAMBRIDGE
UNIVERSITY PRESS

PUBLISHED BY THE PRESS SYNDICATE OF THE UNIVERSITY OF CAMBRIDGE
The Pitt Building, Trumpington Street, Cambridge, United Kingdom

CAMBRIDGE UNIVERSITY PRESS
The Edinburgh Building, Cambridge CB2 2RU, UK
40 West 20th Street, New York, NY 10011-4211, USA
477 Williamstown Road, Port Melbourne, VIC 3207, Australia
Ruiz de Alarcón 13, 28014 Madrid, Spain
Dock House, The Waterfront, Cape Town 8001, South Africa

http://www.cambridge.org

First published 2002

Printed in the United States of America

Typefaces Times Roman 10.5/12.5 pt. and Helvetica   *System* LaTeX 2$_\varepsilon$ [TB]

A catalog record for this book is available from the British Library

Library of Congress Cataloging-in-Publication data available

ISBN 0 521 81342 5 hardback
ISBN 0 521 01313 5 paperback

Contents

Contributors

Michael Boshell, Higher Colleges of Technology, Abu Dhabi Women's College, United Arab Emirates

Jennifer L. Esbenshade, The Pennsylvania State University, University Park

Bob Gibson, Keio University, Japan

Paula R. Golombek, The Pennsylvania State University, University Park

Lynne Doherty Herndon, The Manhattan International School, New York

Suzanne House, Lakeland College, Sheboygan, Wisconsin

Pauline A. G. Johansen, Principal, Richmond School District, British Columbia

Karen E. Johnson, The Pennsylvania State University, University Park

Kimberly A. Johnson, University of Minnesota, Minneapolis

Ling Shi, University of British Columbia, Vancouver

Steve Mann, Language Studies Unit, Aston University, England

Tobie Robison, Boone High School, Orlando, Florida

Patricia Sackville, British Columbia Institute of Technology, Burnaby

Kazuyoshi Sato, Nagoya University of Foreign Studies, Aichi, Japan

Laurie Soltman, Florida Marlins Baseball Club, Florida

Linda Winston, The Pennsylvania State University, University Park

To Glenn and Elizabeth
To Michael, Alex, and Anya

Series editor's preface

Engaging teachers and teachers-in-training in classroom research is now a well-recognized component of teacher development programs, as evidenced by a growing literature on journal writing, case studies, reflective teaching, action research, and other initiatives in which teachers develop "insider" accounts of teaching. Such activities focus on the thinking that teachers employ as the basis for their teaching and decision making, how they frame and problematize issues, and the ways in which they draw on experience, beliefs, and theory in teaching. This book expands what we know about teacher inquiry by describing the philosophy, procedures, and potentials of a less familiar form of teacher inquiry – the use of teachers' narratives – in which teachers write about significant teaching episodes and experiences and, through the process of writing, gain a deeper understanding of the issues they describe as well as of themselves as teachers. Rather than depending on outside sources, narrative inquiry makes use of teacher stories as a source of knowing and as a way of bringing about changes both in themselves and in their teaching practices.

Teacher narratives are similar to case reports. Like case reports, they are a particularly useful form of teacher research because they are relatively easy to obtain and yet can provide a rich source of teacher-generated information that is of great interest both to the teacher-narrator and to others interested in how teachers conduct their practice, the thinking and problem solving they employ, and the sources they draw on in their daily practice. The teacher narratives in this book thus show the following:

- The nature of teacher narratives
- How different forms of teacher research take place
- How teachers theorize their classroom inquiries
- How the professional and theoretical knowledge teachers obtain from academic courses is used in their professional lives
- How teachers struggle to create lessons and courses that reflect their ideals, philosophies, and understandings
- How narrative inquiry can empower teachers

- How narrative inquiry can become a powerful tool in language teacher education
- How collaboration with other teachers enables teachers to develop a better understanding of teaching and of teachers

Many books on teacher education assume that the most interesting parts of a teacher's professional development are what happens during their teacher training. The narratives in this book remind us that teacher development really starts once teachers enter their classrooms and begin teaching. The contributors describe how they addressed very basic issues in teaching, such as using literature in the ESL classroom, giving feedback on writing, the sequencing of classroom activities, conducting classroom discussions, teaching a basic writing class, negotiating student-teacher roles, understanding students' perceptions of learning, and lesson planning. The stories have in common their description of a teaching dilemma, the reasoning the teacher brought to the problem, how the teacher explored the problem and sought to resolve it, and what he or she learned during the process.

The 1986 report by the Carnegie Task Force on Teaching as a Profession, *A Nation Prepared: Teachers in the 21st Century* (New York: Carnegie Forum on Education and the Economy, Carnegie Corporation), proposed the use of teacher-generated case reports as a core resource in teacher education and recommended that "teaching cases illustrating a variety of teaching problems should be developed as a major focus of instruction" (p. 76). *Teachers' Narrative Inquiry as Professional Development* can be regarded as an implementation of this recommendation, expanding the notion of case reporting and providing a rich and powerful set of teacher narratives that will prove to be a valuable resource for language teachers and teacher educators.

Jack C. Richards

Preface

Teachers' Narrative Inquiry as Professional Development is a collection of highly personal, highly contextualized stories of teachers inquiring into their own experiences as learners of language teaching. As such, their stories of inquiry represent the journey of *how* they know as well as *what* they know. In Part I, "Inquiry into Instructional Practices," teachers' stories of inquiry are driven by a sense of dissatisfaction with some aspect of their classroom practice. Yet, as they examine their practice, they are compelled to confront how their understandings of teaching came to be; their own and their students' needs, interests, and objectives; and the institutional constraints within which they work. In Part II, "Inquiry into Language Learners," teachers' stories of inquiry highlight different methods of inquiry, for example, self-reflection, focus groups, journaling, interviews, and discourse analysis, that they have used to come to truly know their students, while at the same time gaining insights into themselves as teachers and their instructional practices. In Part III, "Inquiry into Language Teachers," teachers' stories of inquiry focus on their evolving beliefs and practices as they journey through various contexts, crossing boundaries of different countries, cultures, and roles. And finally, in Part IV, "Inquiry through Professional Collaborations," teachers' stories of inquiry stem from participation in collaborative professional communities, which enables them to learn about themselves as teachers, their students, and the value of being part of a community of teachers.

The purpose of this collection is to bring teachers' ways of knowing into our professional conversations so as to transform our understandings of language teachers and language teaching. By making teachers' ways of knowing public, open to review by others, and accessible to others in this profession, we hope to validate language teachers' ways of knowing and the activity of language teaching in ways afforded to other forms of scholarly work. We expect that readers of this collection will recall, rethink, and reconstruct their own ways of knowing about language teachers and language teaching. We encourage readers to look for multiple interpretations and multiple layers of meaning in these stories. We hope that doing this will change our collective perceptions of what counts as knowledge, who is considered a knower, and what counts as professional development.

As language teachers, teacher educators, and researchers, we are honored to have edited this collection. To the teachers who contributed to this book, we owe our deepest gratitude for their willingness to open up their minds, lives, and classrooms to us and to the entire language teaching profession. We also thank them for their open-mindedness in responding to our seemingly endless queries throughout the revising process, for their patience during the time-consuming review and publishing process, and most of all, for their commitment to the lifelong professional development of language teachers. We would also like to thank Jack C. Richards for his recognition of the value of this collection for the future of the language teaching profession and to Debbie Goldblatt, Mary Sandre, and Olive Collen for their help in the publishing process. As always, our deepest gratitude goes to our families, for their unwavering encouragement and support.

Karen E. Johnson
Paula R. Golombek

1 Inquiry into experience

Teachers' personal and professional growth

Karen E. Johnson
Paula R. Golombek

Shifting views of teachers' knowledge

What is knowledge, and who holds it? The answers to these deceptively simple questions reside at the heart of debates in teaching and learning, and in teacher education in particular. Unfortunately, the traditional answer has been unsatisfying for many teachers. For more than a hundred years, teacher education has been based on the notion that knowledge about teaching and learning can be "transmitted" to teachers by others. In the knowledge transmission model, educational researchers, positioned as outsiders to classroom life, seek to quantify generalizable knowledge about what good teaching is and what good teachers do. Teachers have been viewed as objects of study rather than as knowing professionals or agents of change. Researchers have been privileged in that they create the knowledge, hold it, and bestow it upon teachers. Teachers have been marginalized in that they are told what they should know and how they should use that knowledge. Even though many teachers personally reject this model, most of them continue to work and learn under its powerful hold in teacher education programs and the schools where they teach.

Critics of the knowledge transmission model, although not new (Counts, 1935, reprint 1965), have argued that such a view of knowledge and knower is paternalistic (Goodson & Dowbiggin, 1991; Knoblauch & Brannon, 1988; Schön, 1983), decontextualized (Connelly & Clandinin, 1988; Elbaz, 1983), and, hence, ineffectual (Woods, 1987). Since the early 1980s, ethnographic and second-order investigations of teachers practicing their work in actual classrooms have revealed teachers as constructing their own explanations of teaching and highlighted the messiness that is inherent in the ways in which teachers think about and carry out their work (Elbaz, 1983; Lampert, 1985). The bulk of this research argues that what teachers know about teaching is largely socially constructed out of the experiences and classrooms from which teachers have come. Furthermore, it argues that how teachers actually use their knowledge in classrooms is highly interpretive, socially negotiated, and continually restructured within the classrooms and schools where teachers work (Bullough, 1989; Clandinin, 1986; Grossman, 1990). Such conceptualizations of teacher learning have parallels with sociocultural theories (Leont'ev, 1978; Newman, Griffin, & Cole, 1989; Vygotsky, 1978) that highlight the fundamentally social nature of cognition and learning. Others argue for parallels with theories of situated cognition, which maintain that knowledge entails lived practices, not just accumulated information (Chaiklin & Lave, 1996; Collins, Brown, & Newman, 1989; Lave & Wenger, 1991). Such socially situated views of knowledge and knowing argue that the processes of learning are socially negotiated, constructed through experiences in and with the social practices associated with particular activities, in particular social contexts (Cobb & Bowers, 1999; Wenger, 1998).

When viewed from a socially situated perspective, teachers not only possess knowledge, they can also be creators of that knowledge. What teachers know and how they use their knowledge in classrooms are highly interpretative and contingent on knowledge of self, students, curricula, and setting. Teacher learning is understood as normative and lifelong, built of and through experiences in social contexts: as learners in classrooms and schools, as participants in professional teacher education programs, and as members of communities of practice in the schools where they teach. Professional development emerges from a process of reshaping teachers' existing knowledge, beliefs, and practices rather than simply imposing new theories, methods, or materials on teachers.

It follows, then, that in order to recognize and document the activity of teacher learning and language teaching through the perspective of teachers, it is necessary to gather descriptive accounts of how teachers come to know their knowledge, how they use that knowledge within the contexts where they teach, and how they make sense of and reconfigure their classroom practices in and over time. Since the early 1990s, the reflective teaching movement (Lockhart & Richards, 1994; Schön, 1983, 1987; Zeichner & Liston, 1996), the predominance of action research (Kemmis & McTaggart, 1988; McNiff, 1993; Somekh, 1993), and the teacher research movement (Cochran-Smith & Lytle, 1999; Edge & Richards, 1998; Freeman, 1998) have helped to establish the legitimacy of teachers' experiences and the importance of reflection on and inquiry into those experiences as a mechanism for change in teachers' classroom practices as well as a forum for professional development over time.

Already well established in general educational research, "teachers' ways of knowing" have recently been referred to as the *new scholarship* (Schön, 1995; Zeichner, 1999) or *practitioner research* (Anderson & Herr, 1999).

This new scholarship includes an ongoing struggle to articulate an epistemology of practice that characterizes teachers as legitimate knowers, as producers of legitimate knowledge, and as capable of constructing and sustaining their own professional development over time. The inclusion of a broader epistemological frame reflects a broad-based movement among school professionals to legitimatize knowledge produced out of their own lived realities as professionals. Such work has the potential to fundamentally alter "outsider" or "objective researcher" knowledge, upon which the traditional knowledge base of teacher education is founded, by infusing it with "insider" knowledge: the complex and multilayered understandings of learners, culture, class, gender, literacy, social issues, institutions, communities, and curricula that teachers possess as natives to the settings in which they work (Clandinin & Connelly, 1995; Cochran-Smith & Lytle, 1998).

Much of this new scholarship has been aligned with inquiry-based methods, such as critical, feminist, and reconstructionist approaches to pedagogy and curriculum (Cochran-Smith & Lytle, 1999). Fundamental to these approaches is posing questions, questions that emerge from and are studied in teachers' classrooms. Public recognition of the new scholarship has the emancipatory potential of transforming schools and changing equations of power and control in order to create more equitable social relations between university-generated research and teacher research, and to permit the growth of teachers' personal and professional knowledge and thereby enhance their lifelong professional development.

A compelling example of this new scholarship is the line of research carried out by Clandinin and Connelly (1991, 1995, 2000), in which they view re-storying experiences as essential to teachers' personal and social growth. Their research relies on data that are generated by researcher observation, participant observation, and observations by other participants; the resulting stories are jointly constructed as teachers re-story their experience and researchers offer narrative interpretations based on teachers' stories. In their most recent work, they argue that the value of narrative inquiry lies in its capacity to capture and describe experiences as they occur "in the midst" (2000, p. 63) of other lived experiences, to look *inward, outward, backward,* and *forward* at teachers' experiences in order to capture their temporal nature and their personal and social dimensions, and to see them as situated within the places or sequences of places in which they occur and from which they emerge. Narrative inquiry, then, has the potential to create a "new sense of meaning and significance" (p. 42) for teachers' experiences and thus brings new meaning and significance to the work of teachers within their own professional landscapes.

Although the new scholarship centers on teachers' experiences, in the bulk of this published work, teachers' voices are validated through the collaborations and interpretation of researchers (Connelly & Clandinin, 1988; Golombek, 1998). Although such work is informative for the field as it struggles to articulate an epistemology of practice, Lytle and Cochran-Smith (1992) suggest that systematic inquiry *of* teachers *by* teachers can generate both individual and public knowledge about teaching. Furthermore, having teachers articulate their knowledge and practice in their own voices is one way to respond to calls for the validation of local forms of knowledge (Edge & Richards, 1998; Pennycook, 1989). The end goal of such an endeavor is, of course, the documentation, articulation, and public recognition of teachers' ways of knowing as legitimate knowledge, knowledge that can rightfully stand alongside the disciplinary knowledge that has dominated the traditional knowledge base of language teacher education (Freeman & Johnson, 1998).

Narrative inquiry

We ground our conceptualization of narrative inquiry in Dewey's (1916, 1920, 1933) educational philosophy, which, at its core, argues that we are all knowers who reflect on experience, confront the unknown, make sense of it, and take action. However, not all experiences are informative in that some develop from what Dewey called *habit*, or to make use of an experience to take similar action repeatedly. Rather, inquiry into experience that is educative propels us to not only question the immediate context but to draw connections among experiences – what Dewey calls *continuity of experience* (1938), or how experiences change the conditions under which new experiences are understood so that a person's abilities, desires, and attitudes are changed. Inquiry into experience, in this sense, can be educative if it enables us to reflect on our actions and then act with foresight.

Yet, how we reflect on experience and how we make sense of our experience are often achieved through the stories we tell. Narrative has been constructed as a mode of thinking (Bruner, 1996) and as particularly valuable for representing the richness of human experiences. Through narratives, human beings play an active role in constructing their own lives (Mead, 1977), seeking to make sense of their experiences by imposing order on those experiences (Sarbin, 1986) and by seeing the self as constituted as a story (Bakhtin, 1981). Not surprisingly, narrative has been placed center stage in teacher education as both a method in and an object of inquiry

(Clandinin & Connelly, 1992; Cochran-Smith & Lytle, 1999; Elbaz, 1983; Witherall & Noddings, 1991).

Yet narratives are not simply stories of individuals moving through and reflecting on experiences in isolation. Narratives, by their very nature, are social and relational and gain their meaning from our collective social histories. Therefore, narratives cannot be separated from the sociocultural and sociohistorical contexts from which they emerged. Instead, they are deeply embedded in sociohistorical discourses (Gee, 1999) and thus represent a socially mediated view of experience. For example, when teachers describe a learner as "disadvantaged" or a classroom activity as "successful," such depictions are not neutral but are embedded within sociocultural and sociohistorical notions of what it means to be disadvantaged in a particular society or what constitutes success in a particular educational system. Thus, narrative inquiry allows individuals to look at themselves and their activities as socially and historically situated.

Besides recognizing the social and relational dimensions of narrative inquiry, Dewey's (1933) notion of inquiry into experience as intelligence is not simply cognitive but also moral. Witherall and Noddings (1991) note that "stories represent a journey into the realm of practical ethics" (p. 4). Thus, because classroom dilemmas often serve as catalysts for inquiry, teachers' narratives embody emotions such as frustration, fear, anger, and joy, and they center on the caring emotions and actions of trust, dialogue, feelings, and responding (Noddings, 1984) that permeate the activity of teaching. Likewise, when teachers reflect on, describe, and analyze the factors contributing to a classroom dilemma, they confront their emotions, their moral beliefs, and the consequences of their teaching practices on the students they teach.

In order to make an experience educative, teachers need to approch narrative inquiry not as a set of prescriptive skills or tasks to be carried out but rather as a mind-set – a set of attitudes, what Dewey (1933) called *open-mindedness* (seeking alternatives), *responsibility* (recognizing consequences), and *wholeheartedness* (continual self-examination). When teachers inquire into their experience from this mind-set, they individually and collectively question their own assumptions as they uncover who they are, where they have come from, what they know and believe, and why they teach as they do. Through such inquiry, teachers recognize the consequences of their beliefs, knowledge, and experiences on what and how they teach. They recognize who their students are, where their students have come from, what their students know, and what their students need to know. Through inquiry, teachers question the taken-for-granted definitions of what is and is not possible within the contexts in which they teach. They ask the broader questions of not just whether their practices work but for whom, in what ways, and why. Through inquiry, teachers frame and reframe the issues and problems they face in their professional worlds. As teachers engage in narrative inquiry, they become theorizers in their own right, and as theorizers, they look less for certain answers and more to rethink what they thought they already knew. Thus, we believe that teachers' stories of inquiry are not only *about* professional development; they *are* professional development. Narrative inquiry becomes a means through which teachers actualize their ways of knowing and growing that nourish and sustain their professional development throughout their careers.

Narrative inquiry as professional development

We advance a conceptualization of narrative inquiry as systematic exploration that is conducted *by* teachers and *for* teachers through their own stories and language. We believe that narrative inquiry, conducted by teachers individually or collaboratively, tells the stories of teachers' professional development within their own professional worlds. Such inquiry is driven by teachers' inner desire to understand that experience, to reconcile what is known with that which is hidden, to confirm and affirm, and to construct and reconstruct understandings of themselves as teachers and of their own teaching. What teachers choose to inquire about emerges from their personalities, their emotions, their ethics, their contexts, and their overwhelming concern for their students.

Our view of narrative inquiry as professional development reflects Dewey's (1920) claim that inquiry takes into account:

observation of the detailed makeup of the situation; analysis into its diverse factors; clarification of what is obscure; discounting of the more insistent and vivid traits; tracing the consequences of the various modes of action that suggest themselves; regarding the decision reached as hypothetical and tentative until the anticipated or supposed consequences which led to its adoption have been squared with actual consequences. This inquiry is intelligence. (p. 164)

Thus, inquiry into experience enables teachers to describe the complexities of their practice while stepping back from the hermeneutical processes in which they normally engage. This process of stepping back, description, reflection, and analysis becomes a kind of articulation (Freeman, 1991) or a process through which teachers link and clarify tensions that seem, at first glance, to have no relationship to one another. However, when teachers inquire into their own experiences, such inquiry propels them to question and reinterpret their ways of knowing. Inquiry into experience enables teachers to act with foresight. It gives them increasing control over their thoughts and actions; grants their experiences enriched, deepened meaning; and enables them to be more thoughtful and mindful of their work.

We believe that narrative inquiry enables teachers to organize, articulate, and communicate what they know and believe about teaching and who they have become as teachers. Their stories reveal the knowledge, ideas, perspectives, understandings, and experiences that guide their work. Their stories describe the complexities of their practice, trace professional development over time, and reveal the ways in which they make sense of and reconfigure their work. Their stories reflect the struggles, tensions, triumphs, and rewards of their lives as teachers. We believe that, ultimately, narrative inquiry enables teachers not only to make sense of their professional worlds but also to make significant and worthwhile change within themselves and in their teaching practices.

Teachers who engage in narrative inquiry do not look for simple answers or quick solutions but theorize about their work as they organize, articulate, and communicate what they have come to understand about themselves and the activity of teaching. This is critically important, for teachers often view theory, crafted in the language of the theorist, as a finished product about which they have no right to negotiate (Shor & Freire, 1987). Whereas most researchers frame their inquiry within a review of existing theory and research, teachers tend to frame their inquiry within their experiences, often interweaving their understandings of theory and research throughout. In doing so, teachers theorize in language they feel comfortable using, whether it be narrative descriptions, recounting of specific events, depictions of visual images, metaphors that weave their life stories together, or references to and from theory and research. Their narratives reveal, and allow them to reflect on, their perspectives, understandings, and experiences that guide their conceptions of teaching and their practice and that simultaneously change how they make sense of new experiences. Their narratives often integrate personal and professional worlds in ways that university researchers view as "subjective"; yet it is precisely this integration of the personal and professional that can inform in authentic ways. Their stories are not abstract theory but represent "knowing-in-action" (Schön, 1983) and the dialectical relationship between theory and practice (Clarke, 1994; Edge & Richards, 1998).

Moreover, teachers' theorizing is not linear but, rather, reflects a dynamic interplay between description, reflection, dialogue with self and others, and the implementation of alternative teaching practices. The particular mechanism through which teachers theorize is varied, for example, systematic journaling; continuous reflection; dialogue with others; finding patterns, metaphors, or images as experiences are restoried, and through classroom- and community-based research.

Finally, such theorizing does not necessarily lead to "happy endings." As Edge and Richards (1998) suggest, "dialogues of doubt can be at least as important as the dictates of success, for whereas the former hold out the prospect of development for the sake of improvement, the latter imply that the destination is already decided" (p. 571). At times, teachers try out alternatives that fail, and in that failure, they may or may not recognize more appropriate ways to respond. At times, teachers gain insights into themselves, their students, and their context, and yet fall short of the instructional practices that embody those insights. Inquiry promotes theorizing; yet it captures only moments in teachers' evolving knowledge about themselves and their teaching. We can expect this knowledge, through narrative inquiry, theorizing, and the retelling of stories, to change and grow throughout teachers' professional lives.

The role of theoretical knowledge

Expanding the knowledge base of second language teacher education to acknowledge teachers as learners of teaching and their tacit understandings of the activities of teaching itself does not preclude disciplinary or theoretical knowledge from remaining foundational to the knowledge base of second language teacher education. On the contrary, knowledge of how language is structured, acquired, and used remains fundamental to our understandings of language learning and the activity of language teaching. However, when teacher learning is viewed from a socially situated perspective, it follows that teachers need multiple opportunities to examine the theoretical knowledge they are exposed to in their professional development opportunities within the familiar context of their own learning and teaching experiences. For the purposes of educating language teachers, any theory of second language acquisition, any classroom methodology, or any description of the English language as subject matter must be understood against the backdrop of teachers' professional lives, within the settings where they work, and within the circumstances of that work. When theoretical knowledge is situated within the social contexts where it is to be used, when the interconnectedness of that knowledge is made obvious, and when language teachers have multiple opportunities to use that knowledge in interpretative ways, then theoretical knowledge has relevance for practice. This process of sense making that teachers engage in empowers them to construct justifications for their practices that are grounded in the theories that they understand

and act upon within the complex landscapes in which they work (Johnson, 1996).

Reading this book

What you are about to read are highly personal, highly contextualized stories of teachers inquiring into their own experiences as learners of language teaching. These teachers speak, listen, and respond thoughtfully, carefully, and with professional insight. As you read their stories of inquiry, it becomes obvious that although all these stories emerge from the self, they are fundamentally relational, encompassing the complex social relationships that exist in language teachers' professional worlds. Thus, in each story you will gain a sense of the tangled web of teachers, students, curricula, teaching practices, fellow teachers, administrators, local communities, and theory and research. But as you read on, in each story of inquiry, one dimension seems to be in the forefront. We have, therefore, organized the contributions in this book according to what we feel emerges as center stage.

- Part I, Inquiry into Instructional Practices
- Part II, Inquiry into Language Learners
- Part III, Inquiry into Language Teachers
- Part IV, Inquiry through Professional Collaborations

We recognize that the stories in this collection come from various regions of the world and are written by teachers who have a range of life experiences in different instructional settings. And although not all regions of the world or all types of instructional settings could ever be represented in a single volume, we believe that the stories presented here will resonate with language teachers around the world. The demands of teaching under an exam-driven curriculum, the challenges of giving students' voice in the classroom, the difficulties of recognizing one's limitations as a teacher, and the dilemmas of evaluating student learning cut across regional and instructional boundaries. We suspect that readers will see pieces of themselves or aspects of their professional worlds embedded in these stories of inquiry regardless of the settings from which they have emerged.

And although we have been moved in our own professional thinking by these teachers' stories, their stories are not *the* story. We recognize that narrative inquiry is not the panacea that will miraculously sort out the complexities of preparing language teachers for the work of this profession. We are not proposing that narrative inquiry replace one dominant paradigm with another. We share Carter's (1993) concern not to "sanctify storytelling work" (p. 11), and we recognize that teachers' desire to create a coherent life story out of narratives can be misleading (Johnston, 1997). However, we argue that the objectives of narrative inquiry are many and, thus, do not represent a singular ideological stance. Narrative inquiry is diverse in the changes it seeks to bring about, such as personal and professional growth, empowerment of teachers to change their situations, an epistemological shift, and a change in the relationship between teachers, researchers, and theory. At the same time, we believe that narrative inquiry can provide a transformative quality in teachers' personal and professional lives and in teacher education itself.

As you read these teachers' stories of inquiry, we hope that their stories will prompt you to recall, rethink, and reconstruct your own ways of knowing about language teachers and language teaching. We encourage you to recognize the many ways teachers use to examine themselves and their teaching and to develop alternative conceptions of teaching and alternative instructional practices. Note the ways that teachers acknowledge the consequences of their beliefs and practice on themselves and on their students. We intend for this book to be a "readerly text" (Elbow, 1981), in other words, that it create opportunity and space for you to construct your own meaning and rethink your own understandings of teachers, teaching, and teacher learning. We encourage you to look for multiple interpretations and multiple layers of meaning in these stories and, we hope, change our collective perceptions of what counts as knowledge, who is considered a knower, and what counts as professional development.

Conclusion

In this book, teachers' stories of inquiry are a journey of *how* they know as well as *what* they know. Yet, in language teacher education, there are few professional forums that make teachers' ways of knowing public. The intent of this collection is to bring teachers' ways of knowing into our professional conversations so as to transform our understandings of language teachers and language teaching. By making teachers' ways of knowing public, open to review by others, and accessible to others in the profession, we hope to validate language teachers and the activity of language teaching in ways afforded to other forms of scholarly work. We hope that this collection will transcend the traditional theory-practice dichotomy that has denied teachers' role as theorizers – in essence, allowing teachers to reclaim their own professional development. By making teachers' stories of inquiry public, narrative inquiry stands to become a legitimate and, we hope, a common means of professional development in language teacher education.

References

Anderson, G., & Herr, K. (1999). The new paradigm wars: Is there room for rigorous practitioner knowledge in schools and universities? *Educational Researcher, 28*(5), 12–21.

Bakhtin, M. (1981). *The dialogic imagination*. Austin: University of Texas Press.

Bruner, J. (1996). *The narrative construal of reality*. Boston: Harvard University Press.

Bullough, R. (1989). *First-year teacher: A case study*. New York: Teachers College Press.

Carter, K. (1993). The place of story in the study of teaching and teacher education. *Educational Researcher, 22*(1), 5–12.

Chaiklin, S., & Lave, J. (Eds.). (1996). *Understanding practice: Perspectives on activity and context*. New York: Cambridge University Press.

Clandinin, D. J. (1986). *Classroom practice: Teacher images in action*. London: Falmer Press.

Clandinin, D. J., & Connelly, F. M. (1991). Narrative and story in practice and research. In D. A. Schön (Ed.), *The reflective turn: Case studies in and on educational practice* (pp. 258–283). New York: Teachers College Press.

Clandinin, D. J., & Connelly, F. M. (1992). Teacher as curriculum maker. In P. Jackson (Ed.), *Handbook of research on curriculum* (pp. 363–401). New York: Macmillan.

Clandinin, D. J., & Connelly, F. M. (1995). Teachers' professional knowledge landscapes: Secret, sacred, and cover stories. In F. Connelly & D. Clandinin (Eds.), *Teachers' professional knowledge landscapes* (pp. 1–15). New York: Teachers College Press.

Clandinin, D. J., & Connelly, F. M. (2000). *Narrative inquiry: Experience and story in qualitative research*. San Francisco: Jossey-Bass.

Clarke, M. (1994). The dysfunction of the theory/practice discourse. *TESOL Quarterly, 28*, 9–26.

Cobb, P., & Bowers, J. (1999). Cognitive and situated learning perspectives in theory and practice. *Educational Researcher, 28*(2), 4–15.

Cochran-Smith, M., & Lytle, S. (1998). Teacher research: The question that persists. *International Journal of Leadership in Education, 1*(1), 19–36.

Cochran-Smith, M., & Lytle, S. (1999). The teacher research movement: A decade later. *Educational Researcher, 28*(7), 15–25.

Collins, A., Brown, J. S., & Newman, S. (1989). Cognitive apprenticeship: Teaching the craft of reading, writing, and mathematics. In L. B. Resnick (Ed.), *Cognition and instruction: Issues and agendas* (pp. 453–493). Hillsdale, NJ: Lawrence Erlbaum.

Connelly, F. M., and Clandinin, D. J. (1988). *Teachers as curriculum planners: Narratives of experience*. New York: Teachers College Press.

Counts, G. (1935). Break the teacher training lockstep. *Social Frontier, 1*, 6–7. Reprint in M. L. Borrowman (Ed.), *Teacher education in America* (pp. 218–223). New York: Teachers College Press, 1965.

Dewey, J. (1916). *Democracy and education: An introduction to the philosophy of education*. New York: Macmillan.

Dewey, J. (1920). *Reconstruction and philosophy*. Boston: Beacon; reprint 1962.

Dewey, J. (1933). *How we think*. Chicago: Henry Regnery.

Dewey, J. (1938). *Experience and education*. New York: Collier.

Edge, J., & Richards, K. (1998). Why best practice is not good enough. *TESOL Quarterly, 32*, 569–576.

Elbaz, F. (1983). *Teacher thinking: A study of practical knowledge*. London: Croon Helm.

Elbow, P. (1981). *Writing with power*. New York: Oxford University Press.

Freeman, D. (1991). "To make the tacit explicit": Teacher education, emerging discourse, and conceptions of teaching. *Teaching and Teacher Education, 7*, 439–454.

Freeman, D. (1998). *Doing teacher research: From inquiry to understanding*. Cambridge, MA: Heinle and Heinle.

Freeman, D., & Johnson, K. E. (1998). Reconceptualizing the knowledge-base of language teacher education. *TESOL Quarterly, 32*, 397–417.

Gee, J. (1999). *Introduction to discourse analysis*. London: Routledge.

Golombek, P. (1998). A study of language teachers' personal practical knowledge. *TESOL Quarterly, 32*, 447–464.

Goodson, I. F., & Dowbiggin, I. (1991). Curriculum history, professionalization and the social organization of knowledge. In I. F. Goodson and J. M. Mangan (Eds.), *Qualitative educational research studies: Methodologies in transition* (pp. 231–264). London, Ontario: The Research Unit on Classroom Learning and Computer Use in Schools.

Grossman, P. (1990). *The making of a teacher: Teacher knowledge and teacher education*. New York: Teachers College Press.

Johnson, K. E. (1996). The role of theory in L2 teacher education. *TESOL Quarterly, 30*, 765–771.

Johnston, B. (1997). Do EFL teachers have careers? *TESOL Quarterly, 31*(4), 681–712.

Kemmis, S., & McTaggart, R. (1988). *The action research planner* (3rd ed.). Geelong, Australia: Deakin University Press.

Knoblauch, C. H., & Brannon, L. (1988). Knowing our knowledge: A phenomenological basis for teacher research. In L. Z. Smith (Ed.), *Audits of meaning: A festschrift in honor of Anne E. Berthoff* (pp. 17–28). Portsmouth, NH: Boynton/Cook.

Lampert, M. (1985). How do teachers manage to teach? Perspectives on problems in practice. *Harvard Educational Review, 55*(2), 178–194.

Lave, J., & Wenger, E. (1991). *Situated learning: Legitimate peripheral participation.* New York: Cambridge University Press.

Leont'ev, A. N. (1978). *Activity, consciousness and personality.* Englewood Cliffs: Prentice Hall.

Lockhart, C., & Richards, J. C. (1994). *Reflective teaching in second language classrooms.* New York: Cambridge University Press.

Lytle, S., & Cochran-Smith, M. (1992). Teacher research as a way of knowing. *Harvard Educational Review, 62,* 447–474.

McNiff, J. (1993). *Teaching as learning: An action research approach.* London: Routledge.

Newman, D., Griffin, P., & Cole, M. (1989). *The construction zone: Working for cognitive change in school.* New York: Cambridge University Press.

Noddings, C. (1984). *Caring: A feminine approach to ethics and moral education.* Berkeley: University of California Press.

Pennycook. A. (1989). The concept of method, interested knowledge, and the politics of language teaching. *TESOL Quarterly, 23,* 589–618.

Sarbin, T. (Ed.). (1986). *Narrative psychology: The storied nature of human conduct.* New York: Praeger.

Schön, D. (1983). *The reflective practitioner: How professionals think in action.* New York: Basic Books.

Schön, D. (1987). *Educating the reflective practitioner.* San Francisco: Jossey-Bass.

Schön, D. (1995). The new scholarship requires a new espitemology. *Change: The Magazine of Higher Learning, 27*(6), 27–34.

Shor, I., & Freire, P. (1987). *A pedagogy for liberation.* South Hadley, MA: Bergin and Garvey.

Somekh, B. (1993). Quality in educational research: The contribution of classroom teachers. In J. Edge & K. Richards (Eds.), *Teachers develop, teachers research: Papers on classroom research and teacher development.* (pp. 26–38). Oxford: Heinemann.

Strauss, A. (Ed.). (1977). *George Herbert Mead: On social psychology.* Chicago: University of Chicago Press.

Vygotsky, L. S. (1978). *Mind in society: The development of higher psychological processing.* Cambridge, MA: Harvard University Press. Reprint with an introduction by M. Cole, J. Steiner, S. Scribner, & E. Soubeerman, 1978.

Wenger, E. (1998). *Communities of practice: Learning, meaning, and identity.* Cambridge: Cambridge University Press.

Witherall, C., & Noddings, N. (Eds.). (1991). *Stories lives tell: Narrative and dialogue in education.* New York: Teachers College Press.

Woods, P. (1987). Life histories and teacher knowledge. In J. Smyth (Ed.), *Educating teachers: Changing the nature of pedagogical knowledge* (pp. 121–136). New York: Falmer Press.

Zeichner, K. (1999). The new scholarship in teacher education. *Educational Researcher, 28*(9), 4–15.

Zeichner, K., & Liston, D. (1996). *Reflective teaching: An introduction.* Mahwah, NJ: Lawrence Erlbaum.

PART I:
INQUIRY INTO INSTRUCTIONAL
PRACTICES

Teachers looking into their instructional practices represent a critical component of professional development, as they negotiate their own interests, those of their students, and those of their institutions. In Part I, "Inquiry into Instructional Practices," these stories of inquiry are driven by teachers' sense of dissatisfaction with some aspect of their classroom practice. Yet, as they examine their practice, they are also compelled to examine their beliefs about teaching; how their understandings of teaching came to be; their own and their students' needs, interests, and objectives; and institutional constraints. Pauline Johansen ignores the advice of fellow teachers to wait until her ESL students "can speak and write English" before expecting them to "think about what they are reading." Instead, she struggles to integrate a literature-based curriculum and reader-writer workshops in a secondary school in the Canadian Northwest. Lynne Doherty Herndon recognizes that her love of reading and her passion as a teacher of literature often leave her lessons belonging more to her than to her students. Through reading workshops, a full-class short story unit, and book groups, she learns to let her immigrant students learn to read in a New York City secondary school. Patricia Sackville struggles to help her adult ESL students pass the English requirement for entry into a technology or trades program in the Canadian Northwest. Her choice to allow her students to rewrite graded assignments challenges common notions of grading, fairness, and what constitutes "real" language learning. Kimberly A. Johnson uses exploratory practice to solve the puzzle of how to sequence activities in her adult ESL Developing Fluency course. As a result, she witnesses firsthand the enthusiasm students feel when they are given the opportunity to make decisions about their own classroom experiences.

These teachers' dissatisfaction with their practice motivates them to look at who they are as teachers and people, what kinds of interactions they want to have with students, what kinds of interactions they want students to have with one another, and what they hope students will achieve. As they examine these issues, they describe the rich pedagogical reasoning that serves as the foundation for their practice, as well as the sources of their reasoning and its evolution. For each of these teachers, giving students voice, and allowing them to take ownership of their own language learning experiences, fundamentally alters them, their students, and the entire classroom experience.

Part I Initial reflection

The teachers featured in Part I, "Inquiry into Instructional Practices," explore the types of theoretical and pedagogical concerns reflected in the following questions. As you read their stories of narrative inquiry, reflect on the concerns embedded in these questions and how you have or might have addressed them in your own teaching.

1. How do I align my instructional practices with my knowledge, beliefs, and values about second language learning and teaching?
2. How do I remain true to what I believe in the face of institutional constraints, such as standardized exams, mandated curriculum, and assigning grades?
3. How do I challenge the dominant view that second language learners are somehow deficient and thus work against the common belief that second language instruction is remedial?
4. How do I create instructional opportunities that recognize my students not as remedial learners but as legitimate learners?
5. How do I create instructional opportunities that are truly student-centered, in other words, that go beyond students' interests and needs and entail personal involvement and engagement in their own language learning?
6. How do I develop instructional practices beyond what I am already doing?

2 "And now for something completely different"

Personal meaning making for secondary ESL
students . . . and their teacher

Pauline A. G. Johansen

I love a good story. I think most people do. I'd like to share one with you
that has an intriguing beginning and a complex, action-filled middle. . . . I'm
working on the end. Like all good stories, this one has a rich cast of characters
and a plot with lots of ups and downs. There are questions here as well as
sadness, joy, and excitement that came from exploring new horizons. And I
want to tell you of these times in story because I hope that we can connect
as all human beings do when they hear a familiar story: "Oh yes, I know
what you mean." Through this story I hope to shape meaning out of the
diverse and differing realities that created it.

The scene: An ESL classroom in a suburban secondary school in the
1990s. The main characters: First, there are two groups of sixteen- to
eighteen-year-old Asian ESL students, one group designated as "advanced"
and one as "intermediate." They are funny, sincere, and often bemused. They
all came from either Taiwan or Hong Kong and spoke often (I think with
longing) of their traditional education. One day they were going to school,
hanging out with their friends, being "cool," and the next day they found
themselves on a plane, leaving behind everything they knew and cared
about. Few really wanted to be here. They were lonely, and often alone.
Many with no family here and few friends beyond their ESL classmates,
they were suffering the normal pains of growing up in particularly trying
circumstances. I liked them. We sometimes ate lunch together in our stuffy,
smelly portable classroom. At those times we laughed, shared stories, and,
for a time, connected.

And then there was me, their ESL teacher. Recently arrived from a stint
as a district consultant and just embarking on a master's degree, I felt ready
at this stage in my career to explore some fairly uncharted territory. I had
been an elementary school teacher for twenty-four years, and I believed that
my experience, along with my districtwide work, prepared me for this next
challenge. Well, I was right and I was wrong. You'll see what I mean.

The plot: A year-long journey with these two groups of secondary ESL students. I wanted to explore rich literature with these students. I wanted to make clear for them the value I placed on personal response to reading. It is probably important to understand that my decision to take this path of exploration had not come to me in a "eureka" moment. In fact, the pathway to that point had been rather long and meandering.

I had reached a stage in my career at which I was asking myself some tough questions about what I really cared about in teaching. My beliefs about teaching and learning had developed over a long time, and I knew that they had not developed in a vacuum. There had been thousands of conversations, hundreds of workshops, hour upon hour of working with students and other educators. One thing I felt I knew for certain was that whatever I now believed had developed through those interactions. I am an amalgam of what I have experienced, read, and taught.

Oh, yes, and I had recently fallen in love with a dead Russian. Leonid Vygotsky (1981) and his Zone of Proximal Development. The more I read of him and his ZPD, the more I came to believe in the notion that students can and should be engaged in learning that takes them to a place where they are truly challenged but are supported in their learning. This zone was a place where they would be engaged, and at the same time not frustrated and confused by being expected to perform beyond their current abilities.

This heady mixture of beliefs about the social nature of learning and the notion of carefully scaffolded learning had developed over many years while I was a mainstream intermediate teacher. When I began to learn with ESL students, my belief system came with me. I began to look at my beliefs through the lenses of ESL. There was no sea change in my beliefs. I didn't suddenly throw aside everything that I valued in teaching and learning. But, and it was a big *but*, I suspected that learning an additional language would certainly put a different "spin" on things. Still, I really wasn't prepared for how my beliefs would be tested again and again.

We all have those "if . . . then" propositions in our minds. If, for example, I believe in the social nature of learning, then it follows that students learning English need to be allowed to work in groups in order to talk, share, and clarify issues and ideas together. What I wasn't prepared for was the absolute terror with which my students approached such tasks. They found the notion of group work, with its shared responsibilities and the attendant expectation for dialogue, totally unnerving.

How was I going to support these students as they engaged in group work centered around sharing reading responses and at the same time respect their need for individualism? In addition, I wanted to put into action with these ESL students a way of interacting with print that valued their personal and primary responses to what they were reading. I wanted these responses to occur in their writing, and in their dialogue about what they were reading. That challenge remained throughout the year. This story is about the successes we had together in finding a place for responding. It is also about the struggles and the "miles to go before we sleep."

I was and am attracted to a pedagogy that values and supports students' thoughtfulness. I wanted my students to "own their learning." I wanted them to be motivated not by marks but by the sense of sheer joy gained from interactions with print and the related interactions with others. I wanted to create an environment in which that kind of learning could take place.

The concept of students making personal responses to what they have read is now almost a given in most mainstream classrooms. It is not such an accepted notion in ESL pedagogy. In fact, some colleagues questioned why I would even bother with such activities when there were clearly so many important grammar points to learn, sentence structures to grasp, and verbs tenses to memorize, especially at the secondary level. "When they can speak and write English clearly and effectively," I was told, "then you can take the time to ask them what they think about what they are reading." And, truthfully, my students were saying much the same thing. They ached for grammar sheets; they longed for fill-in-the-blank activities. They didn't want to tell me in their imperfect English what they were thinking.

So, there was definitely a glitch in my "If . . . then" proposition. And so the "search" began: my students the rather unwilling passengers on the voyage to see how and in what ways the notion of personal responses to reading could be made a part of their language learning in a literature-based, response-centered secondary ESL classroom.

Like any good traveler, I consulted the "guides." Much has been written about the use of a reader response approach to reading with students for whom English is a first language (Dias, 1979, 1992; Langer, 1990, 1994; Meek, 1983; Probst, 1988, 1992; Purves, 1972, 1984; Rosenblatt, 1976, 1978). There was no doubt in my mind about the efficacy of this approach. Their research has made it clear that when "all students are treated as thinkers and [we] provide them with the environment as well as the help to reason for themselves, even the most "at risk" students can engage in thoughtful discussions about literature, develop rich and deep understandings, and enjoy it too!" (Langer, 1994, p. 210). Unfortunately, my students and I didn't exist on an island. We were surrounded by a complex environment that included mainstream classroom norms and expectations as well as frequently conflicting school, societal, and family expectations. These pulls were strong, and the students were often torn between the familiar and the unknown.

I am a pragmatist and a realist. I want whatever I do in my ESL classroom to support students' learning English in their mainstream classrooms, where they spend most of their time. These classrooms have cachet and, ultimately, educational power.

I had so many questions. I wanted to know what opinions these students had toward making personal responses, and whether these opinions would change over time. And, ever the teacher, I wondered what approaches or methods might be most useful in helping them make these responses. I was intrigued to find out what forms the student's written responses might take, given the kind of program I was trying to create.

There is an ancient Chinese saying: "May you live in interesting times." Educators in my school district were experiencing very interesting times, indeed. There had been a 2,581 percent increase in ESL students from 1987 to 1994! It is a tribute to the dedication and caring of teachers in the district that, even given the attendant strains and stresses that this amount of increase brought with it, I was still having conversations with mainstream classroom teachers in which they talked about the value of having students learn an additional language in their classrooms.

Of course, all was not rosy. As willing as they were, many teachers felt completely unprepared to work with language-learning students in ways that they believed were supportive of their language needs and at the same time to hold fast to their belief systems. They were questioning their own ability to assess the different linguistic and cultural schemata of their ESL students and their ability to choose suitable teaching methodologies. They wanted to plan learning experiences that were appropriate for their students' intellectual abilities regardless of their language proficiency. I shared their goals. When I looked around my district, I saw wonderful teaching going on in terms of teachers working to support personal meaning making through reading. But somehow, when it came to ESL students, the rules changed. A long history of language instruction that looked and felt different from what was done with students in mainstream classes fostered and maintained a somewhat "us and them" approach.

I felt privileged to have worked in both mainstream and ESL classrooms and was thankful for the broad perspective it gave me. So my beliefs tugged me forward in spite of the swirl of questions and concerns. A goal of a reader response approach that empowered ESL students to take ownership of their learning, encouraged them in their own meaning making, and provided them with a structure within which to experiment and exchange new and developing perceptions was worth pursuing.

Preparing for the trip took me down some interesting roads. I immersed myself in sociocultural learning theories: the mysterious Mr. Vygotsky

(1978, 1981), the profoundly radical and yet, by today's standards tame, Mr. Dewey (1963), the irreverent and always challenging Mr. Smith (1988). I became intrigued with the role of language in a social structure as a resource for meaning making. The social dimension of language was what truly interested me.

The concept that knowledge was constructed in the mind of the individual knower – now this was heady stuff! I had always had a niggling little feeling that the knowledge, the "stuff," that I had wanted to give to my students via a transmission model just wasn't the whole story. Ironically, this transmission model was what my secondary ESL students were most familiar and comfortable with. I think they thought that it was rather tragic to be in a situation in which the teacher who they felt held the key to English was expecting them to behave in ways that were really so very discomforting. They were used to being passive receivers of information. I was asking them to become actively involved. They were terrific at regurgitation. I was asking them to create their own interpretations. These were rocky times, to say the least.

I wanted them to "experience" their learning in the sense that Dewey describes. The experience that he suggests has a special two-pronged quality. First, is the immediate effect of the experience, and second, more important, is the nature of this experience as it causes the learner to connect with future learning. "Just as no man lives or dies himself, so no experience lives and dies to itself. Wholly independent of desire or intent, every experience lives on in further experiences" (Dewey, 1963, p. 27). That was what I wanted for my students: connections. Connections to one another, connections to other learning, and connections to their inner selves and what was vital to them in their lives. I wanted these connections to come through and be sparked by their reading and their responses to it.

I knew that the students would need a great deal of nurturing as they worked in these unfamiliar ways. Vygotsky and his perspective on the social nature of learning provided me with great comfort. I clung to the notion that what was once an external, group process could, with support, become an internal, individual one. An acceptance of the power of social learning brings with it great responsibilities in terms of creating a learning environment in which students can flourish. So, rather than looking only at what students are able to accomplish on their own, now I would consider "their zone of proximal development": "those functions that have not yet matured but are in the process of maturation, functions that will mature tomorrow but are currently in an embryonic state" (1978, p. 86). I believed in my students' potential as learners. Now it was up to me to co-create with them a situation in which this socially mediated learning could take place.

So now you have a sense of the players, the setting, and some of the dilemmas we faced. At this point I would like to paint in broad strokes the backdrop that existed in the classroom in terms of the frameworks or "superstructures" I had initiated. They were:

- The use of a literature-based curriculum
- Thematic units and content-based instruction
- Dialogue journals
- Readers' workshops and response journals
- Writers' workshops

Frameworks or "superstructures"

I think that my students felt betrayed by the reading and writing activities I asked them to do in my classroom. I was not playing by ESL rules. I had broken a powerful unspoken pact, according to which the teacher agrees to run the classroom in such a way as to avoid asking the students to make personal meaning of what is being read or to share perceptions with others, a classroom in which the students agree to answer reams of questions to which there are already answers, and both parties agree to call this "reading."

Well, I didn't buy into that pact. Early in the school year, I had the students complete a reading survey. I was not surprised that most students said they did not read well in English. What did concern me were their responses as to the purposes for reading. Most of their responses indicated that they viewed reading as the act of getting information – basically an efferent activity. They did not read for pleasure. I quote: "We read to get information." "People read because learning things will improve their knowledge and hobbies." "People can get some reference and knowledge from the book." I sighed and realized that the notion of reading as an aesthetic activity was not part of my students' current thinking. But I love and trust good literature and believe in its power to transform.

Literature-based curriculum

At this point I would like to stand tall on my soapbox. High-interest, low-vocabulary books, Scientific Reading Approach (SRA) kits, and the wide range of programmed materials "created" for ESL students to read are not what will cause students to pause and consider, to go back and reread, or to think again about what they have read and what it means to them. I believed that it would have been meaningless to introduce a response-based reading program that wasn't predicated on the use of literature. How could I expect these ESL students to care about and to make personal choices about rich literature if they were being served Pablum on the page?

There is, of course, a lot of support in the literature for a skill-based view of reading. There seems to be a "commonsense" view of reading that can be thought of as the manipulation of parts into a whole. The very strong belief persists that simplification is the answer to reading experiences for ESL students. Many lessons suggest breaking down reading into small, easily digested pieces in order to make for more effective reading. However, reading is much too complex an act to be amenable to this approach. Instead, I wanted to guide the students in making choices that would provide them with satisfying reading experiences. I wanted to highlight the role of literature "in the development of a sharp and critical mind" (Langer, 1990, p. 182). Literature, I felt, was a source of ideas, impressions, feelings, and emotions. At some point, I hoped that it could provide an impetus for students to create their own writing. I wanted them to get in touch with and to have insights into their own behavior based on encounters with a broad range of other humans' behavior. I wanted them to be touched by the humanity of literature and to experience other living things, ideas, and events. The language that they needed was there on the page in all its wonderful structural complexity. Good literature allows students to see, in a deeply contextualized way, how to use the rules of grammar for effective communication.

The possibilities of human life are illuminated, both the good and the evil, and we are free to explore, to take sides, to experience, to learn, but without the dire consequences we sometimes encounter in our physical world. When we read a story we truly merge heart and intellect. (Peterson & Eeds, 1990, p. 16)

Thematic units and content-based instruction

Language learning takes time. My own experience told me this, as did my reading of the work of researchers such as Collier (1987) and Wong-Fillmore (1989). But oh, my students felt the tyranny of time. These students arrived at the age of sixteen or seventeen, and their parents expected them to graduate with their peers and then go on to university. However, there were secondary school English requirements to be met first. And the entrance into those courses was dependent on successful completion of their ESL courses. So, unfortunately, the ESL class became in their minds a barrier to true success rather than a support.

I felt that relevancy might hold the key to lowering the affective filter that was getting in the way of students' active engagement. I decided to draw upon my many years in elementary classrooms and what I had learned there in terms of using themes to satisfy students' needs for content learning and at the same time contextualize their language learning experiences. For the most part, learning language through useful, transferable content appealed to the students. It was a successful framework and a valuable piece of language teaching data I have relied upon again and again.

Dialogue journals

I was eager to create an avenue of communication between the students and myself, and dialogue journals seemed to be a good place to begin. There were many opportunities for the students to write during the early months of the year, but what I was particularly interested in was accessing the students' higher-order thinking. I wanted to provide an outlet for expressive writing. And, although my main incentive was not an evaluative one, I was able to see at what stage my students were able to use language in terms of fluency of ideas and appropriate structures. My main focus, however, was to help the students find their own voice. "Correctness is not the point; the learner's internal dialogue is. When students write to learn, they construct knowledge by writing about a subject in their own words and connecting what they are learning with what they already know" (Patterson & Shannon, 1993, p. 187). I was hoping to create a learning environment that would, in conjunction with the other structures I was putting in place, be instrumental in creating a community of learners – a place where students would feel safe in expressing their ideas, asking questions, stating opinions, and relating when and however they could.

I used the dialogue journals only with the intermediate students. In retrospect, I see that not using them with the advanced students had a negative impact in terms of their willingness to engage in personal meaning making around literature. The advanced group never really bought into the idea that they could express opinions in print. So when the time came to use our reader response journals, they hadn't had the "rehearsal time" through the use of dialogue journals. I regret that decision. If I were given that year again, I would initiate dialogue journals with all my students as a valuable way to build trust and openness and to begin the communication process that is at the heart of writing.

Readers' and writers' workshops

READERS' WORKSHOPS AND RESPONSE JOURNALS

When I put readers' and writers' workshops in place, my intention was to provide an environment that would support a community of literate learners. I feel as do Meek (1983) and Smith (1988), that in order for reading to be fostered, students must collaborate with others interested in reading, especially a knowledgeable adult. "[F]or all the reading research we have financed, we are certain only that good readers pick their own way to literacy in the company of friends who encourage and sustain them and that . . . the enthusiasm of a trusted adult can make the difference" (Meek, 1983, p. 193).

Readers' workshops provide just such an environment of learning together: a "literacy club." Twice-weekly, hour-long sessions provided students with the opportunity to select reading material and to make personal responses in their reading journals about what they were reading in ways that made sense to them. Response journals were meant to show tangible, ongoing evidence of their thinking about their reading. The journals were not a test of knowledge; rather, they provided another way for me to "dialogue" with the students. But, rather than being free writing or personal writing, the writing in this journal was meant to provide a focus for the students' questions, wonderings, reflections, and predictions about what they had chosen to read during our reading workshop time. I had also selected stories and poems for them to read or to be read aloud to them, and the response journal was a place to write about those literary experiences. The students handed in these journals once a week, and we used them as an additional communication tool and as a way to measure their growing literary understanding.

There was a powerful message I wanted my students to receive: "You are readers and writers. I believe in you and I trust you." The response journal was meant to be a physical artifact that made tangible my belief in the interactive and reciprocal nature of literature. But the fear of risk taking made it difficult for the students to make choices about what to read. As Probst (1988) firmly states, the making of these choices "places a tremendous burden of responsibility on the student – it demands that the student think and decide, and those are awesome tasks. But there is not much point in working for less in the schools" (p. 47). I hoped that the use of organizational structures such as readers' and writers' workshops would make powerful explicit statements to these ESL students. I felt that they needed to believe that they were ready and able to be successful readers with the support of other students and a knowledgeable adult. I wanted them to think about what was important to do during reading time and who had the power that real reading confers, as Frank Smith says (1988) so clearly: "[E]very reading/writing teacher should be a member of the literacy club. Many teachers are surprised when they reflect upon what they actually demonstrate about reading and writing during the day" (p. 12).

Reading involves social relationships among teachers and students, among students and students, and among students and authors. I know that the social relationships needed for reading do not just happen. I hoped that by using these workshop formats, I would be able to create opportunities for social interaction with others around a common activity: reading, writing, and talking about books.

WRITERS' WORKSHOPS

The structure of a writers' workshop approach in my classroom was founded on basic principles gleaned from writers such as Atwell (1987) and Graves (1978, 1983). Much has been written about this approach, which values and makes a space for students to select topics to pursue in their writing. Ironically, this structured approach results in tremendous flexibility. The notion of using this approach with ESL learners held great appeal for me because at its heart the workshops provided three essential elements. First, there was invaluable *time* to think, create, and re-create. Second, student *ownership of topic* provided a rich element of commitment. And finally, students were able to receive timely and important *responses* from fellow students and their teacher. The intermediate students appreciated the predictable, twice-weekly, hour-long segments. This space of time made it possible for ideas to develop, to be shared, changed, and revised.

There is a built-in open-endedness in the workshop approach that invites writers to begin where they are and encourages them to go as far as their imaginations can take them. There was value in attending to the minilessons on grammar, structure, and syntax issues that were a part of these workshops. These minilessons were attempts to address the issue of contextualization of language concepts. I was able, over time, to note the type and frequency of written errors my students were making, and then to approach them in short, meaningful, and if necessary, repeated learning sessions.

I believe that the issue of ownership of topic is at the heart of a writing workshop approach. Over and over the students said how much they liked being able to choose their own topics and how much easier their freedom to choose made it possible for them to pursue their writing to a satisfactory conclusion.

I was able through the workshop approach to respond to students' writing in authentic and meaningful ways. These responses were both structured and unstructured. The students were able to see editing modeled – either by listening in as I worked with one student on a piece of writing or more formally as I took an unidentified author's work and modeled, using the overhead projector, how one could comment specifically and helpfully to a fellow writer. The students were drawn to the opportunities to share their writing with peers and me. The workshop was founded on the elements of listening and being listened to and a quiet respect for one another that connected to and was part of the building of a sense of community of learners. An ethos of respect for one anothers' ideas as well as a deeper understanding of the need for sharing these new insights grew as we met for nine hours each week. This sense of community, so essential to creating a working and learning environment, developed with the intermediate-level students. Sadly, the advanced students never really came to that place of willing commitment to the joint tasks of reading and writing in a community of learners. In the next and concluding section, I will paint in broad strokes what I feel were some of the influences or factors at work in creating this resistance from the advanced students.

"I've got some good news and some bad news"

I've always been fascinated by kaleidoscopes. The other day in a store I picked one up to look through and was once again struck by the beauty and mystery of the glass configuration that takes the everyday and makes it magical. I turned the tube, and the lights in the store refracted, multiplied, and picked up color to create something new and no longer familiar.

Considering the time spent with ESL students reminds me of the kaleidoscope: I find myself looking, twisting and turning, and examining in different lights several interacting elements. None of these bright and fascinating issues is really more vital than any other. Rather, they worked together to create a set of circumstances, some of which were tremendously heartening and some of which still haunt me. In particular, I want to describe what I call the *environmental factors, systemic elements*, and *teacher-controlled factors*.

Under the rather large and perhaps nebulous heading of *environmental factors*, I group matters such as the students' educational background and age on arrival in Canada and their concern about time spent in the ESL program. I am very leery of any literature that claims to describe a culture. "All [fill in the blank with a culture] like/don't like . . ." So I won't. What I will say is that both groups of Asian students I worked with had a definite reticence to make personal responses orally in response to their reading. I still blush and feel foolish looking back at the times when I tried to orchestrate opportunities for oral responses to what had been read. It was painful for the students and for me. It was at this point that my journal began to take on a rather desperate tone. I tried before-response strategies, during-response strategies, after-response strategies. I had very little success with either the intermediate or the advanced students. I knew them well enough to know that they had the "words" and were bright students. But the notion of verbally sharing personal thoughts about what they had read was just too foreign and too discomforting and not part of their past educational experiences.

The time element, which I consider part of environmental issues, really accentuated what a driven group these students were. Sadly, much of the motivation was external. Explicit demands from their parents to exit the ESL program sooner than was realistic created great tension. Arriving as they did at age sixteen or seventeen precluded the possibility of graduating with their peers, although the students never really accepted this and bore the burden of unfulfilled expectations. I can only imagine what possibilities might have existed for these students had the time frame been more relaxed and realistic. Still, considering all I have said about environmental factors, they were not as powerful as I initially thought they would be. After all, I had to admit that even though the advanced students had not shown great gains in their written responses, there had been success for the intermediate students in terms of their written responses, and the environmental factors were similar for both groups of students. No, now I feel that it was much more a matter of the combining of environmental factors with other factors that needs to be attended to.

Schools are organisms. They live, they breathe, they evolve, and at times they devolve. At work within this system is a clash of conflicting interests that often seem at odds with our stated goal of student success, for example, the systemic elements such as testing methods used with ESL students, the scheduling of classes for these students, and the overall issue of time spent with one teacher.

Students had received language level designations through initial testing, and many, arriving at age sixteen or seventeen, were designated intermediate or advanced. Their expectation then became to exit the program within one year. Any time beyond this was seen as "marking time." A palpable sense of frustration grew among the students, a frustration that was difficult to ignore. Ultimately, this frustration led to a deep unrest and an unwillingness on the part of some of the advanced students to engage in any meaningful way in their classroom activities, especially in terms of personal response. Leveling tests, which were used beyond initial testing to move students from one level to another, also held great currency. The message was clear: There is one right answer. Find it and you can move on and up. There was a disturbing incongruity between the goal of these tests, the one right answer, and my daily encouragement to share their personal responses in either written or oral form. Dissonance and confusion were certainly powerful negative forces affecting the advanced students.

Something as seemingly innocuous as the systemic problem of scheduling made it difficult for the advanced students to make a commitment to the type of program I was suggesting in my classroom. The schedule resulted in the students' having a fractured ESL timetable divided between two ESL teachers. Furthermore, I was unable (in the shortened time we were together) to develop the readers' and writers' workshops in a satisfying way. Of course, differences in teaching style and approach are natural, and in any school setting shouldn't be such a problem. However, in this case the differences between reading programs were so pronounced that the incongruity was too much for students to overcome. Their other class required a very efferent approach to their reading: Read, gather the facts, report the answers, remember the details, give them back. Doing these things was their ticket out. And in my class, I was asking them to relish the words, the images, the entire sensory experience that reading could provide. What I failed to do, however, was to *teach* the difference between an aesthetic and an efferent stance to reading. I failed to *acknowledge* that both types of reading are important and that both types have currency. My failure to make these differences clear to the students meant that they became good at regurgitation but never really bought into the value of personal meaning making, at least not in terms of their verbal responses.

I had no control over the timetables or environmental circumstances. However, there were elements I could have controlled. It still saddens me to think that those issues over which I did have the greatest teacher control were the ones I ultimately had the least success with.

As a teacher, I often said I felt that grammar and surface features in writing were important as the *carriers* of the message but not the message itself. However, in my work with the advanced group of students, all my beliefs went out the window as I fought and lost the "battle for correctness." Both the intermediate and the advanced students struggled with written English, and both groups made a myriad of errors in their writing. I can still remember reading the pieces created by the intermediate students. I viewed their errors as a natural reflection of individuals who were actually engaged in what they were reading. They had important things to say, and I could ignore the surface features to focus on the message. They consistently wrote more, took more risks, and tried to put into practice the many ways of responding we had discussed. In fact, their errors became ways for me to judge the students' increasing confidence and, where necessary, to use these errors as focal points for focused miniwriting lessons.

What a difference I perceived with the advanced students' writing. Most of their writing seemed to me to be "going through the motions." Their writing didn't increase in complexity, or length for that matter, throughout the entire year. I felt a sense of hopelessness with these students that affected my interactions with them. I didn't recognize that my challenge was to direct their energies. I saw them as the "enemy." They were resisting me at every stage, and they knew that ultimately it didn't matter. They would pass through the ESL gates into freedom whether or not they ever made a personal reading response verbally or in written form. They knew the game. They knew the structure of the tests and for the most part would be able to jump through the hoop. Many, in fact, had already – by strange and circuitous means – been able to pass a test that let them take a mainstream English course in the evening. So some of these advanced students were taking my course concurrently with an English course that certainly held more power for them than their ESL course.

My residual feeling about this group is one of missed opportunities. I think that the advanced students felt my uneasiness, my sense that all was not well. I imagine that it was hard for them to have confidence in someone who was obviously struggling but, and this is the tricky part, was trying to hide that struggle. I kept a journal throughout that year, and reading through it now, I certainly hear the voice of desperation. I felt as teachers often do that, if I could "just find the right strategy," all would be well. I had forgotten what years in a mainstream classroom had taught me: All the strategies in the world are nothing more than props on an empty stage unless they are connected to a deeper, common understanding about the purposes of the endeavor.

The creation of a common understanding, sometimes called a "community of learners," was an element over which I did have control but didn't enact. In fairness to myself and with gratitude to the intermediate students, I must say that they reached the vibrant place where learning can take place for all the reasons I have described. But sadly, the mixture of factors that affected the advanced students created a critical mass of uneasiness I could not overcome.

Sometimes the vast array of ESL methodologies can be daunting. Teachers seeking a "best method" with good intentions and hard work often wander down lonely paths to failure. Maybe what is needed is not another methodology, another strategy, another better way. Maybe it's as simple as making a connection between ourselves and our students in a truly human way, in a way that says, I know this is hard work, let's do the work together, let's learn together, let's muck about in the messy place of learning together.

All the research literature on language learning talks about the key element of risk taking as being vital to success. And yet it seems so hard for us as teachers to take those risks. We ask questions we know the answers to and create learning opportunities that engage only half of the equation, the students. It's scary not knowing how things will turn out, and I'm not suggesting that we enter into "experiments" with our students that aren't based on our best thinking and personal background knowledge. What I am suggesting is that it's good and right that we not always know the end, that we don't always need to know exactly how things will turn out.

And I don't think we need to take this voyage alone. We strive so hard to structure classrooms in which social interaction and learning can take place, and yet we do so little to support our own interactions. Do you have a safe place in which to talk about the triumphs, the questions, the failures that take place between you and your students? Do you feel as if you belong to a community of teacher-learners? When did we stop thinking of ourselves as learners and start to imagine that we needed to have all the answers?

I said in the beginning that this story doesn't have an end. It doesn't. In my current role as a vice principal/ESL teacher, I am focusing on creating environments in which we can move beyond the niceties we often engage in to a place where we can all see ourselves as learners – a place where an intellectual environment will support risk taking, a safe place to tell our stories, even the ones with sad endings. I believe in that for students, and I dream of it for teachers.

References

Atwell, N. (1987). *In the middle: Writing, reading and learning with adolescents*. Portsmouth, NH: Boyton/Cook.

Collier, V. P. (1987). Age and rate of acquisition of second language for academic purposes. *TESOL Quarterly, 21,* 617–641.

Dewey, J. (1963). *Experience and education.* New York: Collier.

Dias, P. (1979). Developing independent readers of poetry: An approach in the high school. *McGill Journal of Education, 14,* 199–214.

Dias, P. (1992). Literary reading and classroom constraints: Aligning practice with theory. In Judith Langer (Ed.), *Literature instruction: A focus on student response.* Urbana, IL: National Council of Teachers of English.

Graves, D. H. (1978). *Balance the basics: Let them write.* New York: Ford Foundation.

Graves, D. H. (1983). *Writing: Teachers and children at work.* London: Heinemann Educational Books.

Langer, J. A. (1990). Understanding literature. *Language Arts, 67,* 812–816.

Langer, J. A. (1994). A response-based approach to reading literature. *Language Arts, 71,* 203–211.

Meek, M. (1983). *Achieving literacy.* London: Routledge & Kegan Paul.

Patterson, L., & Shannon, P. (1993). Reflection, inquiry, action. In L. Patterson, C. M. Santa, K. G. Short, & K. Smith (Eds.), *Teachers are researchers: Reflection and action,* Newark, NY: International Reading Association.

Peterson, R., & Eeds, M. (1990). *Grand conversations: Literature groups in action.* Ontario: Scholastic-TAB.

Probst, R. E. (1988). *Response and analysis: Teaching literature in junior and senior high school.* Portsmouth, NH: Boyton/Cook.

Probst, R. E. (1992). Five kinds of literary knowing. In J. Langer (Ed.), *Literature instruction: A focus on student response* (pp. 54–77). Urbana, IL: National Council of Teachers of English.

Purves, A. (Ed.) . (1972). *How porcupines make love: Notes on a response-centered curriculum.* New York: Wiley.

Purves, A. (1984). The challenge to education to produce literate citizens. In A. Purves & O. Niles (Eds.), *Becoming readers in a complex society.* (83rd Yearbook of the National Society for the Study of Education, P. 1). Chicago: The University of Chicago Press.

Rosenblatt, L. M. (1976). *Literature as exploration.* New York: Noble and Noble.

Rosenblatt, L. M. (1978). *The Reader, the text, the poem: The transactional theory of the literary work.* Carbondale, IL: Southern Illinois University Press.

Smith, F. (1988). *Joining the literacy club.* London: Heinemann.

Vygotsky, L. (1978). *Mind in society: The development of higher psychological Processing.* Cambridge, MA: Harvard University Press. Reprint with an introduction by M. Cole, J. Steiner, S. Scribner, & E. Souberman, 1978.

Vygotsky, L. (1981). The genesis of higher mental functions. In J. V. Wertch (Ed.), *The concept of activity in Soviet psychology*. Armonk, NY: Sharpe.

Wong-Fillmore, L. (1989). Teaching English through content: Instructional reform in programs for language minority students. In J. H. Esling (Ed.), *Multicultural education and policy: ESL in the 1990's*. Toronto: O.I.S.E. Press.

3 Putting theory into practice
Letting my students learn to read

Lynne Doherty Herndon

New job. New semester. New curriculum. A new opportunity to reenvision my teaching. A chance to put into practice the insights I had gleaned from my previous teaching experiences as well as the theory I had absorbed during my intensive MATESOL program the summer before. But how?

I had been teaching English to mainstream and ESL students in private and public schools for several years. Although I was well practiced as a teacher of writing, my real love was reading, and my students and colleagues generally appreciated my skills as a literature teacher. I had learned how to choose literary works that the students enjoyed, how to craft study guides that delved into the key themes of a text, and how to lead students in provocative class discussions. I was an effective teacher, no doubt, but somehow my teaching didn't feel right to me.

My training had emphasized the importance of allowing students ownership over the reading and writing process, a philosophical orientation that I embraced in theory but failed to follow fully in practice. Perhaps my love of literature was part of the problem. As I prepared a lesson plan, my excitement about a reading would sweep over me and thoughts would begin to race through my head. In the classroom, my ideas too often predominated, and my voice was too often the most assured in the room. Although students generally enjoyed and benefited from my classes, in the end the literature we studied belonged more to me than it did to them. My new teaching position provided me with a chance to shift the balance. But how?

There were certain givens. I would teach two 100-minute periods of English a day, four days a week, at the New York City public high school for immigrant students whose staff I had joined the previous fall. Given the diversity of the school's population, my classes would be heterogeneous in every sense of the word: Each class of twenty-five students would reflect an intentional mixture of races, nationalities, languages, educational backgrounds, levels of English proficiency, gender, grades, ages, and dates of arrival in the United States. To encounter such vast diversity in one classroom was a major change for me, having taught more traditionally leveled classes in the past. This diversity would be one of my greatest challenges, as well as my greatest impetus for change.

There would be new experiences for my students as well. Although English credits had, throughout the school's two-year existence, always been awarded in the context of interdisciplinary humanities courses, this semester we would for the first time offer English as a freestanding class. A close colleague and I were charged with designing and teaching this course. We would each draw upon our backgrounds in whole language methodologies and student-centered curriculum as we developed and implemented a semester-long, thematically based reading and writing course.

Our conception of English as a distinct course, related to but independent from the history curriculum, was significant. For most of the students (and many of their teachers), the word *English* had until this time referred only to the second language they were learning; they didn't realize that this term could also refer to a specific area of study, like math, science, or social studies, with a distinct set of academic structures, intellectual patterns, and points of view. Because English as an academic discipline offers especially powerful methods of understanding human experience, we wanted the pursuit of this understanding to be one of the organizing principles of our course. By choosing literature that focused on individual experiences, by encouraging students to draw upon their own experiences in their responses to their reading, and by asking them to evaluate those responses in relation to the literature and to one another, we hoped to lead students toward more complex understandings of their own and one anothers' viewpoints, and of their places in the larger world. But how?

Curriculum planning and implementation

Before approaching the task of curriculum planning, we needed to articulate our goals. First of all, we wanted to develop reading fluency in our students by requiring sizable amounts of reading and exposing them to a broad range of literary texts. Second, we hoped to inspire in our students a love of reading for reading's sake. We wanted to give them the opportunity to experience literature as literature – as an end in itself, rather than solely as a vehicle for learning about other subjects. Third, we sought to facilitate the exchange of ideas through full-class discussion, a format that was often overlooked at our school because of its emphasis on task-oriented, small-group projects. Finally, we wished to introduce our students to specific comprehension-aiding techniques that would support them in all of their reading, by creating reading guidelines that could be used with a wide variety of texts.

Satisfying all these objectives proved to be impossible within the context of a single reading unit, however, and we found ourselves experimenting with various methods as the semester progressed. Our three major approaches – reading workshop, a full-class short story unit, and book groups – and what we learned from each of them are outlined in the sections that follow.

Reading workshop: Independent reading and response

We began the semester by introducing students to the structures and expectations of reading workshop, which we based on a model created by Nancie Atwell (1987). Aiming to transfer the principles of writing process theory (see Calkins, 1986; Graves, 1983) to the teaching of reading, Atwell developed a format in which students engage in sustained, silent reading of self-chosen books for entire class periods and respond to their reading in "literary letters" that are exchanged with their teacher and peers. In addition to demonstrating greater personal investment in their reading, Atwell's students achieved increased reading rates, improved comprehension levels, and stronger vocabulary skills, results we wished our students to obtain as well.

From a theoretical perspective, reading workshop has great potential for multilevel ESL classes. Similar to the "reading lab approach" described by Eskey and Grabe (1988), it addresses three factors they define as integral to effective reading instruction: quantity of reading, appropriate materials, and the judgment of the teacher, who plays an important role in matching students to texts (p. 228). The reading workshop model also gives priority to text authenticity, reader interest, and the match between the schemata of the reader and the text, factors that have been determined to be critical to successful reading in a second language (Barnett, 1989, p. 144). When students are allowed to read authentic literature of their own choosing, as they are in a reading workshop format, they are free to pursue their own interests and to select texts that match their schemata to the degree that they desire.

This highly individualized approach struck us as ideal for our heterogeneous ESL classes, which reflected a broad range of English proficiency levels and reading skills. To permit students easy access to reading materials, we used our textbook budget to stock our rooms with a variety of literary texts: picture books, adolescent fiction, historical fiction, short story collections, and a variety of contemporary and classic novels covering a wide range of topics and genres. Because abridged and "high-interest, low-vocabulary" texts often seem less overwhelming to low-beginners, we decided to have some of these materials on hand as well. We encouraged students who elected to read abridged books at the start of the semester, however, to move on to unabridged literature within the first few weeks.

The primary method for students to respond to the literature was through reading journals, in which they were encouraged to write their thoughts, feelings, and questions about what they had read. Although not written in letter form, their journal entries were responded to in writing by either the teacher or a peer. One of our challenges as teachers was to help students move from superficial plot summaries to deeper responses; some students made this shift easily, but others tended to remain stuck in summary mode. Mohammed, a low-beginner still struggling with the English alphabet and sound system, wrote the following journal entry after struggling through the first several pages of an abridged text:

I read *The Prince and the Pauper*. Author is Mark Twain. This book is two boys, one boy is rich, other is poor. One boy see other boy and they thing to be frend.

Summarizing seemed to serve as a way for less proficient readers to master the factual content of a text, and for students like Mohammed, we felt that summarizing was a necessary precursor to the formulation of a personal or analytical response. Through follow-up questions to which these students responded in writing, we attempted, with varying degrees of success, to move them toward more complex responses to what they had read. In reply to my written query, "How would you feel if you were the poor boy? Would you want the prince to be your friend?" for example, Mohammed wrote, "I thing poor boy life so sad. Yes, I want prince to be my frend." Although some students' initial responses were rudimentary at best, they began to get the idea that, in the context of our English classes, their personal reactions to their reading were as important as the reading itself.

Reading workshop helped us to achieve several positive outcomes in our classes. We observed increased reading rates and levels of comprehension in many students, as demonstrated by the number of books they read and the quality of their written responses. We also found that independent reading fostered a love of literature in a significant number of students, who began to see themselves as capable readers of English, both inside and outside school. Several students read five to ten full-length novels over the course of the semester, and almost every student successfully completed at least one unadapted literary text. Although some students eventually tired of the silent reading format, others found it to be a welcome oasis – a time for peaceful reflection in the midst of a noisy, commotion-filled school day.

We found several drawbacks to reading workshop, however. As Eskey and Grabe (1988) have noted, this model tends to isolate reading from the rest of the academic curriculum, offering few connections to other disciplines, topics, and themes. Because of its highly individualized nature, this model overlooks the social aspects of meaning making, providing limited opportunities for purposeful student interaction and small-group work. As a result, we as teachers tended to remain center stage. We also found that students' written responses to their independent reading tended to wear rather thin. Because students lacked shared knowledge and experience, their journal exchanges often remained at a superficial level; as a teacher, I too was often stymied as to how to respond meaningfully to students' inchoate reactions to books I had never read. Although reading workshop helped us to meet some of our objectives, we sought an approach that would foster greater levels of student interaction and more meaningful exchanges of ideas.

Short story unit: Full-class reading, discussion, and response

One of our stated aims was to develop our students' discussion skills, an area we felt was neglected in many of their other classes. Since class discussion constitutes a significant portion of many college courses, we considered it important to give our students experience in listening to, responding to, and building upon one anothers' ideas. We believed, moreover, that by sharing their ideas with others in extended conversations, students would arrive at deeper, more complex understandings of literary texts. Full-class discussion, of course, requires that the entire class have something in common to discuss – and so we set out to create a short story unit that would provide a common core of readings for our students to explore individually, in small groups, and as an entire class.

Given the heterogeneity of our classes, making the same texts accessible to all our students constituted a significant challenge. Acknowledging that no author can take into account the multitude of variations among individual readers, Carrell and Eisterhold (1983) propose that teachers "can approach the problem by manipulating either one of the two variables: the text and/or the reader" (p. 566). We discovered, however, that in order to address the inherent heterogeneity of our classes, to foster increased levels of reading comprehension, and to develop our students' independent reading skills, we could more profitably "manipulate" a third variable: the reading process.

The development of our short story unit was in keeping with this point of view. Rather than build reading activities around the content of particular stories (which we did not, in fact, choose in advance), we decided to create a set of content-free guidelines that students could use to approach each of the stories we would read as a class. Rather than provide students with specific background information before they began reading, we allowed them to wrestle with unfamiliar ideas, individually and with the support of their classmates, as a natural part of the reading process. Rather than preview content in order to develop a uniform level of reading comprehension, we encouraged students to use a variety of comprehension strategies while they were reading, as they worked to craft individual meanings from each of the texts they read.

Although we did not engage in overt schema building prior to reading, we did not overlook the importance of background knowledge when we chose stories for our students to read. Our hope was that each story would provide enough recognizable content to make it accessible to our students, while also presenting them with new information and encouraging them to entertain new ideas. We selected texts that we felt would leave room for a variety of interpretations, so that provocative student-generated discussions could take place.

Throughout the reading unit, we operated on the assumption that students' understandings would evolve as a result of several types of inter-actions with each story. An important part of the process was the use of story maps: graphic organizers that allow students to represent visually the meanings they derive from a text (see Hanf, 1971; Hyerle, 1996). Many reading theorists (Barnett, 1989; Grabe, 1991; Hudson, 1982; Mikulecky, 1984) have noted the effects of formal discourse structures on reading comprehension, as well as the importance of providing students with at least a basic orientation toward unfamiliar texts. In our short story unit, mapping proved to be an effective means of addressing these concerns. Before reading, students knew that they would be responsible for filling in a simple bubble map, provided by the teacher, that included spaces for the story's "who, when, where, what, why, and how" information. They were given several days to read the story and were required to complete their maps independently and to bring them to class. On a practical level, the story maps served as an effective homework check, while also providing a glimpse of students' initial understandings of the text.

Mapping proved to be a useful method for students on all points of the linguistic spectrum, both supporting and demonstrating their varying levels of comprehension. Finding the factual information (who, when, and where) was a manageable task for even the least proficient readers, and formulating critical interpretations related to the story's conflict and resolution (what, why, and how) offered an additional challenge for students who were prepared to work at this level from the start. As students compared their story maps with their classmates, they were able to confirm or to revise their factual understandings and to compare their personal interpretations, extending and building upon their initial readings of the text.

Group work played an essential role at virtually every stage of the process. Eskey and Grabe (1988) have described reading as entailing two levels of interaction: the interaction between the reader and the text, and the simultaneous interaction of various processing strategies within the reader. In our classrooms, we wished to add to this conception at least one other level: the social interactions of different readers as they worked together to make sense out of what they had read. While respecting the varying interpretations of individual readers, we attempted to structure group tasks that would encourage students to share their linguistic and cultural knowledge with one another as they engaged in the acts of reading, rereading, and deriving meaning from the texts.

We found it essential, as we charged students with the responsibility of constructing meaning together, to accept a range of approximative readings on their parts and to trust them to work toward more accurate understandings of the story within and among themselves. Maintaining such a stance toward the reading process required great discipline on my part. I often wanted to jump in and "correct" students' initial misinterpretations but soon saw how much more effective it was to let students work out as much as possible for themselves. Although they tended at first to look to me for answers when they disagreed with one another, students soon accepted their roles as co-teachers and called on me only when they were truly unable to work out an answer among themselves. On the rare occasions when a group arrived at a serious factual misinterpretation, I intervened with a provocative question intended to move them to another track. By encouraging students to work together, I was able to give them the space they needed to work out their own interpretations, while feeling confident that I had not left them completely "alone" with the text.

After building factual comprehension through reading, mapping, and comparing their understandings of the story at least twice in their small groups, we shifted our emphasis to interpretation, as students composed "opinion" questions that could be discussed by the entire class. As they moved toward critical analysis by generating interpretive questions, students continued to solidify their comprehension of the text. Advanced readers were often able to pose more complex questions, but less proficient readers also benefited from taking part in the question-composing process. (If one group member asked why a certain character fought with another one, for instance, another reader might learn, for the first time, that a fight had taken place.) Although my students sometimes asked surface-level comprehension or textbook-type questions about the readings, more often they generated meaningful, thought-provoking questions that they were genuinely interested in discussing with the rest of the class.

The importance of the students' questions was reinforced in the next stage of the process: the full-class discussion. Adapting methods presented by Gantzer (1995), we implemented a model of student-directed short story discussions in which we as teachers took little or no part. Rather, students discussed the literature freely among themselves, by posing and responding to the interpretive questions they had composed in their small groups. Any student could ask a question, and any student who wished to could respond. The teacher's role was to sit on the sidelines and to take notes on the conversation, paying particular attention to the students' levels and types of participation. It was difficult at times to resist the urge to take over in these discussions, particularly in the early stages as students struggled to establish a group process, and I often had to remind myself of Bartholomae and Petrosky's (1986) wise advice: "A course in reading and writing whose goal is to empower students must begin with silence, a silence that students must fill" (p. 7). Fostering increased participation on the part of our students means that we as teachers need to get out of the way. As Salvatori (1986) has noted, "[W]e must be prepared to be silent and they must be prepared to speak" (p. 154).

In our first discussions, students presented their questions in seemingly random order and tended to jump erratically from one idea to the next. We later discovered that the quality of the discussion improved considerably when we first reviewed, combined, and categorized the groups' questions together as a class; the questions were then publicly posted for easy reference during the discussion. This process fostered a sense of shared ownership of the questions and resulted in more balanced and coherent exchanges of ideas. Less vocal students could participate by simply reading a question from the list at the appropriate moment, and more active participants seemed less worried about getting "their" questions heard and showed more interest in listening to and building upon other students' ideas.

Although I initially worried about whether these student-based discussions would work effectively, I was generally pleased by the results. I was able, for the most part, to stay completely outside of the discussions and was impressed by the students' maturity as they articulated complex literary ideas. Because I wasn't worried about my own part in the discussion, moreover, I found myself able to attend more fully to the students, noticing interactions that I would likely have missed had I been caught up in the role of facilitator. One of the liveliest discussions was about "Alien Turf," an excerpt from Piri Thomas's *Down These Mean Streets*. Twenty-one of twenty-six students participated verbally, many of them connecting personally to the issues of racial prejudice and urban violence that are central to the story. As the end of the period approached, I pointed out that a few students had not yet spoken and wondered whether any of them wished to share their ideas. It was at this point that Desmond, an intense but quiet boy who had been listening attentively but silently throughout the forty-five-minute discussion, spoke up:

Everybody talking about gangs and violence, and I see that, too. But in my mind, that's not what the story's all about. When I was reading, I keep thinking what Piri really want is love from his father. Like when he was fighting and he was thinking what would his father say. Then at the end he knew his father loved him. When he say he'll bring the rollerskates, it's like he's saying that he really love his son.

Had I planned and led this discussion, I might or might not have pointed out the father-son relationship that is at the heart of the story. If I had, however, my introduction of this theme would not have carried nearly the same weight as Desmond's contribution did, for him personally as well for the rest of the class. Although I gave no response other than an impressed nod in Desmond's direction, there was a feeling throughout the classroom that the conversation had progressed to a different level as a result of his astute observation.

In general, students were extremely excited about the full-class discussion process, which was unlike anything they had experienced before; in their course evaluations, several of them cited these discussions as one of the semester's most worthwhile activities. A visiting teacher who sat in on one class was genuinely amazed by what she observed; she reported that it was the most sophisticated level of discussion she had ever heard among high school students, let alone students who were learning English as a second language. At the end of their final discussion, when I congratulated the students in one of my classes on their levels of participation and the depth of the ideas they had exchanged, they burst into a spontaneous round of applause for themselves!

The next step in the process was for students to write personal responses to each story in their reading journals. I found it effective to have students begin these responses just before our full-class discussions, as a way of focusing their attention and encouraging them to formulate ideas that they could then share with the rest of the class. They returned to their written responses after the discussion, using their journals to explore their reactions not only to the story but to the discussion itself. What was most striking was that every student, regardless of his or her level of English language proficiency, was able to formulate a two-page response to each story. Although some of these students would have been hard-pressed to write more than a few words after their initial readings, they were able to achieve solid understandings of the stories through the process of reading, rereading, and discussing each text.

After reflecting on the stories in their reading journals, students also wrote creative responses to them. Once they had read each story, they were given the options of writing an alternative ending, imagining the next chapter, or retelling the events of the story from another character's point of view. At the end of the short story unit, each student chose one creative response to revise, edit, and publish in final draft form. These creative writing assignments allowed students to demonstrate their understandings of the stories through yet another medium, and sharing them with their classmates contributed to the further broadening of each student's point of view. When we foster new kinds of reading-writing connections and allow students to use their imaginations, their creative responses contribute vitally to their understandings of the literature and help them to further develop their writing skills.

The process outlined here was time-consuming; we spent almost two weeks working through each short story. Most students were helped by the extended time and careful attention given to each of the stories; others, however, found the process somewhat repetitive. Although most students benefited from repeating familiar activities, we realized that we could guard against student restlessness in the future by varying the process slightly from text to text. Each group could be made responsible for the in-depth development of a particular section of a story map, for instance, which could then be presented to the rest of the class. Rather than relying exclusively on teacher-generated mapping strategies, students could also devise their own methods of responding graphically or pictorially to each text.

On the whole, we felt that the short story unit was successful in helping us to meet our major teaching objectives. Students became more confident readers and thinkers, as they read and interpreted a variety of challenging literary texts. They experienced literature as literature and acquired a working knowledge of basic literary elements: character, setting, conflict, and theme. Through full-class discussions, they developed skills in articulating and responding to ideas. Our guidelines had introduced a variety of reading strategies that could be used in approaching a range of literary texts. As the semester progressed, however, it became clear that our students were ready to apply similar processes more independently to a wider selection of texts. In our final reading unit, then, we sought a balance between the complete autonomy of reading workshop and the full-class orientation of the short story unit described above.

Book groups: Small-group reading and response

In our final reading unit, students were assigned to groups of three to five students who would all read the same novel. Students made their selections from an assortment of ten novels that reflected a range of reading levels, historical periods, and cultural perspectives. After hearing brief descriptions of the novels and looking them over in class, each student submitted a list of his or her top three choices. Assignments were made on the basis of reading level, group dynamics, and text availability.

Content-specific reading activities would be virtually impossible to design and implement with so many different books being read in each class. Just as we had created flexible guidelines that could be used with any short story in the previous reading unit, we now devised content-free activity guides that could be applied to any novel. Because of end-of-year time constraints, we could not give the same amount of time to the novels as we had to the short stories – a challenge for some of the less proficient readers but a relief for some of the upper-level students who were ready to forge ahead on their own. The novels' variations in length and linguistic complexity accommodated the different reading paces and language levels of individual readers; although the most advanced students had to read eighty pages of a full-length novel per week, the least advanced students were required to read only fifteen to twenty pages per week of a simpler text.

Group work remained an important component of the reading process, as did several other techniques that we had used in the short story unit. After reading the opening sections of their novels, for example, students made story maps that they compared and revised with the other members of their groups. Subsequent group activities included detailed character profiles and story timelines on which students graphed the positive or negative effects of five to ten significant events from the novel. In general, we found that visual activities, such as the story maps and timelines, made for more effective group work than tasks that were primarily language-based. The character profile, which involved a great deal of writing, proved to be cumbersome and unduly time-consuming; it would have been more effective and efficient, we felt, for students to represent similar information about the characters in graphic form.

The processes of question posing and journal writing were repeated in the novel unit as well. By this time, most students had become skilled at composing thoughtful questions about the deeper meanings of what they had read. I sensed, moreover, that they had internalized this strategy as part of the reading process. At the start of the short story unit, students sometimes took an entire period to come up with eight questions; during the novel unit, most groups were able to compose their questions much more quickly, suggesting that prior to consulting with their classmates, students had already begun to formulate interpretive questions, consciously or subconsciously, on their own.

These interpretive questions became the basis for students' journal entries, each of which was exchanged with and responded to by another member of the group. The quality of their written responses also improved, and their journals became places in which they could truly share and build upon one anothers' ideas. I found that the quality of my responses to students' journals improved as well, as a result of their more coherent thinking about their reading and my own familiarity with each of the texts being read. Rather than struggling to formulate a coherent reply (as I often did during reading workshop) or repeating ideas from one journal to the next (as was sometimes the case during the short story unit), I was able to engage in more varied and substantive written exchanges with each student. The fact that I read the students' journals only after they had exchanged them among themselves often added a layer to my observations, for I was able to comment on their interactions with one another, as well as their interpretations of the texts.

One of my most revealing teaching moments occurred toward the end of the semester, when I was reading journal responses that two students had written to the first several chapters of *Year of Impossible Goodbyes* by Sook Nyul Choi. Set in 1945, this autobiographical novel describes the Japanese occupation of North Korea during World War II through the eyes of its ten-year-old narrator, Sookan. Reflecting on the cruel treatment Sookan and her family received at the hands of the Japanese army, one student, Therese, wrote:

I don't think I would be as brave as Sookan if these things happened to me. I would hate the Japanese for taking away my language and making me speak Japanese. They wouldn't even let the family practice their Catholic religion. . . . Haiwon is lucky that she is safe at the convent. I wonder why the rest of the family don't go there so they could be safe too.

Responding to Therese's journal entry, her classmate Preema wrote:

I agree with you that this time was terrible for Sookan and her family. I also don't think I would be as brave as Sookan. . . . I have one question about your journal. You say Sookan's family is Catholic, but it is my understanding that they are Buddhist. I don't know, maybe this is my mistake. . . .

I was struck by the fact that two readers, both of them advanced ESL students with strong reading skills, could arrive at such different factual understandings of the same book. "It sounds as if you and Preema need to talk this over," I wrote in the margin of Therese's journal. "Maybe you should discuss your opinions about the family's religion in class." After returning their journals to them during the next class, I encouraged them to share their ideas further, each one showing the other evidence from the novel to support her point of view.

In fact, one generation of Sookan's family is Catholic and the other is Buddhist, and references to both religions occur frequently throughout the opening section of the book. Each student was amazed to discover what she had overlooked. After they had sorted through the textual information, I followed up by asking them what religious traditions their families observe. "I am Catholic," answered Therese. "Hindu and Buddhist," Preema replied, a smile of understanding spreading slowly across her face. It's remarkable, we agreed, how our individual experiences and values can influence our understandings of what we read.

Even more remarkable to me was the degree to which my students had learned to engage with literary texts, and with one another, in such a genuine and substantive fashion. Most remarkable of all, however, was the sheer delight I took in seeing them achieve these results with so little direct input from me. After "teaching" literature for several years, I was learning how to let my students learn to read.

Conclusion

We found great potential in each of the reading units described in this chapter and felt that the semester-long reading curriculum was successful on many levels. Through independent reading, full-class experiences, and book groups, we satisfied many of Grabe's (1991) recommendations for effective reading instruction, among them the development of content-centered, integrated curriculum – "the practice of silent, sustained reading; the reinforcement of specific reading skills and strategies; the use of group work and cooperative learning; and extensive reading" (p. 396).

This multiunit reading curriculum ultimately satisfied our stated teaching objectives as well. Students gained increased levels of fluency and competence as readers, discovering themselves capable of reading and responding to a wide range of authentic literary texts. The degree to which the readings contributed to our students' love of literature is harder to quantify; most of them, however, voiced positive responses to the stories and novels they read.

Through small-group activities and full-class discussions, students developed their conceptual abilities and learned to articulate, exchange, and build upon meaningful ideas. The steps outlined in our reading guidelines offered viable reading strategies for students at all levels and were transferable to a variety of literary texts.

My own growth as a teacher of reading, as I learned to step aside, allowing my students and their learning to take center stage, was as significant as my students' growth as readers over the course of the semester. The size and heterogeneity of my classes, although challenging at times, helped me to make this shift. Faced with twenty-five students at such varying levels of linguistic proficiency, I had no choice but to abandon the teacher-centered methods that had worked well enough in my leveled ESL classes in the past. I was compelled to relinquish my old approach for a new one – one that would prove, over time, to be much more satisfying to me and my students.

In subsequent classes, I have used similar approaches to the ones outlined in this chapter, adapting and refining them in relation to the demands of the curriculum and the needs of the students. The content-free guidelines developed for the short story unit have inspired similar sets of guidelines for full-class poetry and novel units. Student-generated questions now form the basis of almost all of my class discussions – about social studies content as well as literature – and I am continually amazed as I watch students in each new class establish their own unique methods of negotiating the discussion process among themselves. Although reading workshop and full-class literature units play notable roles in most of my classes, however, it is the use of book groups that has most transformed my teaching.

Book groups have come to form the heart of my teaching, and of my students' learning, each semester. By selecting groups of novels related to a common theme ("coming to America," "equalities and inequalities," or "adventure and survival"), I am able to meet the needs and interests of the wide range of students I encounter while still providing opportunities for full-class exchanges of ideas. With several different novels being read simultaneously in each of my classes, I can no longer be the primary owner of each text. As I circulate from group to group, helping students to address the issues they bring to my attention, I become a mentor and guide rather than a final authority. The use of book groups encourages – in fact, requires – me to take this role, thereby allowing my students to become expert advisers to one another as they establish their sense of ownership over a wide variety of literary texts.

Although group interactions play an important role in my students' literary experiences, perhaps most significant are the opportunities provided for students to derive intellectual satisfaction and personal meanings from the stories they read. I was particularly impressed by the opening paragraph of one student's final response to Rudolfo Anaya's *Bless Me, Ultima:*

This is the first big book I ever read in English. At first, I thought it is too long and hard for me, but after some time I became to really like the story. The people are Mexican like me, and some parts of the story were in Spanish. Sometimes I was confuse about what happen, but my group always help me to understand. I felt so good after I finish it, that I can read a book of 262 pages!

I, too, had originally feared that this novel would be too difficult for her, but Maria read consistently, participated enthusiastically in small-group activities, and wrote thoughtful journal responses to each section of the book. In her final essay, she offered a highly original analysis of the effects of World War II on each of the characters' lives. These connections were in no way explicit in the novel, and some of Maria's more advanced classmates struggled to meet the challenge. Buoyed by a sense of intellectual investment, personal, connection, and the support of her classmates, however, Maria was able to construct her own meaning from a demanding literary text. It is not too much, I have learned, to expect all our ESL students to do the same.

References

Atwell, N. (1987). *In the middle: Writing, reading and learning with adolescents.* Portsmouth, NH: Boynton/Cook.

Barnett, M. A. (1989). *More than meets the eye: Foreign language teaching theory and practice.* Englewood Cliffs, NJ: Prentice Hall Regents.

Bartholomae, D., & Petrosky, A. R. (1986). Facts, artifacts and counterfacts: A basic reading and writing course for the college curriculum. In D. Bartholomae & A. R. Petrosky (Eds.), *Facts, artifacts and counterfacts* (pp. 3–43). Portsmouth, NH: Boynton/Cook.

Calkins, L. M. (1986). *The art of teaching writing.* Portsmouth, NH: Heinemann Educational Books.

Carrell, P. L., & Eisterhold, J. C. (1983). Schema theory and ESL reading pedagogy. *TESOL Quarterly, 17*(4), 553–573.

Eskey, D. E., & Grabe, W. (1988). Interactive models for second language learning. In P. L. Carrell, J. Devine, & D. E. Eskey (Eds.), *Interactive approaches to second language learning* (pp. 223–238). New York: Cambridge University Press.

Gantzer, J. (1995). Lecture/presentation at the School for International Training. Brattleboro, VT.

Grabe, W. (1991). Current developments in second language reading research. *TESOL Quarterly, 25* (3), 375–399.

Graves, D. H. (1983). *Writing: Teachers and children at work.* Portsmouth, NH: Heinemann Educational Books.

Hanf, B. M. (1971). Mapping: A technique for translating reading into thinking. *Journal of Reading, 6*, 225–230.

Hudson, T. (1982). The effects of induced schemata on the "short circuit" in L2 reading: No-decoding factors in L2 reading performance. *Language Learning, 32*(1), 3–31.

Hyerle, D. (1996). Thinking maps: Seeing is understanding. *Educational Leadership, 53*(4), 85–89.

Mikulecky, B. S. (1984). Reading skills instruction in ESL. *On TESOL 84.* Alexanderia, VA: TESOL.

Salvatori, M. (1986). The dialogical nature of basic reading and writing. In D. Bartholomae & A. R. Petrosky (Eds.), *Facts, artifacts and counterfacts* (pp. 137–166). Portsmouth, NH: Boynton/Cook.

Suggested readings

Carrell, P. L., Devine, J., & Eskey, D. E. (Eds.) (1988). *Interactive approaches to second language learning.* New York: Cambridge University Press. See in particular the following chapters in this volume: J. Devine, A case study of two readers: Models of reading and reading performance, pp. 127–139; J. Devine, The relationship between general language competence and second language reading proficiency: Implications for teaching, pp. 260–277; D. E. Eskey, Holding in the bottom: An interactive approach to the language problems of second language readers, pp. 93–100; W. Grabe, Reassessing the term "interactive," pp. 56–70; P. Rigg, The miscue-ESL project, pp. 206–219.

Dixon, C. N., and Nessel, D. N. (1992). *Meaning making: Directed reading and thinking activities for second language students.* Englewood Cliffs, NJ: Prentice Hall Regents.

Freeman, Y. S., and Freeman, D. E. (1992). *Whole language for second language learners.* Portsmouth, NH: Heinemann.

Gajdusek, L. (1988). Toward wider use of literature in ESL: Why and how. *TESOL Quarterly, 22*(2), 227–257.

Goodman, K. S. (1992). I didn't find whole language; whole language found me. *The Reading Teacher, 46*, 188–199.

Halliday, M. (1984). Three aspects of children's language development: Learning language, learning through language, and learning about language. In M. Halliday (Ed.), *Oral and written language development research: Implications for instruction.* Urbana, IL: NCTE.

Krashen, S. (1982). *Principles and practice in second language acquisition.* New York: Pergamon Press.

Oster, J. (1989). Seeing with different eyes: Another view of literature in the ESL class. *TESOL Quarterly, 23*(1), 85–103.

Probst, R. E. (1988). *Response and analysis: Teaching literature in the junior and senior high school.* Portsmouth, NH: Heinemann Educational Books.

Rigg, P. (1991). Whole language in TESOL. *TESOL Quarterly, 25*(3), 521–539.

Rosenblatt, L. (1983). *Literature as exploration* (4th ed.). New York: The Modern Language Association of America.

Silberstein, S. (1994). *Techniques and resources in teaching reading.* New York: Oxford University Press.

Smith, F. (1985). *Reading without nonsense.* New York: Teachers College Press.

Spack, R. (1985). Literature, reading, writing, and ESL: Bridging the gaps. *TESOL Quarterly, 19*(4), 703–724.

Stanovich, K. E. (1980). Toward an interactive-compensatory model of individual differences in the development of reading fluency. *Reading Research Quarterly, 16*, 32–71.

4 Rewriting is more than just writing again

Patricia Sackville

If you walk into my classroom, you will probably think that it isn't very high-tech for an institute of technology. This white room contains blue rectangular tables and gray plastic and metal chairs. There are a white board, windows, and brown curtains, and the walls are made of bricks painted a smooth, glossy white. There are an overhead projector and a pull-down screen hanging at the front of the room. There are people too – twenty students ranging from nineteen to fifty years old. Some are from Asia, some from the Middle East, one from Africa, and a couple from South America, for a total of fifteen men and five women. And, of course, there is me, the teacher who comes from Vancouver by way of Japan.

I teach business and technical writing to adult students who have English as an additional language (EAL). My students at the British Columbia Institute of Technology (BCIT) are in a preentry program that prepares them to meet the English requirement for entry into a full-time technology or trades program at BCIT.

I have been teaching at BCIT for ten years. In this formal educational institution, I have to keep attendance and give grades. These are parts of my job that do not come naturally for me. Grading feels like a huge responsibility because grades greatly affect students, opening them to or closing them off from future opportunities. After many years of struggle, trying to figure out what was expected of me as a teacher and what felt right to me in the classroom, I have recently let students rewrite graded assignments as many times as they want to do so. It means more work for them and for me, but I think it increases their learning by engaging them in what Lave and Wenger (1991) refer to as "authentic practice," the practice of ordinary techniques used by writers in the workplace. Also, it makes me feel more comfortable with the grades I give to the students. In this chapter, I reflect on the experience of allowing students to rewrite graded work as often as they choose to do so. I describe my teaching context and trace my thinking during the ten years that I have taught at BCIT. I use situated learning theory to support my argument: By rewriting work that counts, students become writers.

BC college and institute system

The "college and institute" system in British Columbia (BC) is made up of four types of institutions: community colleges, university colleges, technical institutes, and the Open Learning Agency (Ministry of Education, Skills, and Training, 1996). Institutes like BCIT, with a provincewide market, have a mandate to be on the leading edge in their respective fields, and BCIT prides itself in equipping graduates with job-ready skills. BCIT, which opened in 1964, offers certificate (one-year programs), diploma (two-year programs), advanced diploma (specialty programs for people with diplomas), and degree programs (those articulated with university programs) in business, engineering, and health technologies and in trades. In recent years, 6,000 full-time students and 36,000 part-time students have been enrolled in BCIT. The preentry program in which I teach has more than 800 part-time students a year, and courses are taught by twelve to fifteen part-time studies contract instructors (Vance, Fitzpatrick, & Sackville, 1998).

The preentry program

The preentry program of BCIT's Communication Department helps students meet the English requirement for full-time study at BCIT. Courses in this program are geared to teaching primarily EAL students the language skills they need to succeed in BCIT full-time programs, and they focus on business and technical English for the workplace. One of my courses (Comm 0004) focuses on the writing of paragraphs using cause and effect, comparison, classification, and other rhetorical devices commonly used to support main ideas in business and technical writing. The next course in the progression (Comm 0005) focuses on the writing of memos and letters. These are the two courses I will discuss in this chapter.

Students meet either for six hours on Saturdays or for four hours on each of two evenings during the week. A course runs for eleven to fourteen weeks, depending on the schedule, for a total of eighty-four hours. Every class involves a bit of lecture, some group work, individual writing time, and sharing of written work for peer and teacher feedback. Students are expected to write approximately one graded assignment per week.

My professional development

I'm standing on the train platform at busy Shinjuku station in Tokyo when a foreigner like me comes up with a look of desperation on her face. Thinking she's going to ask for directions, I make a mental note of where the various exits are and where they lead. "Do you want to teach an English class? I'm leaving the country and need to find a replacement," she says.

I never planned to be a teacher. I acquired my first teaching experience rather accidentally while I was in Japan. Teaching English was just a way to make money while traveling. None of my classes was very formal, some being just "conversation" over dinner in a restaurant or company cafeteria. But I discovered that I really liked teaching. It was engaging and even fun. I was a foreign "expert," and students seemed to want to learn to use English the way I did.

After two and a half years in Japan, I returned to Canada and began teaching at BCIT. I started as an eager beaver teacher wanting to fit in at BCIT, but I was young and inexperienced. Actually, I felt like a fake and did not want my colleagues to know how ad hoc my teaching had been in Japan where my white skin and Canadian accent were my selling points. I did not want them to know that a Japanese interviewer had said that he wanted to hire me because I was female and my students would be young male engineers who needed female company.

At BCIT, I was not very comfortable calling myself a teacher, for I did not really know what I was doing or why I was doing it. I just copied others. For example, at BCIT, grading is an important part of a teacher's job. This was new to me; in Japan I did not assign or evaluate work. In learning to copy other teachers at BCIT I had to master the "local dialect" for grading; I learned "pass," "fail," "satisfactory," "unsatisfactory," the difference between 50 percent, 55 percent, and 60 percent, and other technical terms. Dialogue about grading seemed to dominate my experience in those first few years, and I saw my task as learning to be tough enough with students so that I was not passing people who were not ready to meet the difficult demands of their future full-time programs.

In my early years at BCIT, I wanted to avoid giving failing grades, so I asked students to rewrite work as a way to postpone grading until the work was acceptable. But I found that I was passing students who weren't really as capable as they seemed, because I told them how to correct their work. They just did what I told them, often without knowing why. I then gave up allowing rewriting altogether because it was too hard to help students without giving them answers. I began to believe that if students did not understand how to write, they did not belong at BCIT. Several colleagues had voiced that opinion, and I was worried that they would think I was too soft and that I did not understand the grading standards.

In my mind, I had made it over some kind of hurdle: I had become tough enough to maintain BCIT standards by giving failing grades. You see, officially, BCIT does not teach EAL. Students are expected to have well-developed language skills before they arrive, so they are not taught English language skills. They are taught technical writing skills, and many instructors in the Communication Department view these skills as being quite distinct from language skills. "Writing standards" are couched in terms of maintaining workplace writing standards as dictated by employers; the support of EAL students does not have a place in this scheme. EAL students are seen as belonging in the preentry program, where they study language until they are ready for real-world writing.

Because of budget cutbacks and the cost-recovery requirement of the program I taught in, there seemed to be no way I could get a permanent position at the institute. I got discouraged and put the minimum effort into my job. The ratings I received on student course evaluations seemed to be going down along with my enthusiasm. I felt like a failure.

The student evaluations I received at the end of one term really stand out in my mind. Comments like "unfair," "full of mean tricks," and "hard on EAL students" really hurt me. I did not like the person I had become. One night I dreamed I was yelling at students and they were refusing to do what I wanted. They began to stand on their heads, and I screamed, "Those with legs up in the air will fail." I woke up saddened but with the vague feeling that there was something insightful to be learned about the importance of students in the teaching process.

In order to keep teaching in the preentry program, I needed to get certification as an EAL instructor, and I returned to university to get a diploma. Ironically, while upgrading my education to better enable me to teach language skills, I began to question the distinction between language skills and technical-writing skills. Through my research, I no longer thought that students had to reach a certain level of English proficiency before they could engage in technical writing. I began to view language acquisition as a more integrated process that involved learning about grammar and mechanics at the same time as learning to write letters, memos, and other technical documents. When I read about the Whole Language philosophy, which views the whole as more than the sum of its parts (Goodman, 1986), I was very excited to find that I was not the only one opposed to the isolation of language skills.

I continued studying to get my master's degree in education and was introduced to many theories that expanded my thinking about teaching and learning. Situated learning theory, in particular, stood out because of its underlying belief that learning is something that takes place in social interactions rather than in the mind (Brown & Duguid, 1993). It was this emphasis on social context that interested me as I was trying to make the classroom experience feel right. Indeed, if practice was such an important resource to learning (Lave & Wenger, 1991), then rewriting could be justified on educational grounds.

Something inside me had changed. I shifted my focus from maintaining standards to interacting with students. I wanted students to be satisfied with my course, and I wanted to enjoy what I was doing. I wanted to share my ideas, ideas I developed by struggling with theory and trying to test it all out for myself in my work context. I didn't want to focus on whether a student belonged in my course. I wanted to engage all students, no matter what level they were at. I wanted to allow each student to participate more fully in the class. I wanted to create a rich and productive environment so that all students could be writers. I didn't want them to think that they had to wait until their English was good enough before they could engage in the practice of technical writing.

I decided to try rewriting again because it was the most authentic activity that I could think of for a writer. According to situated learning theory, learning focuses on building connections from learners to the world of practice, where the learning is actually applied (Lave & Wenger, 1991). If EAL students are to learn to become workplace writers, they need the opportunity to sit down with a more experienced colleague and discuss their writing. I am trying to be that more experienced colleague for them. Working with students, no matter how low their level of English, has become the focus of the class rather than the nuisance I had come to view it as.

Recently, I have been mentoring student teachers who need classroom experience as part of their university linguistics degree. As a mentor, I want to open myself up to scrutiny – here is what I do, here is what I struggle with, here is what I believe, here is what I don't know – reflecting on it all myself while sharing it with . . . you.

The rewriting process

Here is what I have been doing lately and why I think it works.

Making expert knowledge explicit

The first time I read an assignment, I do so aloud with an individual student. I circle problems, underline unclear parts, and make general comments about the organization of the writing. I do not name the errors, and I do not grade the writing. I discuss my comments with the student, asking what he or she is trying to say in the unclear parts. We discuss grammar as well as organization. For example, many students make errors in verb tense, so our discussion focuses on the problems I face as a reader trying to understand the timing of events in the writing.

Discussion about organization often includes information about the standard patterns of English paragraphs and how these patterns differ from common patterns in other languages. I get students to verbalize what they do when they write to help make their thinking more explicit. And then I can share my thought processes when I write, helping them to understand the expectations of readers in a Canadian workplace.

First-draft discussion involves making my "expert" knowledge explicit to the student. We talk about the student's writing and my reactions to it as a reader, and the student learns more about the discourse associated with workplace writing in English. For example, the student learns the importance of gearing writing to a certain audience and purpose in a business memo and how this involves more than knowledge of grammar. Swales (1990) refers to learning a discourse as a means of being initiated into a group, a way for a novice to learn to talk like an experienced practitioner.

For example, I might tell a student that an idea is underdeveloped in a paragraph. I would describe how I had expected certain points to be discussed because they were mentioned in the opening sentence. Because they were not elaborated on, I was confused when I read the paragraph. I would mention that in technical writing the English reader may seem lazy compared to readers of other languages because everything has to be described directly and completely rather than only alluded to. Through this discussion, the student learns how English readers think and why it is important for a writer to know how English readers think.

After I clarify what it is students are trying to say, I ask how else they might express their ideas. Often the words they use verbally are better than the words they have written. The act of verbalizing an idea seems to improve the expression of it, so I tell them to write what they told me.

Full access to practice

Because BCIT communication courses focus on business and technical writing, it makes sense to me to treat students as if they were employees in the workplace. When writing at work, employees share drafts with others and rely on this feedback to make their written documents clear and correct. In fact, many companies hire in-house technical writers or editors to help with this feedback function. I have tried to duplicate this process in my EAL classroom.

After we discuss their first drafts, students then work on improving the piece of writing either in class if there is time or at home. I read the second version and give feedback again. If the writing is acceptable, I give it a passing grade. If it still needs more work to meet the minimum passing standard for the course, I give comments once again and talk to the students, and the rewriting process continues. In my classes, many students choose to keep rewriting so that they can improve even a passing grade. Like experienced writers, my students learn that there may never be an end to the revision process. A writer can always change and improve the work, but there are deadlines. My students run out of time when the course finishes.

When discussing a draft assignment, I legitimate a student's knowledge and understanding of writing, and this allows the student to engage more fully in a real and complex activity that experienced writers engage in – sharing drafts with colleagues for feedback. Moving from peripheral activities to more complex elements of a practice is how Lave and Wenger (1991) would explain this process. My students move from studying language (that is, English grammar and sentence structure) to learning to struggle with the production of a piece of writing that communicates to a real reader.

After useful feedback and many chances to get the writing as good as they can, my students seem to feel better about the grading process. They seem to have a better understanding of how I go about judging their work. My thinking becomes more visible to them. By learning to think like more professional writers, students learn to be more like experts, what situated learning theorists call *becoming progressively more involved in a community of practice* (see Lave & Wenger, 1991). Rewriting allows students the opportunity to become more and more engaged in the practice of communicating clearly.

Final thoughts

One evening, a student teacher I was mentoring said, "You really enjoy teaching!" I stood there, my face flushed from the energy generated by the discussion I had just had with a student about his writing, and I thought about how true it is. I enjoy teaching! I have found my way back to the feelings I had in Japan when I first started.

Rewriting, as part of a structured process of dialogue, allows students to learn from their mistakes in time for it to make a difference to their grades. Because structured rewriting provides students with the opportunity to discuss their work with an expert reader, they engage in an authentic practice of writers in the workplace who share drafts with colleagues in order to get useful feedback. Rewriting involves so much more than just writing again.

References

Brown, J. S., & Duguid, P. (1993). Stolen knowledge. *Educational Technology, 33*(3),10–15. With an introduction by Hilary McLellan, guest editor.

Goodman, K. (1986). *What's whole in whole language?* Portsmouth, NH: Heinemann.

Lave, J., & Wenger, E. (1991). *Situated learning: legitimate peripheral participation*. Cambridge: Cambridge University Press.

Ministry of Education, Skills, and Training (1996). *Charting a new course: A strategic plan for the future of British Columbia's College, Institute and Agency system*. Victoria, BC: Ministry of Education, Skills, and Training (MEST), March.

Swales, J. M. (1990). *Genre analysis: English in academic and research settings*. Cambridge: Cambridge University Press.

Vance, K., Fitzpatrick, D., & Sackville, P. (1998). Computer mediated communication inside a classroom: An experiment using CMC technology with ELT students. *Canadian Journal of Educational Communication, 26*(3), 175–188.

5 Action for understanding

A study in teacher research with exploratory practice

Kimberly A. Johnson

Teachers doing research is not a new idea. Teachers draw upon knowledge, training, and the experiences of teaching to construct their own theories of teaching and to understand or improve their practice (Richards & Lockhart, 1994); hence classroom research is a potentially important component of both personal and professional development. Rather than relying solely on generalizations or input provided by outside researchers, teachers can re-search for resolution of problems or increased understanding in the context of an individual class or situation. In fact, many teachers are researching ideas all the time, whether they are aware of it or not. "If . . . one of your goals is to improve the quality of your teaching, then you will ask some relevant questions, hypothesize some possible answers or solutions, put the solutions to a practical tryout in the classroom, look for certain results, and weigh those results in some manner to determine whether your hypothesized answer held up or not" (Brown, 1994, p. 437). Since one goal of professional development is to improve the quality of classroom practice and another is to improve the working lives of teachers, it stands to reason that exposure to more formal methods of teacher research, in addition to Brown's example of unconscious or informal research, would serve teachers well.

By doing classroom research, teachers can make valuable contributions in personal and professional development as well as beyond the classroom in "both the creation of knowledge and the development, monitoring and maintenance of innovations, in teaching methods as well as in classroom organization and curriculum development, materials and institutional cultures" (McDonough & McDonough, 1997, p. 233–234). In this chapter, I will focus on my own experience with exploratory practice in the classroom to solve my dilemma with the sequencing of activities, and I will use my experience to illustrate the ease with which I was able to increase my understanding of this one aspect of classroom practice. Finally, I will express the enthusiasm that exploratory practice has brought to my own teaching and the implications it has for other language teachers.

60

Exploratory practice

Exploratory practice encourages teachers to reflect on and identify an area that they wish to better understand, but it recognizes that reflection and contemplation may in and of themselves not lead to "understanding." "Exploratory practice is a step toward a serious attempt to understand the current situation *before* an innovation is tried out" (Allwright, 1992, p. 15). Not everyone agrees with this, of course. Donald Schön (1983) argues that change and understanding are inexorably linked to one another and that understanding is oriented by interest in change and change is what enhances understanding. Exploratory practice argues that action for understanding, *without the addition of extra burdens on the teacher*, should precede change, for it is possible that increased understanding will lead a teacher to the conclusion that no changes are necessary at all. On the other hand, increased understanding may lead the teacher to conclude that change is desirable, in which case the teacher can formulate and initiate an action research plan.

Exploratory practice begins with the identification of a puzzle that involves questioning, thought, and discussion to gauge the degree of understanding reached (Allwright & Lenzuen, 1997, p. 74). The notion of puzzling over something is far less threatening; a *puzzle* is, by its very nature, less clear-cut and more open-ended, and puzzles are suited for discussion of successes as well as failures. Exploring successful ideas (puzzling, for example, about why something seems to work so well) may shed light on just what makes good teaching good, and that will be beneficial for increased understanding for that teacher and could have positive implications for the larger teaching community when that insight is shared (Allwright & Bailey, 1991).

Once the puzzle is identified, teachers need to formulate the puzzle into a question, look for plausible or alternative ways of thinking about that question, and then ask what can be done to gain more insight. An important characteristic of exploratory practice is that insight should be attained without disruption to the established routine, and this can be achieved using familiar classroom procedures and strategies that complement the things teachers do normally in the classroom (Allwright, 1992; Richards & Lockhart, 1994).

Exploratory practice also encourages teachers to create or alter activities to generate data, if needed, to provide the means of understanding the puzzle. Even videotaping a class session to collect data to reflect on may be disruptive and time-consuming (Richards & Lockhart, 1994, p. 11).

Exploratory practice encourages teachers to collect data in a way that is unintrusive and will not hinder teaching or learning (Allwright, 1999b), and this, in my opinion, is one of the real strengths of exploratory practice. Data can be generated by building monitoring into regular classroom activities, "where ordinary and familiar classroom language learning activities are adapted and developed for their investigative potential, without losing any of their potential for language development" (Allwright, 1999a, p. 10). It is possible to exploit the language benefit of an activity that will also generate data which teachers can use to increase understanding and/or evaluate the need for any changes. The advantage of collecting such data in the language classroom arises, of course, from the fact that activities regularly conducted in the classroom, utilizing the target language, can themselves become ways of monitoring to research the "puzzle." These include learner diaries or journals, group discussion work, note taking on relevant discussion topics, poster sessions, surveys, and problem-solving activities (Allwright, 1991; Allwright & Bailey, 1991).

Personal experience

The puzzle and action for understanding

In the spring of 1999, I taught an advanced adult ESL course entitled Developing Fluency that met two evenings a week for two-and-a-half hour lessons at the University of Minnesota. The primary focus of the course was the improvement of speaking and listening skills utilizing a textbook and authentic reading and listening materials that included audio, video, and guest speakers. During the initial needs analysis, the students themselves had identified discussion skills as a priority, and at the students' request I also included work on aspects of pronunciation in the course.

The class consisted of fourteen adult students from Azerbaijan, the People's Republic of China, Guadalupe, Japan, Korea, Poland, Russia, and Spain. It was a mixed group of au pairs, businesspeople working full time in the community, and postdoctoral fellows in various departments at the university. All had regular interactions with English speakers in their workplaces or at the university, and many participated regularly in meetings, discussions, and seminars. To complement our work on discussion strategies and language (for giving opinions, interrupting, and so on), each student was expected to lead a class discussion on a topic of his or her choosing beginning during the third week of the course. All selected a reading that they copied and distributed to their classmates during the class period before they were to lead the discussion, and the leaders were expected to begin, facilitate, and conclude the discussion.

My puzzle sprang from my concerns about the sequencing of activities, specifically the scheduling of the student-led discussions. Activity sequencing was partly determined by outside factors – the availability of the audio language lab, for example – and I was comfortable with my conscious as well as intuitive sense of how to arrange the lessons. In previous courses I had felt comfortable that lessons and the sequencing of activities seemed to work well.

But the student-led discussions were different, and did indeed puzzle me. They were a separate thirty-minute "chunk" that could be dropped anywhere into the lesson. Given the late hour and busy lives of the students (all of whom came to class following a busy workday), the students were "freshest" and less fatigued at the beginning of the two-and-a-half hour lesson, so it made sense to start with new or difficult material at the beginning. Common sense led me to sequence activities in the following manner: grammar or introduction of new ideas at the beginning of class, practice and review of new material and material from previous lessons, and then student-led discussion as the final activity. This had seemed to work during the previous term, during which I had initially scheduled student-led discussions at different times during the lessons for various reasons but finally settled into a routine of doing the discussions as the final activity. So what was the puzzle?

I had a nagging sense lingering from the previous term that I was not being fair to the students. I worried that scheduling the student-led discussions for the end of class time was doing a disservice to the students by asking them to engage their classmates and to practice what they had learned, and be evaluated for their performance, at the time in class when they were most fatigued. This nagging worry pushed me to reflect critically on my reasons for sequencing activities as I had, pondering not only what worked best, but why.

But reflection alone didn't seem to settle the puzzle. I hesitated to launch into an action research project because I wasn't convinced that the current sequencing was a problem. Until I felt that was warranted, I did not want to disrupt the class. Exploratory practice offered me something between the two, providing the means to "research" this question on my own by incorporating it directly into the lesson plan. My puzzle was well suited to the two basic principles of exploratory practice: Understanding is necessary before change, and teaching and learning must not be disrupted but, rather, promoted, if possible (Allwright, 1999a). To begin, I formulated a specific research question from my puzzle: Given the circumstances of the busy lives of these students, who often come to class weary after having already completed a full day at work or research, when is the best time to schedule the student-led discussion required of each student?

Now into the second week of a ten-week term, the students had worked on giving and sharing opinions. During the third week, in a lesson that focused on discussion phrases and effective discussion tactics, I broke the class (twelve students present) into four groups of three students. Following our discussion of tactics and the language of "rephrasing," "conceding a point," "agreeing," and "disagreeing," we did a short, structured exercise that asked students to practice as many of these tactics as possible and to consciously monitor themselves and their use of these tactics. This worked well, with students consciously attempting to utilize many of the phrases that we had identified earlier.

I followed this with a less-structured exercise, designed to gather data for my own puzzle (see Appendix). With the student-led discussions scheduled to begin during the following class period, I provided each group of three with a list of the activities scheduled for the next class and asked them to organize the activities. Because I wanted the activities to "promote thoughtful articulation . . . rather than the thoughtless provision of instant answers" (Allwright, 1992, p. 1), I asked them to think carefully about their reasons for choosing to sequence the activities the way they did. I asked them to practice the discussion techniques we had been learning in an authentic situation – to discuss and form a consensus on the sequence of activities for the following lesson. After each group had finished, I combined the groups to form two groups of six. Each group reviewed the schedule that each of the smaller groups had created and attempted to form a consensus as a larger group. This larger grouping generated a great deal of discussion (continuing for the most part to use the tactics we had practiced) as they voiced opinions and discussed how to form a consensus, which they then listed on posters, for example:

Group A	Group B
Pronunciation warm-up	Pronunciation warm-up
Enunciation of vowel sounds	Enunciation of vowel sounds
Finish Tape Assignment 1	Finish Tape Assignment 1
Student-led discussion	Unit 4: Listening Exercise 1
Break	Unit 4: Listening Exercise 2
Unit 4: Listening Exercise 1	Break
Unit 4: Listening Exercise 2	Unit 4: Specialized adjectives
Unit 4: Specialized adjectives	Discussion to prepare for speaker
Discussion to prepare for speaker	Student-led discussion

Afterward, each poster was mounted at the front of the class, and we discussed the schedules and any differences that existed. Because I had asked them to also think of *why* they would schedule activities when they did, we had a whole-class discussion on why groups scheduled the activities as they did. After ten minutes of discussion, and with class ending, we were unable to agree on all eight activities, including the student-led discussion. I had learned, however, that all the students wanted the discussions held either as the final activity before the break or as the final activity of the day. I felt that I had gained some insight into the factors deemed most important by the students: fatigue, logistics, and logical sequencing of activities. Fatigue was understandable, and everyone (teacher included!) was tired after a long day. Logistics was an issue because of the scheduled hour in the audio lab. I found the logic of keeping activities together very interesting. One student commented that it was "logical to start with pronunciation" prior to any speaking tasks, and there was unanimous consensus on that issue. Another aspect of sequencing things logically involved keeping the textbook exercises, in the order they appear in the text, together in the lesson. Although I indicated that students could arrange the schedule any way that they chose to, none wanted to break the textbook exercises apart. I am not certain why students felt it important to keep the exercises together; perhaps it is consistency or familiarity, perhaps a recognition that the textbook exercises build on one another.

Student "ownership" of the class also entered into the discussion, and although it may not have figured directly into their decisions about the sequencing of the lesson, I believe that it certainly affected the students and the course of the discussion. Their interest in the lesson was heightened by an understanding of their stake in it. I believe that it contributed to the interested atmosphere and the nature of the discussion as they attempted to form a consensus as a class. This was an exciting and unanticipated benefit of my exploratory practice project, and I will return to this in the following section.

When sequencing the activities for the next lesson, I used all that was agreed upon and based my decisions about the remaining activities on the priorities the students had set in our discussion:

Pronunciation warm-up
Enunciation of vowel sounds
Finish Tape Assignment 1
Unit 4: Listening Exercise 1
Break
Unit 4: Listening Exercise 2
Unit 4: Specialized adjectives
Discussion to prepare for speaker
Student-led discussion

In the end, the student-led discussion remained as the final activity, just as I'd done the previous term. The difference was that the students realized that they themselves had a say in how the class was organized, and I now felt confident that they were most comfortable with that schedule. I had also gained insight into what factors the students considered relevant when sequencing activities, and I came to a surprising realization of the importance of their understanding of their own role in the class as well.

The analysis and interpretation

Although there was no consensus, I feel that the discussion was valuable and the results were positive. The animated, lively, and sometimes argumentative discussions in progressively larger groups, on a topic that concerned them directly, not only provided me with data for my own "research" but served a legitimate, and obvious, linguistic purpose itself. Because the students were able to tell me *why* they scheduled activities when they did and articulated factors to consider such as fatigue, logical sequencing, and logistical considerations, I felt more in tune with their concerns and priorities. In the end, I decided when we would do the student-led discussion, leaving it at the end of each lesson as I'd done before, but I now knew that the learners preferred to have it at the end of a lesson, or at least as the final activity before the break, and I understood why. Having listened to their discussion and made notes for myself and recorded my impressions immediately after class, I had what I assumed was a good idea of what was important to the learners in general, as well as the specifics of scheduling activities. They seemed to enjoy the lesson very much, and I sought confirmation on that as well. I wanted feedback.

To accomplish this, I began our next lesson (the one that they had scheduled) with an overhead transparency outlining the schedule of activities for the day. I explained the changes that I had made and my reasons for doing so. One of our first activities was to complete an audiotape assignment that we had begun the week before. The first part required students to practice pronouncing unfamiliar words by using the pronunciation keys in their dictionaries. The second part of the assignment listed two questions eliciting opinions on topics we had discussed in class and required students to record these on their audiocassettes. The point of this part of the assignment was to allow me to evaluate their pronunciation and to permit them to practice impromptu speaking. I saw this as a perfect opportunity to get the feedback on the lesson-scheduling activity from the previous class. I added a third opinion question for those students who finished early to include on their tape. This question asked them to comment on whether they enjoyed the discussion activity and to reflect on what factors were most important in determining where they placed activities. As it turned out, only six of the fourteen students had time to answer this final question, but I believe that it was sufficient for my purposes.

The taped opinions confirmed my impression that they had liked the activity. All were positive about the practice with discussion skills, and some liked it because it gave them the opportunity to use those skills in a "real" situation. One student remarked enthusiastically that it was "fun and I liked to discuss a real thing," and another commented, "I liked the discussion we had because it was nice to be involved in what's going on in the class. It's a very good thing." Giving students an opportunity to make decisions about what occurred in the classroom through this simple activity not only provided me with insight but also fostered in them the awareness that they were an integral part of the class. During their discussions, I had heard two students disagreeing about the placement of a listening activity in the lesson, one arguing that they should schedule it as we had done in prior lessons because "that's Kimberly's way." When I intervened to reassure the group that they needn't do things the way we had always done them, but that this was their opportunity to schedule things the way they wanted, it seemed to really open up the discussion. I believe that this experience, in which I took their opinions seriously and asked them for input on how to structure the lesson, helped the students realize that this was *our* class, not just mine, and that their input was valuable and important to me.

Student awareness of the importance of their role in the classroom is a lesson I will take with me from this experience. Although this insight was not part of my motivation or expectations when I began this research, I found it to be surprising and valuable. Although I do negotiate syllabi and have often adjusted a syllabus to adapt to learners' needs or wishes, it seemed to have a different impact when they saw immediate results. Other students in the past have commented positively on my flexibility, but I wonder whether some students have viewed that flexibility as arbitrary, or maybe my catering to particular students over others. One of the lessons that I have drawn from this project is the importance of being honest with students, telling them specifically that I respect their wishes and then demonstrating that I do by allowing them the freedom to make some of the decisions about the class. And asking them to form a consensus puts the onus on them – they have a vested interest in participating and being heard because they will all have to live with the result. As a teacher, I am freed, too, to an extent, from feeling that I may indeed be shortchanging someone in the class because I cannot do everything for everyone.

All the students named fatigue as an important factor in their decision to schedule activities as they had. There was discussion about logical sequencing (keeping all the activities from the book together, for example), staggering various skill activities (breaking up listening with speaking, for example), and keeping an eye on the logistics of time and space (what we should do in the audio lab or what should come before and after the break). This provided me with some insight into the issues deemed relevant by the students.

Regarding my initial puzzle about where to place the student-led discussion, this activity and the feedback provided me with an answer to one of my questions: No, students did not feel that the discussion should come at the beginning of the class when they were freshest. Both in the whole class discussion and in the feedback from the audiotapes, nearly every student indicated fatigue as a vital factor in the sequencing of activities. But although I worried that students would be better served to lead discussion when they were least tired, none of the students felt the same way. On the contrary, they all felt that the discussion was an interesting and interactive activity that should come at the end *precisely* because that was when they were most tired. They stated that such an activity "wakes them up" and is a good way to end the lesson. This provided me with the understanding I sought, and I felt that my puzzle was solved and anything more (in this context, anyway) was unnecessary.

Conclusion

Teachers are very busy, and the prospect of launching into the realm of researcher, on top of the many things that a teacher already does, can be quite intimidating. Exploratory practice is a vital step that I believe many teachers would welcome as they attempt to research what happens in their own classrooms. As a busy teacher myself, and from this simple foray into exploratory practice, I am encouraged and excited at the prospect of what I can learn in my own classroom. Exposure to exploratory practice has provided me with a way to articulate my questions, and a means to investigate them, without feeling that they must be "problems" to warrant investigation. I found that the rather seamless way I was able to integrate my "research" into the actual lesson to be stimulating and interesting. Rather than feeling overwhelmed by my attempts to gather evidence and understand my classroom better, I actually enjoyed the exercise and now feel very confident about attempting to solve other puzzles in future classes. In addition, the students were very enthusiastic about the exercise, and I feel that all of us benefited from it. I recognize that the answer I got from the class on this issue isn't necessarily one that will hold true in future classes, but it has provided me with an increased awareness of the importance of learner involvement and "ownership" in the class. The ease with which I was able to investigate this puzzle encourages me to try something similar in another class.

At the same time, I must acknowledge the fact that all my classroom puzzles may not be so easily solved. What would I have done, for example, if the students had chosen to sequence activities in a way that I felt was inappropriate, based on my own experience and training? With future puzzles it is possible that students will not enjoy activities designed to generate data to investigate questions, or that the data generated will be insufficient to solve a puzzle, or that I may not be happy about the results. Despite this, my enthusiasm for exploratory practice is unflagging. Because exploratory practice entails the utilization of pedagogically sound activities as the means to solve the puzzle, activities can be rationalized for their pedagogical value, even if the results seem insufficient or unsatisfactory.

The lessons for me as a teacher from this one experience are many. I had my initial puzzle solved and scheduled the student-led discussions at the conclusion of the lesson. I found this "research" to be manageable in terms of the added work required; I was able to learn about something in my class on my own, with little extra work (other than reflection and the thought put into how to generate data that would help me solve the puzzle) and with little disruption to the class. In addition, I witnessed firsthand the enthusiasm with which students greeted the opportunity to make decisions about their own class.

Most important, however, is the personal and professional satisfaction of the experience. I feel good that I have taken some kind of action to solve an issue that nagged at me. I feel that I have grown and benefited from increased understanding of how my own research can help me to learn more about the students and my role in the classroom. I am enthusiastic that I was able to "research" without disruption to the class, while furthering the goals and objectives of the course. During this experience, I truly facilitated their learning as I learned some things myself; I provided the students with tools (the language and tactics), and they used them to successfully negotiate and form a consensus while I gathered data to solve my puzzle. I leave this experience with an increased understanding of myself and my role in the classroom, another means to collaborate effectively with students, and a new faith in my own power to grow and learn as a teacher.

Appendix   Sample lesson for integration of data generation and classroom activity

Dev Flu 0326
S 99
K Saylor

Group discussion – Lesson schedule

To practice group discussion skills in a real and meaningful way, work in small groups to decide how we should organize the activities for class on Thursday. Try to use the discussion tactics we have talked about in class as you attempt to form a consensus. *Important: You must be able to explain why you organize the lesson the way you do!*

The lesson components and approximate times for each activity:

* Unit 4, "Toast to the Tap," Listening Exercise 1, "Interview with a Master Water Taster," 15 minutes
* Unit 4, Listening Exercise 2, "Poison in the Well," 10 minutes
* Unit 4, Specialized adjectives, 15 minutes
* Pronunciation warm-up, 5 minutes
* Enunciation of vowel sounds, 25 minutes
* Student-led class discussion, 20 minutes
* Break, 10 minutes
* Finish Tape Assignment 1, 15 minutes
* Discussion to prepare for speaker on Tuesday, 30 minutes (sharing information about water quality in the Twin Cities and creating questions)

Remember the following: We are scheduled to be in the language lab from 6:20 to 7:30, but the only activity we will do during this time is the tape assignment.

ESL 0326   Schedule for Thursday, April 29, 1999
6:20–8:50 p.m.

Activity Time
Greetings and announcements   6:20–6:25

References

Allwright, D. (1991). *Potentially exploitable pedagogic activities.* Unpublished handout from workshop, Rio de Janeiro.

Allwright, D. (1992). *Exploratory teaching: The advantages of talking about 'puzzles' rather than 'problems'.* Unpublished handout from workshop, Bratislava.

Allwright, D. (1999a). *Putting learning on the classroom agenda: A case for learner-based 'Exploratory Practice'.* Paper presented at the National Congress of English, Conferentiecentrum Woudshoten, The Netherlands, January.

Allwright, D. (1999b). *Three major processes and the appropriate design criteria for developing and using them.* Working Papers: Center for Advanced Research on Language Acquisition. Minneapolis: University of Minnesota.

Allwright, D., & Bailey K. M. (1991). *Focus on the language classroom.* Cambridge: Cambridge University Press.

Allwright, D., & Lenzuen, R. (1997). Exploratory practice: Work at the Cultura Inglesa, Rio de Janeiro, Brazil. *Language Teaching Research, 1*(1), 73–79.

Brown, H. D. (1994). *Teaching by principles: An interactive approach to language pedagogy.* Englewood Cliffs, NJ: Prentice Hall.

McDonough, J., & McDonough, S. (1997). *Research methods for English language teachers.* New York: St. Martin's.

Richards, J. C., & Lockhart, C. (1994). *Reflective teaching in second language classrooms.* Cambridge: Cambridge University Press.

Schön, D. A. (1983). *The reflective turn: Case studies in and on educational practice* (pp. 1–12). New York: Teachers College Press.

Part I Discussion

1. To what extent have these teachers begun to align their instructional practices to match their knowledge, beliefs, and values about second language learning and teaching? How did they accomplish this? What did they need to overcome to do this? What changes in their perceptions and their practices occurred as a result?
2. How have these teachers created instructional opportunities that recognize their students not as remedial learners but as legitimate learners? What did they need to do to accomplish this? What changes in their perceptions and their practices occurred as a result?
3. How did the very notion of what it means to create a student-centered classroom change for these teachers? What were the consequences for these teachers when students became personally invested in the daily activities of the classroom?
4. In what ways has narrative inquiry enabled these teachers to develop their instructional practices beyond what they already do?

Part I Reflection

1. Keep a reflective journal in which you describe dimensions about yourself that you recognize and wish to maintain in your teaching and learning. In addition, describe dimensions about yourself that you recognize and wish to alter in your teaching and learning. Finally, describe dimensions about teaching and learning that represent your greatest challenges.
2. Brainstorm some key concepts that are important to your instructional practice. Create a conceptual map that shows the relationships between these concepts. If this activity helps you to identify any tensions in your practice, determine how you might inquire further into them.
3. Select one of the reflection questions from the beginning of Part I, "Inquiry into Instructional Practices." Write a short (two- or three-page) position paper on how you have or might have addressed the theoretical and pedagogical concerns embedded in these questions in your current or future instructional practices as a language teacher.

Part I Action

1. Keep a reflective journal for at least two weeks in which you focus on your daily practices for a class that you are currently teaching. Describe

the sequence of activities within each class and the rationale behind your choices. Then, do any of the following:
- Describe how you felt about each class
- Describe any interactions with students or between students that you did not feel comfortable about
- Describe any aspects of your practice that were in conflict with one another (for example, time constraints versus sufficient explanations)
- Describe how an institutional constraint seems to affect your teaching
- Describe any moral issue that seems to affect your teaching (for example, trying to encourage a quiet student to participate while not squelching the enthusiasm of more outgoing students)

Reread your journal and try to identify any themes or patterns that emerge. Reflect on and write about:
- How these themes or patterns embody your experiences as a student, language learner, and/or language teacher
- How these themes embody your principles of instructional practice
- How these themes embody any tensions that might exist between your practice and your beliefs about language learning and language teaching

2. Identify a "puzzle" (Allwright & Bailey, 1991) and conduct some exploratory practice (see Johnson, this volume). In other words, identify an area of inquiry through questioning, reflection, and discussion with others, reformulate the puzzle into a question, identify ways of looking at the question, and collect data to investigate the question without disruption to the class. On the basis of the understanding you reach, determine whether you should develop alternative instructional practices or conduct further research.

3. Audiotape or videotape a single class or a series of classes that you are teaching. Before or after listening to or watching the tape, identify an issue in your practice that you would like to listen or watch for. Then, do any of the following:
- Identify a critical incident
- Describe the extent to which you have aligned your instructional practices with your knowledge, beliefs, and values about second language learning and teaching
- Describe the extent to which you have created instructional opportunities that recognize your students as legitimate learners

Suggested readings

Allwright, D., and Bailey, K. M. (1991). *Focus on the language classroom.* Cambridge: Cambridge University Press.

Allwright, D., and Lenzuen, R. (1997). Exploratory practice: Work at the Cultura Inglesa, Rio de Janiero, Brazil. *Language Teaching Research Journal, 1*(1), 73–79.

Dobbs, J. (1995). Assessing our own patterns of discourse. *TESOL Journal, 4*(3), 24–26.

Kemmis, S., & McTaggart, R. (Eds.). (1988). *The action research planner* (3rd ed.). Geelong, Australia: Deakin University Press.

McNiff, J. (1988). *Action research: Principles and practice.* New York: Macmillian.

Patterson, L., Santa, C. M., Short, K. G., & Smith, K. (Eds.). (1993). *Teachers are researchers: Reflection and action.* Newark, NY: International Reading Association.

Richards, J. C., & Lockhart, C. (1994). *Reflective teaching in second language classrooms.* Cambridge: Cambridge University Press.

Tsui, A. (1993). Helping teachers to conduct action research in their classrooms. In D. Freeman & S. Cornwell (Eds.), *New ways in teacher education* (pp.171–175). Alexandria, VA: TESOL.

Wallace, M. J. (1991). *Training foreign language teachers: A reflective approach.* Cambridge: Cambridge University Press.

Zeichner, K., & Liston, D. (1996). *Reflective teaching: An introduction.* Mahwah, NJ: Lawrence Erlbaum Associates.

PART II:
INQUIRY INTO LANGUAGE
LEARNERS

Another critical component of professional development is teachers' inquiry into language learners. In Part II, "Inquiry into Language Learners," each teacher's story occurs in an ESL or EFL university setting, but how the story is generated and analyzed differs, for example, through self-reflection, focus groups, journaling, interviews, and discourse analysis. These teachers use these methods of inquiry to learn about their students' needs, interests, and objectives, and yet gain insights into themselves as teachers and their practice. Suzanne House, writing about a volunteerism elective class in an intensive English program in the United States, learns about her students as individuals and gains insight into the cultural assumptions and values they hold. In realizing that "students and teachers share the shaping of any class," she recognizes that how students understand class content and what they learn differs from student to student and from what the teacher expects. Bob Gibson writes about the use of focus groups with freshman EFL students at a Japanese university. He discovers that students' interpretations of classroom interactions can differ significantly from those of the teacher, and credits the use of focus groups as a way to uncover feelings that students may be reluctant to discuss. Jennifer L. Esbenshade writes, after a semester of reflection and journaling, about her undergraduate ESL students in a basic-level composition course at a large university in the United States. Through her journaling, she not only comes to understand herself and her interactions with students better but also articulates key aspects of her conceptions of teaching and the sources of her beliefs. Linda Winston and Laurie Soltman, in a community-based research project, give voice to the wives of international graduate students as they struggle alone and with support to adjust to a new culture and a new identity as unemployed professionals, mothers, and/or homemakers. As they reflect on their interviews, these teachers identify their own struggles to adjust to new identities and seek community-based ways to assist others as they adjust, thus bridging the personal and professional lives of both teachers and students. By seeing themselves as part of, and empathizing with, this "hidden" ESL population, these teachers are changed in how they view themselves, as well as how they view their students, their students' living environments, and the resources available to address students' needs.

Each of these stories points to the influence of what learners bring to the classroom – their knowledge, beliefs, and cultural assumptions – on how class members interact with one another and with the teacher and how teachers struggle to adjust their instructional practice to meet individuals' needs within a particular context. Inquiring into learners' knowledge, beliefs, assumptions, and experiences changes teachers, giving them insights into themselves, their students, and their practice, and, sometimes, an ability to change their instructional practice.

Part II   Initial reflection

The teachers featured in Part II, "Inquiry into Language Learners," explore the types of theoretical and pedagogical concerns reflected in the following questions. As you read their stories of narrative inquiry, reflect on the concerns embedded in these questions and how you have or might have addressed them in your own teaching.

1. How do my students influence what I do and say in the classroom?
2. How do I develop a deeper understanding of who my students are?
3. How do I adjust my instructional practices to recognize who my students are?
4. How does developing a deeper understanding of individual students alter my view of students in general and alter me as a teacher?
5. How do I recognize that teachers and students experience instruction differently?
6. How do I deal with the consequences of recognizing that teachers and students experience instruction differently?
7. How can I create instructional opportunities that are relevant to the personal and professional lives of my students?

6 Who is in this classroom with me?

Suzanne House

When I set out to design and pilot a new volunteerism elective class in the intensive English program (IEP) at a large Midwestern university, I was thinking mainly of the pedagogical and linguistic knowledge I would need to make the class a success. I thought about ordinary teaching concerns like integrating skills, having students journal in class, and preteaching vocabulary they would encounter in their volunteer experiences. As the pieces fell into place, however, the reality of a volunteerism elective, so simple as a plan in my mind, pushed me to use knowledge I had not considered in the initial stages. The complexity of the organizational, experiential, and personal knowledge I found myself using transformed the class into a much bigger project than I had anticipated. Most important, this class was a dramatic reminder that knowing what students bring to the class – their own knowledge, their experiences, their expectations, their work ethic – is an essential element that must be fully explored every time a teacher enters a classroom to teach.

The instructional setting

Most students enrolled in this program were studying English in preparation for undergraduate or graduate study at the university; others attended for business or personal study. The students viewed the IEP instruction as a valuable step on their way to a bigger goal: academic classes. In the six-level IEP, students studied reading, writing, speaking, listening, grammar, and vocabulary in a range of integrated content-based classes for three or four hours each day. An additional optional hour of study in a half-term elective class was encouraged. These electives offered focused study of a specific subject, such as pronunciation, TOEFL preparation, academic speaking skills, or American film. The elective lineup was flexible, and teachers were welcome to propose and pilot new electives.

Why volunteerism?

I endeavored to take advantage of this opportunity and teach a five-week elective on volunteerism for personal and professional reasons. My personal reasons arose in part from my belief in volunteering as a humanitarian activity, my desire for students to see beyond their own often privileged experiences, and a strictly personal interest in seeing whether I could put together and pull off such a class. I had often experienced the satisfaction that comes from the actual work of volunteerism, the feeling of helping another person, and – most important in terms of language teaching – the bonding that occurs when volunteers with a common interest join together to accomplish something concrete. The language learning experience I strive to provide in my classes is one that recognizes each student as an individual and honors these individuals as they struggle with the gulf between who they are and what they are able to articulate. Because of my own experiences as a second language learner in a foreign country, I am sensitive to students' frustration as they search for ways to express their personalities and talents within the limitations of restricted language proficiency. Activities like volunteering offer opportunities for language learners to move beyond their limited classroom roles and function as multifaceted people in a larger context. I want to facilitate opportunities like these as often as I can, and so I eagerly anticipated joining students in five weeks of volunteering.

As a language teacher, I knew that volunteering in the community could be a valuable task-based activity providing authentic opportunities to interact with native speakers. Volunteer experiences could be expanded into reading, writing, speaking, and listening activities as students explored the issues of poverty, hunger, homelessness, and aging. Surely, as students sorted food and clothing at a local pantry, painted sheds for the volunteer house-building organization Habitat for Humanity, and chatted with residents of a retirement community, they would be able to meet people and see situations not normally found in typical life on an American campus. These pedagogical reasons formed a convincing plan, and based on my written proposal and informal meetings, I was given the go-ahead by the IEP's director to prepare for the class.

On a deeper level, my beliefs about teaching and learning have been informed by critical pedagogy. When I began my ESL teaching career, I strove to integrate my composition courses with tenets of critical pedagogy that resonated with what my students needed in their writing: a refusal to accept unconditionally what is given, a questioning perspective, and the ability to write and think with an awareness of what lay beyond their immediate experience. Although I have veered from more emancipatory aspects of critical pedagogy, I still work to deliberately stress thinking and questioning over perceiving and accepting (Recchio, 1994). Shor (1987) defines a critical pedagogy as one that is "participatory, critical, values-oriented, multicultural, student-centered, experiential, research-minded, and interdisciplinary" (p. 22). Although we had only five weeks to work together, I hoped that bringing discussions of homelessness, poverty, aging, and civic responsibility into a classroom could offer a rich (if brief) opportunity for critical pedagogy, allowing students to hear and evaluate other perspectives and then to practice appraising their own beliefs. The hands-on volunteering would provide tangible openings to help students begin to identify some of the social forces that shaped their beliefs in the first place, and with the resulting classroom dialogues, I hoped to create opportunities for students to educate one another and broaden their own perspectives, ensuring a "continual contact with reality" (Dewey, 1990, p. 56). Although the class interaction would require more speaking than writing, I wanted to adopt Elbow's two goals of "[producing] active and questioning students who inquire and make meaning rather than just [receiving] information" and welcoming "difference of opinion and view . . . in a classroom" (1990, p. 41).

The students

The dozen students who chose to take the class were a mixed group, very ready to provide differences of opinion and view. Half of them were traditional intermediate- and advanced-level IEP students whose native countries were Japan, Kuwait, Mexico, Saudi Arabia, Taiwan, and Venezuela. The other half were English teachers from Japan who were studying in a special program in the IEP. The Japanese teachers' proficiency was significantly beyond the level of the other students, so the class dynamics vacillated between the more proficient students taking the less proficient students under their collective wing, and the more proficient students monopolizing class conversations and critiquing the organization, teaching, and purpose of the class. The students chose to take the class for a wide variety of reasons, including a genuine interest in volunteering, a desire for more chances to talk with native speakers, and simple curiosity about trying something different.

Knowledge I needed

The weeks I spent planning the class had prepared me for some of the types of knowledge I would need. I knew that I would require pedagogical knowledge to arrange the lessons, integrate skills within the activities, introduce and follow up on the issues we would discuss, ground the issues at hand with students' own experiences, and plan for a poster session to allow students to bring together and show off what they had learned. I would need linguistic knowledge to teach the vocabulary and discourse structures students would use in the course of their volunteering. Finally, I would draw on the knowledge of experience to allow me to determine students' levels of linguistic and situational comfort, guide student interaction, and manage the time and communication in a class with such a range of English proficiency. My teacher training, my linguistic education, and my teaching experiences are the basis of these types of knowledge. They would not come as a surprise to a bystander observing the process of teaching.

I had not considered, however, other kinds of knowledge I would need to draw on as I taught the class. On a strictly pragmatic level, my powers of organization were called upon and tested as I fought to juggle students' schedules, my schedule, the schedules of the organizations that allowed us to help, the transportation needs faced by thirteen people with only two cars, city bus schedules, and the process of acquiring a university van for a trip to the local food shelter. The phone calls alone ate up huge chunks of time, and the seemingly simple task of renting a van became an afternoon spent with the phone book, calling one rental agency after another. My research skills, especially my Internet skills, became important as I searched for definitions of *poverty*, demographic information for the city and state, and poverty and economic statistics for countries around the world. And the question of liability – what if a student had an unfortunate meeting with a hammer while helping to rebuild a home for Habitat for Humanity? What if we had an accident while I transported students to the food pantry? – sent me on a search to learn about the university's legal policies.

Even with these skills and background information, my preparation for teaching the volunteerism class was incomplete. The most important knowledge I needed for this class was information about the perspectives and values of the students, and this was the most difficult knowledge to obtain. In any class, the interaction and actual learning are shaped by what the students bring to the classroom, and this seemed doubly so for a class based on the idea of helping others. Kutz and Roskelly contend that "[T]eachers and students bring lots of 'outside' knowledge to the classroom, and the classroom needs to be a place where such knowledge is valued, and where it's connected to the learning that goes on within the classroom" (1991, p. 250). Why was each student there? What was his or her experience with volunteering? What cultural ideas and attitudes concerning volunteering did each person hold?

Learning about students

I spent a substantial amount of time trying to gather information about the students' backgrounds and opinions because I knew that my understanding of them could inform their understanding of the issues at hand. I used journals, conversations, group discussions, and talking to colleagues familiar with my students' cultures to gain this essential information: knowledge of the student. Without this knowledge, I would be operating in the dark; I would be giving information to students without being able to predict its effect or effectiveness. I did not need the students' personal histories, their private feelings, or information they were not comfortable sharing, but I could not teach well without drawing out of them the reasons behind their comfort or discomfort with our work and their frustration with or enthusiasm for the act of volunteering. They had chosen to forgo more traditional electives like TOEFL preparation and advanced conversation to learn about volunteering, and I believed that they must have had some grounds for being in my classroom beyond a chance check mark on the elective form at the beginning of the term.

One of the dangers of attempting to learn about students was that I didn't always know what to do with the information I gathered. Some things I noted, such as students' unwillingness to take the initiative in their individual projects, frustrated me and tempted me to kick office furniture. Other, more significant discoveries, such as a few students' eagerness to disparage American society and American people regularly, diminished my enthusiasm for the class. There were times when I backed off on discussion ideas because I didn't feel equipped to deal with harsh condemnation from students whose language skills – or cultural discourse styles – kept them from using any semblance of tact.

Knowledge of my students often came through class discussions. For example, from the outset questions arose regarding who deserves to be helped. I was unprepared for the reaction of most of the Japanese teachers, who strongly believed that with education and effort, very few people would actually need the services we explored. Their questioning of the worthiness of our actions was valuable to shaping the class, but it was also an obstacle for which I had not been prepared. On the other hand, students from poorer countries, who brought with them alternative understandings of volunteering, approached the class from an entirely different perspective. They had volunteered before, or they knew people who needed help, and they were much more inclined to accept the idea that the people we met were not entirely responsible for their difficulties and situations.

I gained additional perceptions of the students through the assigned weekly journals, in which further differences among the students appeared. Here, the class members who were easygoing with our volunteer work generally skimmed over questions about who deserves what, writing blithely about the sheds they had painted or the nice people they had met. The Japanese teachers, on the other hand, delved into complicated reflections on the murky issues they were uncovering in the class. This gap was partly due to proficiency disparities, but it also reflected the earnestness with which the teachers approached the course. They were eager to analyze complex issues, though almost all rejected questioning what had shaped their perspectives.

These differences between students became clear during a budgeting activity we did in one of our classroom lessons. This activity followed our Habitat for Humanity outing, when some of the students had raised doubts about how many people in society actually need help. The students worked in groups to prepare a budget for a family of four, using categories that I provided (rent, food, transportation, insurance, clothing, and so on) and resources that included classified ads from the city newspaper, insurance quotes, and local child care prices. The students were told that the father in this hypothetical family had lost a decent job for which he had technical training when the business was forced to close by competition, so both parents currently had jobs paying only slightly above minimum wage. Among the budgetary decisions they had to make, the students had to think about the logistics of sending one of the parents back to college to finish a degree as an investment in the future. Most of the class worked enthusiastically on the challenges of stretching limited dollars, trying to decide whether the cost of child care was worth having both parents work, dealing with the complexities and frustrations of health insurance, and struggling to make hard-earned wages meet expenses. However, some of the Japanese students spent the class period insisting that this couple should never have had children they could not afford, brushing aside my reminder that the father's training was rendered useless because his job had been terminated through no fault of his own. They seemed unable to grasp the idea of a competent worker being laid off, and the concept of people's lives being affected by forces beyond their control was equally unpalatable to them. Instead of working within the structure of the activity to expand their understanding, they used their time to judge people and a society that would allow this kind of situation to occur. In their eyes, the only explanation for being poor was personal failure – and they often asserted that there are no poor people in Japan, despite many indications to the contrary. These attitudes affected the dynamics of class work and discussions, and the frustration I felt as a result affected how I planned other activities.

Clearly, we all approached the volunteering experiences wrapped in our own cultural assumptions. The Japanese teachers were coming from a society in which lifelong employment was taken for granted, and they found it difficult to understand the forces of unemployment and a changing job market. Their previous experiences with volunteering had involved group activities like cleaning their schools and picking up trash. They worked hard when we volunteered, but they struggled with the principles involved in packing food boxes to be distributed to the homeless, people who had, they assumed, made the choice not to work. These students engaged the American volunteers they met in serious conversations about how often and why they came to the shelter, and they were understandably angered by the benefiting Habitat for Humanity family who sat inside the house, watching us paint their shed.

Conversely, the Venezuelan student talked about her personal knowledge of poverty and teen mothers as she cheerfully painted the shed. Her ideas of helping others came in part from her religious beliefs, and she was enthusiastic about our activities and the issues we discussed in class. She valued the opportunity to meet new people and, while acknowledging the complications involved in social issues, she was willing to trust in our ability to help.

Learning from students

How did learning about such disparities in the students' backgrounds and attitudes change my teaching? Sometimes it simply affected the way I listened to the students. A clear example involved the Japanese teachers. Knowing that they were accustomed to being in front of their own classes allowed me to understand the tension that resulted as they struggled to reconcile the different roles of student and teacher. This did not mean that I was always graceful when they chose to critique my teaching methods during class time, but it did give me a window on the reasons behind their actions. Sometimes my knowledge of students meant grouping students in different ways to encourage discussion. Once I realized which of the students refused to consider perspectives outside their own experiences, I alternated between grouping those students together to allow the others freedom to explore ideas and pairing the recalcitrant students with other strong students who wouldn't be intimidated by them. Some students displayed a lack of tact in criticizing American society, reminding me that, for ESL learners, it is not enough to simply speak their minds without knowledge of discourse conventions. Mindful that "competence in classrooms means interactional competence . . . when and how and with whom to speak and act in order to create and display knowledge" (Hull, Rose, Fraser, & Castellano, 1991, p. 301), I encouraged speakers to express their opinions taking into account their audience and the audience's level of defensiveness. Possibly because I did not begin the class with the intention of teaching tact, I was not very successful in conveying the need for sensitivity. In the discussions that involved looking at a single issue (poverty, housing, or how families treat elderly members) across multiple cultures, many students were blissfully unaware of the subjectivity involved in lambasting the United States while presenting their own countries as models of social perfection. In the course of these discussions I also learned about my own beliefs – and that sometimes the only way to squelch my patriotic defensiveness was to change the subject.

The natural process of getting to know the class as individuals instead of as a group also affected my teaching. Realizing that students' interest in the class was affected but not determined by language proficiency freed me to treat different individuals differently. As I grew to know them better, I began to ask each student different questions, push each toward different choices in class discussions and individual projects, and develop different expectations for what each could gain from the class. For some, the class was simply a matter of language practice. For others, the class and volunteering opened the door of American culture a bit wider. With the first group, I concentrated more on vocabulary and conversation skills; with the latter, I spent my time stoking their enthusiasm and helping them find volunteer opportunities. The more knowledge I gathered about each student, the more able I was to focus the class activities in ways that were useful for the group and the individuals in it.

It sometimes happens that a student's expectations about the role of the teacher clash with the teacher's expectations, and this class provided a splendid example of this collision. My teaching style involves, as much as possible in the natural educational power structure, sharing control of the classroom with the students (Ellsworth, 1989). As I headed into the class, I perceived my role to be that of a teacher and fellow volunteer who could offer some cultural and linguistic knowledge and was prepared to use pedagogical knowledge to provide a learning experience for the students. Half of the class, on the other hand, expected me to be a cultural expert who had explanations for the actions of all American citizens as well as the American government. They also expected me to be able to answer unanswerable questions about the role of government and individual citizens in society and to provide solutions for the quagmires of poverty, homelessness, and corruption in American culture. As I slowly recognized these expectations, I worked to provide more facts and possible solutions, all the while becoming frustrated at my lack of answers and the students' unwillingness to listen to my repeated insistence that some questions simply have no clear answers. Although I remained wary of the risk of imposing my own values and political ideologies on the students, I was compelled to acknowledge that sometimes it was all right for me simply to bring ideas to the class instead of attempting to provide sets of data-based answers. This allowed me to push the students to practice linguistic and cultural negotiation even more than if I had been able to offer solutions to universal problems. This realization influenced the way I led class discussions and responded to students' questions, a change that could not have happened had I remained unaware of the students' expectations.

The poster session on the final day of class, which was the culmination of the individual projects, reminded me that much of the best learning must take place outside of my control and that much of students' learning depends on choices they make alone. The Kuwaiti student took the initiative with enthusiasm. After working through his low oral proficiency to arrange his individual volunteer activity, he got up early one Sunday morning and helped serve breakfast to homeless people at a local church. He was the only nonnative English speaker present, and he thoroughly enjoyed his entire biscuit-making experience. One Japanese student volunteered at a high school cross-country meet with his conversation partner and came back with enthusiasm and exciting pictures of the runners and the day's activities. Other students participated in a campus cleanup day; although they did not go beyond the campus environment, they did feel comfortable with what they did. A final group of four students made plans to help with children's activities at a local elementary school's after-school program, but their contact person didn't meet them at the school on the appointed day. Instead of giving up, they returned to the food pantry, where we had all worked together. They gained valuable practice at communicating and negotiating in English, and they had great stories to tell afterward. The poster session that came out of these experiences provided an excellent depiction of the broad range of interests and personalities contained in a class of just twelve students. Listening to the students explain their posters to visitors confirmed my conviction that if I expect students to learn from me, I must take the time to learn from them.

Reflecting on the volunteerism course

After our five weeks together, the class ended on a vague note of success – not the dramatic finale I had envisioned but a more realistic blend of new vocabulary, new experiences, writing practice, and a successful poster session. The students and I all gained new information about ourselves, one another, and the social issues that inevitably become a part of discussions about helping other people. We had achieved my critical pedagogal goal, to "discover complexity where there appeared to be simplicity" (Kutz, Groden, & Zamel, 1993, p. 178). We stretched one another's awareness, and, as a result, we were different from what we would have been if we had volunteered alone or with a like-minded group.

For the students, these differences meant new views of Americans and American culture, an expanded consideration of issues surrounding need and volunteering, and, less intellectually significant but certainly useful, improved painting techniques.

For me, the awareness stretching came as I considered and reconsidered the quality of what had happened in our classroom and in the community. My belief in the value of the class did not change, but I realized that my initial hopes for the class, though unarticulated, had not taken into consideration the limitations, detours, and struggles that would naturally accompany such an undertaking. This was not a grammar class with prewritten rules I could give to students, nor was it a pronunciation class in which the goal was a standard articulation of the /th/ sound. It was, despite my frustration, exactly the kind of class I value: more easily conceived than carried out, but tremendously worthwhile. Every one of us in the classroom had been forced to think outside what we had previously known and believed, and we had negotiated and disagreed with purpose. I was reminded that encouraging critical thinking is almost always more difficult than encouraging the correct use of the present progressive, but that the two have in common the teacher's task of planting idea seeds and trusting that they will grow. Eight months after the end of the volunteerism elective, I received a gift from one of the students who had been in the class. I had taught her in two other courses, a lengthy advanced integrated skills class and a TOEFL preparation class, but her note of thanks specifically emphasized the value she had found in the volunteering experiences. This encouraged me in my eternal teaching hope: that the students take away from each course more than is immediately visible, just as they add more than is apparent on the first day of class.

In the course of planning, organizing, teaching, and evaluating the class, I used pedagogical, linguistic, organizational, experiential, and research knowledge. More important, I gained and made use of knowledge about my students as learners and as people. As a teacher, I am constantly drawing on an extensive range of ways of knowing that I have acquired, and it is tempting to believe that this makes me unique in my classroom. If I could simply impart hard-earned wisdom to students who all want and need the same information, teaching would be an easy art. I know, however, that the complexity of what I bring into a classroom is matched by the complexity of what students bring to the same room. As Delpit (1988) affirms, the instructor is not the lone expert in the classroom; students come bearing as much information and as many ideas as the instructor does. Not only do the students possess a multitude of experiences, beliefs, and goals, but each student will – must – make decisions and choices that may or may not have anything to do with the influence of the teacher or the class. Students and teacher share the shaping of any class, and losing sight of that reality in the race of everyday activities means missing chances to teach in a meaningful and lasting manner.

References

Delpit, L. D. (1988). The silenced dialogue: Power and pedagogy in educating other people's children. *Harvard Educational Review, 58*, 280–298.

Dewey, J. (1990). *The school and society* (expanded ed.). Chicago: University of Chicago Press.

Elbow, P. (1990). *What is English?* New York: Modern Language Association of America.

Ellsworth, E. (1989). Why doesn't this feel empowering? Working through the repressive myths of critical pedagogy. *Harvard Educational Review, 59*, 297–324.

Hull, G., Rose, M., Fraser, K. L., Castellano, M. (1991). Remedial as social construct: Perspectives from an analysis of classroom discourse. *College Composition and Communication, 42*, 299–329.

Kutz, E., Groden, S. Q., & Zamel, V. (1993). *The discovery of competence: Teaching and learning with diverse student writers.* Portsmouth, NH: Boynton/Cook.

Kutz, E., & Roskelly, H. (1991). *An unquiet pedagogy: Transforming practice in the English classroom.* Portsmouth, NH: Boynton/Cook.

Recchio, T. (1994). On the critical necessity of "Essaying." In L. Tobin & T. Newkirk (Eds.), *Taking stock: The writing process movement in the '90s* (pp. 219–235). Portsmouth, NH: Boynton/Cook.

Shor, I. (1987). Educating the educators: A Freirean approach to the crisis in teacher education. In I. Shor (Ed.), *Freire for the classroom* (pp. 7–32). Portsmouth, NH: Boynton/Cook.

7 Talking at length and depth
Learning from focus group discussions

Bob Gibson

I suspect that I'm not the only language teacher in the world who has felt just a little uneasy at the mention of *reflective practice* (Schön, 1983), for a good deal of what I 'know' about teaching seems to take the form of intuitions that haven't been reflected upon in any real depth. What do these – for want of a better phrase – 'ongoing hypotheses' stem from? Can they be verified, or at least firmed up, and if so how? In this chapter I describe an ongoing attempt to access a less-exploited seam of information, that of students' considered opinions about their needs and aspirations in their particular learning circumstances. In the Japanese university context discussed here, mining this seam has helped me to understand what my students believe about the language education they're receiving, and how they feel about the experience. The process of getting at these beliefs and reactions, moreover, has benefitted my relationship with my students, their relationship to their studies, and my relationship to my teaching.

Receiving wisdom

Nearly all 'qualified' language teachers nowadays have been down the professional training route and have taken on board at least some of the received wisdom of the field. But certification courses are only one of the inputs we're exposed to. Just as important, and in some ways more effective, is the informal, in-service education – sometimes explicit, sometimes implied – that we pick up in conversation with colleagues. In my first teaching post in Japan, I gleaned a whole range of useful pointers that hadn't surfaced in the school's formal teacher-orientation sessions: "Key point: Remember that your students expect you to act like a teacher. Take control." "Another thing. They don't want you to be all carey and sharey. Strict but fair is what works here."

Like every other 'chalkface' instructor, I digested the advice I received, and by some route arrived at what seemed to be at least provisionally true for my own teaching context and style. This 'knowledge' sustained me, with occasional doubts, for several years.

Active versus passive

I left Japan in 1992 and went to Britain to do a postgraduate degree in applied linguistics, and after this I was offered a limited-term EFL teaching post at Berlin's Free University. I didn't feel ready to return to Japan just yet, and since the artist I'm married to felt that her work might be better received in Germany than in her native Japan, she had no objections to my taking the job.

Given that university study in Germany is comparatively inexpensive, the Free University attracts students from other European countries, Asia, and Africa, as well as from all over Germany itself. I thus found myself teaching students from many linguistic and cultural backgrounds. After years in essentially monolingual/monocultural Japan, this called for some mental and methodological readjustment on my part. What struck me most was that my students in Berlin expected far more involvement in their English language studies than had been the case for my Japanese students. And they felt refreshingly free to vent their opinions. (In Germany, anyone who earns the *Abitur* high school diploma has historically been eligible for university education, but because universities may impose a lengthy waiting period for applicants, German undergraduates as a population tend to be older than their peers elsewhere.)

My students in Berlin explicitly questioned aspects of what Holliday (1994) refers to as *BANA models*, the British–Australian–North American paradigms and assumptions that structure (or 'dominate', depending on your point of view) EFL education in many parts of the world. Things that many BANA-trained EFL/ESL teachers accept as 'natural' may, in some cultural contexts, need to be explained and even defended. These can include even such methodologically basic procedures as information-gap pair work: More than one student from the former East Germany asked me why I was asking her to converse with someone whose English was no better than her own. How was this more beneficial than listening to me, a native speaker? Others wanted to know why I spent so little time on translation and grammatical analysis, which for students planning to be EFL teachers might be key skills. I could rationalise these aspects of 'modern' pedagogy fairly readily, but it was considerably more difficult to convince my writing course students of the benefits of the thesis statement-topic–sentence-conclusion essay structure. (I hadn't even heard of thesis statements myself until after I graduated, for in my day it was assumed – by no means accurately – that anyone making it into a British university could already put together a coherent essay!) I explained that anyone planning to do postgraduate work in the United States or Britain needed to know the writing conventions of those academic cultures, but this didn't persuade many of my students. I then suggested that the skill of organising an essay in this way would be useful in composing English language reports and memorandums in later working life. This argument appeared to be more convincing, for no one could seriously question the hegemony of 'Anglo-Saxon' conventions in the business world. Yet some students were clearly reluctant to accept that their native modes of argumentation couldn't simply be transposed into English, as though they were somehow outmoded or inadequate to the English-dominated modern era.

Back to my future

I thoroughly enjoyed the questioning, at times mildly combative, attitude of students in Berlin, but after three years I realised that my return to Japan had to be then or never. Back in the Tokyo area, I quickly realised that Japan was not the same place it had been during my previous stay. For one thing, the economic 'bubble' had well and truly burst, and Japanese certainties like lifelong employment were slowly going by the wayside. Students, too, seemed different, although the old passivity was still fairly widespread. It is still true of many Japanese universities that, once a student is enrolled, and in the absence of serious misdemeanors, graduation is more or less automatic. But it had dawned on at least some undergraduates that merely graduating from even a 'name' university no longer guaranteed a dream job. Even the (to me at least) curious student habit of taking little or no active part in communication-oriented college English classes, while also attending an expensive English conversation class, appeared to have declined along with disposable income.

I could see that some of my old teaching nostrums would have to be revised, if not abandoned, but I wasn't at all sure which were candidates. Moreover, there simply wasn't the same old certainty among teachers as to what worked now and what didn't. The only consensus I encountered – fittingly in the postmodern era – was that, for better or worse, Japanese learners were a very much more varied population than they had been.

After a year I landed a post teaching an elective course in one of Japan's best universities. This course, with double the regular class load in Britain, is intended for freshmen and sophomores who have not lived overseas but whose current English ability is such as to allow them to benefit from – for want of a technical term, if there is one – a communicative approach to English for Academic and Special (legal studies) Purposes. Not only do students have to opt for this course, they also have to pass an entry test that assesses motivation as well as ability. Those students who make it are not only conspicuously keener than the average undergraduate in Japan, but many also have definite ideas about what a language course should offer. This was a novelty in my experience of Japan, but I quickly realised that it offered a golden opportunity to test what I found myself 'knowing' and wondering about what Japanese language learners today actually need and want. Did Japanese students, for example, share the doubts about classroom practices that students in Germany had aired? Did they actually care about how various language skills were weighted in the course? I surprised myself with how many questions I wanted to ask.

First steps and missteps

My first step was to administer an anonymous end-of-semester survey to all my freshman classes, asking for their views about various aspects of the course. Was there too much, enough, or too little homework, for example? On a scale of 1 to 6, how interesting was the lesson content? Which of the following words would you use to describe the atmosphere in your classes? The results of this survey were, as survey results so often are, less than clear. A minority of students claimed to be very satisfied with the course, another minority was dissatisfied, and the majority was apparently more or less content. Findings like these carry the risk of simply nourishing complacency: It's 'common sense' after all, that you can't please all of the people all of the time, and if most appear to be content, then why change anything?

The compilation of unbiased and effective questionnaires is a subtle art, of course, and the more I looked at my little survey, the more I began to wonder not only whether the questions could be improved in a technical sense but whether they even came close to tapping my students' areas of concern. In an attempt to get at these concerns, I suggested that students write their own questionnaires during class time. For reasons that so far haven't become clear, however, the task was not at all well received, and the resulting product was of little value. My best guess is that the questionnaire was seen not so much as an opportunity for self-expression as just another teacher-imposed classroom task (in Japanese culture, a 'suggestion' from someone in a higher position is perceived as an order) in which students had little investment.

Reluctant to give up my enquiry, during the following semester I set up in-class group discussion activities in which both freshmen and sopho-mores were invited to list the good and bad points of their classes and suggest changes. Here again, however, the results were inconsistent and offered few clear directions for improving the course. Some students felt that teachers didn't allow them enough talking time, and others felt that teachers themselves didn't talk enough. Whether as an aid to comprehension or as a source of entertainment, a few even wanted foreign teachers to speak Japanese in class! This time around, moreover, some respondents expressed a good-natured but definite skepticism about whether their efforts would lead to any real change in the way the course was run. I could offer no guarantees in that respect, of course, and many of the proposed changes were practically or financially out of the question anyway.

This skepticism, and the impracticality of some of the suggested course improvements, made me wonder whether my students might be on the verge of 'consultation fatigue'. Then again, it's not unusual for critiquing activities like this to produce 'wish lists' whose compilers feel little pressure to confine their ideas to the realm of the feasible – if indeed they have any way of knowing where the boundary falls. But I did rather like the suggestion that the university should "hire only really good teachers and pay them really high salaries so they'll teach well."

In yet another effort to delve more deeply into students' concerns, I tried interviewing individuals at random. By no means were all students keen or even willing to help, however, and I had to fall back on volunteer informants. A self-selecting informant group, of course, brought the risk that interviews might be used to advance particular positions. If, for example, the keenest students pressed for a more demanding course, this could only compromise my efforts in the eyes of their less enthusiastic peers – leading perhaps to even narrower participation in the next opinion survey. (I was already aware that marked differences of opinion existed among my students about how teachers ought to be dealing with aspects of classroom discipline such as lateness, the use of Japanese in class, and failure to prepare for group work.) It was clear, too, that volunteer interviewees were more likely to be from the 'striver' end of the spectrum, leaving the 'coasters' relatively voiceless. Although this is inevitable to a degree – if you didn't vote, you can't complain about the government – I still wanted to tap into the views of less vocal students.

The usual suspects

After some thought, I decided to employ what advertising agencies and political campaign-managers call *focus groups*. Small groups of individuals, representing customers and voters as a whole, are asked to discuss various products or issues, and their comments are recorded. I could see at least three benefits of this format. First of all, my ongoing investigations into test-taking behaviours via introspective procedures suggest that, for Japanese subjects at least, a group 'talk-aloud' can be much more productive than the conventional interviewer-solo interviewee format. Second, I anticipated that participants' comments would be more authentic in a peer-group context – it is, after all, much harder to dissemble in front of your peers. Last but not least, I felt that the strength of the group's agreement or disagreement with individual comments might offer some insight into the likely reactions of the student body as a whole.

I was reasonably confident that the information I got from my informants would be honest, but how complete would it be? After all, although I felt that I had demonstrated a willingness to accept adverse student reaction, I had always made a point of ensuring that such reactions were delivered anonymously. Would group participants feel able to deliver criticisms face-to-face? I couldn't think of any further 'trust-building' steps I could take that wouldn't feel somehow artificial to me at least: If trust wasn't already there, I would simply have to hope that it would develop during the group discussions.

Discussion, I decided, would most usefully be based on 'defocused' products of the freshman students' in-class discussions. For example, rather than taking up the specific comments that had come up in the earlier survey, such as "Some teachers make us angry by treating us like children," "Teacher X's lessons never have anything useful in them," or "There are too many semester assignments too close together," I tried to develop more general 'umbrella topics' from these comments, such as "How much freedom and responsibility do you think teachers should give their students in deciding how the class should be run?" "What kinds of things do you think a good English course would help you to do?" and "What do you think are fair ways to assess students' performance?"

I augmented these looser topics – which I anticipated would allow the group to return to points from the initial survey about which they felt strongly while also permitting them to go beyond specific grievances – by a few topics of my own choosing. These focused on points that hadn't been included in the earlier surveys – either because of considerations of questionnaire length or uncertainty on my part about how to phrase the question in a clear and concise form. I wanted to know whether the right amount of time was being spent on individual lesson topics, how smoothly topics 'flowed' from one to the other, and whether topics adequately built upon or recycled those that had come before. I also tried to include a few points to which responses in my initial survey had been unclear. For example, were the content areas of students' major subjects (in this case either law or political science) being adequately reflected – if indeed this was desirable – in course work? Were there any subareas of these fields that needed a stronger focus?

I distributed topics for discussion as far in advance as possible of the focus group meetings, but I strongly emphasised that members were free to raise any other issues they saw fit to bring up. "These are only a starting point for discussions," I noted on each set of questions. "We don't have to discuss every topic on this page, and you are welcome to bring up any other points that you think are useful or interesting."

Not surprisingly, the sixteen students who initially volunteered were among the best motivated, though by no means all were especially fluent in English. Owing to students' fluid part-time work commitments, it was decided that meetings (which were to take place after the last class of the day) would be arranged a few days in advance, and that anyone who could attend on any given day would be welcome. As a result, sessions could have as many as nine participants or as few as three or four. The average attendance was five or so, which is perhaps close to the maximum size for 'intimate' group discussion. One student dropped out completely after the first meetings, claiming lack of time, and although I was unhappy to lose her input, I was pleased that excuses of work pressure and club activities allowed anyone who wished to drop out to do so without loss of face. Although it appeared that the volunteer pool would include several freshmen, they somehow melted away when it became clear that sophomores would be in the majority. This was unfortunate, for I particularly valued the opinions of newer, less 'acclimatized' entrants to the program. Just like most other Japanese institutions, universities use the semiformal *senpai-kohai* system, in which freshmen (*kohai*) are mentored by more senior *senpai*, and it's plausible that freshmen felt uneasy about expressing critical opinions in the presence of mentors. Discussions kicked off with an 'active' pool of eleven or twelve sophomore participants.

Discussion, I had emphasized, could be in English, in Japanese, or in an ad hoc mix of both languages. The consensus, however (some volunteers inevitably saw the exercise as an opportunity for extra language practice), was that Japanese should be used only when members were unable to express themselves in English. In order to be able to take part in discussions, I asked for and received the participants' permission to tape-record the proceedings, with the understanding that once I had extracted the relevant information (with identifying codes instead of names), the tapes would be erased. I made clear that not only participants themselves but all individuals mentioned in the course of discussions would remain anonymous through codes. Thus, if an individual student or teacher was mentioned by name, he or she should never know. In the event, participants were typically restrained about naming names, referring instead to "a certain teacher," or "a male student in my class."

Record keeping

In order to keep track of what had been said while still actively taking part in the discussion, I needed to have a real-time record of points raised. I utilised a set of captioned Likert scales to record consensus (when it emerged) in areas that I had predicted would come up or that I planned to raise as being important to me as a course teacher-cum-coordinator. 'Blank' scales, captioned ad hoc, did the same for points that I hadn't anticipated, for example, that of whether students should be able to make oral presentations in small groups rather than individually.

Allow							Disallow
1	2	3	4	5	6	7	8

Nonnumerical response ranges, left blank until used ad hoc, allowed me to approximate individual participants' views on various topics. In this way I could quickly note on another question, which arose unexpectedly but which clearly merited recording: Were returnee students (Japanese who had lived and been educated overseas for a number of years) perceived as being held to a different standard of performance?

No difference ———✓——+——+—✓✓—+———+—✓—— Clear difference

Two participants claim to have noted a clear difference in expected standards, two noted some difference, and one noted no real difference.

Even with a set of 'agenda' topics (which were anyway no more than a starting point), it was unrealistic to anticipate more than a fraction of the discussion, and I relied extensively on handwritten notes as supplements to the devices described above. If you have a very good memory, and can write clearly at speed, you may have no need of little tricks like these, but I found them invaluable. If you can do it consistently, noting the number on the tape counter helps to quickly locate interesting moments on an audiotape, whether during the discussion or afterwards. There are even recorders with a push-button 'memo' function that marks selected points on the tape with a special tone and allows the user to 'search' for them. Already overloaded with detailed transcriptions of audio data for my doctoral research, I was simply unable to transcribe verbatim (but see comments in the next paragraph) the full product of our discussions, and in the end did so only for contributions that I found particularly germane, succinct, or amusing. I chose to set down the remainder of the discussion in a fairly economical 'minutes' format, with my own comments alongside: FP2 (female participant 2) pointed out that students in this course were taking double the required number of hours of English and suggested that some might feel that they should be rewarded just for this. MP1 (male participant 1) said that he had heard a male student actually express this opinion. I asked (open question to group) how group members felt about this idea. Some amusement and embarrassment. No one wanted to answer directly, but MP2 said, "I think I can understand their [opinion]." A few nods of apparent agreement.

Verbatim transcription, I noted, can actually impinge on the informants' anonymity. When I raised a point myself in discussions, I would typically elicit comments from participants by name, but when participants spoke among themselves they often didn't use names at all. Although I could always identify speakers by their voices, I also noticed that I could readily identify individuals by idiosyncrasies in their use of English. One participant, for example, used the phrase "up to a point" with great enthusiasm, and it seemed likely that if I could identify him so easily by this trait, others could do so too. In order to preserve anonymity, I resorted to editing transcribed remarks when doing so wouldn't affect meaning. I also edited out linguistic errors – again, potential identifiers – and glossed Japanese interjections. Anyone undertaking informal research along these lines simply has to decide in how detailed and/or pristine a form data should be captured and how best to balance the preservation of individual voices with the time available for compiling a record. The procedure I have described meets my own need for a summary of what was said in group discussions and will allow me to safely use my transcriptions as a stimulus for future discussions among students and colleagues.

Two cultural peculiarities

As a gentle introduction to the discussion process, our little group first took up some genuine questions I had concerning typical Japanese student behaviours and attitudes: Why can it be so hard to get male and female students to work together in pair work, and why do even weak students complain when they don't pull an A semester grade? Here are extracts from a discussion of the (in my view) problem of nonmingling of genders (verbatim comments are in quotation marks):

Me: Umm . . . another thing I've noticed is that even today women students and men often don't really mix in pair work, especially in freshman year. Is that a habit left over from school, where boys and girls hardly ever work together in lessons?

Note, however, that, thanks in part to the Japan English Teacher (JET) program's introduction of English-speaking teaching assistants into Japanese junior high and senior high schools, there has been an enormous expansion of 'communicative' pedagogy. JET teachers have also brought a much stronger BANA expectation that male and female students will work together in class.

After pointing out that my observation was an overgeneralization and probably outdated, one woman participant said:

FP4: It depends on the boys [sic]. Some boys just don't seem very interested, so I think girls don't want to work with them.

Now this was interesting. Could it be that what I'd taken to be a negative classroom behaviour actually had a pedagogically positive rationale? I replied that I could see that it would be hard to work with someone who didn't seem very interested. The same student continued:

FP4: [Right!] And you told us that our grades depend on our effort in class, but it's hard to make a good effort when your partner doesn't want to speak much.

Well, self-interest is seldom far below the surface. Yet this female student's opinion doesn't explain why many male students appeared reluctant to work with women. On further enquiry, it became clear that some male participants – and hence probably a good number of their peers – had been unaware of these grounds for some women students' reluctance to work with males. They had assumed (as indeed I had myself, along with many of my colleagues) that the reluctance was based merely on a partner's gender, rather than on what we might call his or her communicative (or grade!) potential. Far from being the reflexive hangover from schooldays that I had assumed, this preference among women students for partners of their own gender – and of course if most or all of the women choose female partners, then males will typically be stuck with one another – makes good sense from a (female) language learner's point of view.

I next took up the question of grades, pointing out that, although this didn't apply to anyone in the room, students would soon descend on me to complain about their semester grades. Why, I wondered, did even rather lazy students appear to seriously expect an A? One participant explained that the difficulty lay in the fact that many lecturers awarded A grades to all students who attended class regularly and carried out the basic requirements of the course. Confronted with a course that awarded A grades only to those who performed exceptionally well, many students felt rather put upon. One male participant in the discussion mentioned that some (male) students he had talked to prior to our meeting had pressed him to bring up just this question of disparate grading standards and teacher expectations.

I knew that in Japan professors are typically free to award grades much as they see fit (Aoki, 1999), but I hadn't been aware that expectations of my courses were markedly in conflict with those of at least some other courses. Japanese undergraduate degrees are conventionally awarded on a simple pass-fail basis, so the award of a high grade to everyone who meets a professor's criterion of 'good enough' isn't entirely unreasonable. And yet the participants in the discussion were clearly unhappy with the idea of extra effort going unrewarded, with one maintaining that this was a factor in his decision to join the elective course, in which grading standards – he understood – were largely set by Western-educated Japanese faculty and by non-Japanese teachers.

MP2 said that in one of his courses the teacher spoke almost all the time, and students had to answer only very occasional questions. He added that, in that kind of class ("It's too much like a lecture!"), a teacher could base semester grades only on whether students were, first, present, and, second, awake. Laughter around the table, nods of agreement.

Me: "The rest of you have classes like that too?" Most nod.

The group agreed that this was a short-term problem anyhow, in that word would soon get around that in my classes I was stricter about grade standards, and so only more dedicated students would elect to join. This was fine with me, but I explicitly asked participants to help make clear to next year's intake that grades depended as much on effort to improve as on improvement itself. Students everywhere trust what they hear from their peers, and I anticipated that the focus group might be a useful means of feeding back information to the wider student body.

Classroom power

Having acclimatized my informants to an atmosphere of open discussion, and myself to the need to avoid even the appearance of reacting defensively to critical comments, I returned in a subsequent meeting to the topic of the 'balance of power' in the classroom:

Me: I've mentioned before the controversy in teaching about whether class should be teacher-centered, which means that the teacher is very much in charge of what goes on, or student-centered, which means that the students themselves have a lot of say in what happens in the class. Now, you've experienced both styles this semester. Do you have any thoughts about them?

A participant asked whether I wanted to know whether students preferred teacher X's way or my own way of conducting lessons. I had hoped to avoid discussing colleagues directly, so I fudged.

Me: I know that different teachers have different teaching styles. But I've tried to use both ways in my own classes this year. How did you feel about that?

Participants responded with:

FP4: Things work better if the teacher really takes charge. We get more done in less time. When we have to find a partner, it's better if the teacher tells us who to work with, 'cause we need a lot of time to choose, sometimes.

MP1: And some people try to choose the same partners all the time. Returnees sometimes try to work with [other returnees]. So shy students don't get a chance to work with people who can speak well.

It appeared that, as far as 'classroom mechanics' went, a more teacher-directive style could make class work not only more efficient in students' eyes, but also 'fairer'. But why couldn't motivated and able students solve this for themselves? I wondered.

Me: Okay, but why don't shyer people just choose more fluent people as partners? I've never seen a returnee student, for example, refuse to work with someone at a lower level. I would make them [sic] if I saw that happening.

MP2: Sometimes we feel too embarrassed to do that.

Me: Because you feel your English is weaker than theirs?

FP3: We sometimes feel that it's unfair to ask a returnee student to work with us because they [sic] might get bored.

This (to my mind) excessive 'self-denial' out of concern for the feelings of others is a common feature of interpersonal relations in Japan, but was it open to change? I agreed that I could understand this feeling but pointed out that one or two returnees, by their own admission, had opted for my class in the expectation that it would provide a good semester grade without too much effort, at least compared to what was required in the courses intended especially for returnees. Shouldn't these guys be expected to work with everyone in the class? I wondered.

Participants' uneasy responses to that question suggested that their reluctance to 'impose on' peers was too deeply rooted to be easily overcome. When teachers themselves allocate partners in pair work, individual students are absolved of responsibility for any imposition that might be felt. Although this basic teacher control may undermine the goal of student 'empowerment' (Pennycook, 1989) in the sense of self-management, the affective benefit of removing this burden may be considerable.

"The nail that sticks up gets hammered down"

This Japanese proverb holds true today, and not only in the workplace and in school. At one stage, the natural flow of the discussion brought us to the topic of the relationships within a class, particularly those between the class as a whole and individual 'nonconformists'. Not only was I probing, here, into one of the darker corners of Japanese culture, but I was also conscious of trespassing on what Holliday (1994) calls the 'classroom culture'. In addition to reflecting the wider national and institutional traditions, individual classes have a culture that is to some degree their own. Some groups, for example, are very accepting of classroom clowns, or those who fail to prepare adequately for class work; others seem much less tolerant of those who deviate from the group's expectations. This can be a particularly sensitive area in Japanese culture, with its emphasis on at least the appearance of harmony. Despite that, however, I genuinely wanted guidance about how to deal with one particular case:

Me: We had a case the other week in which a guy who hadn't done his homework just got up and left the room without saying anything.

A participant said she thought that the student in question had felt ashamed.

Me: Because he hadn't done the preparation? He hasn't come to class at all this week. He may be ill, but if he's just too embarrassed to come back, what should I do?

I noted subdued, perhaps embarrassed, giggling and shrugging of shoulders around the table.

Me: You don't mind if he doesn't come back?
FP2: *Shoganai, ne* ["It can't be helped"]. He's not so interested in what we do in class. Many of us try to encourage him, but it doesn't do any good.

There was a general nodding of heads by participants who knew the individual in question. Now, Japanese pedagogical tradition honours the teacher who spares no effort to bring the stray back to the fold; yet here was a group of students more or less telling me to let a classmate sink or swim. Although no one said as much directly, it soon became clear that participants felt that, within reasonable limits, individuals should be allowed to make their own decisions and take the consequences. They seemed to feel that teachers who fell over themselves to prevent a student from dropping out were in a real sense undermining other students' claim to adulthood and self-direction. One participant argued – naively, in my view, for graduation from college is a prerequisite for almost any white collar position in Japan – that no one *had* to enroll in a university. By this point the discussion had acquired a definite edginess, and some participants were exchanging whispers in Japanese. I couldn't tell how much of the ill feeling around the table was directed at the (clearly unpopular) student we'd been discussing, and how much at my stubborn digging at the question of how the situation should be handled. I backed away and switched the focus of the discussion.

Me: I've seen some of you talking with little groups of your classmates. Were you asking their opinions about the questions we were going to discuss here? [Nodding of heads.]
Me: What did they tell you? [All around the table, Japanese body language meaning *That's a sensitive point.* Embarrassed smiles.]
MP2: Some people said that we shouldn't be talking to you. They said that [whenever] teachers try to improve things it means more work for the students.

I suddenly remembered that this had been true when I was a student: Every 'improvement' to a course seemed to lengthen the reading lists even more. "Well, maybe the same amount of work, but more useful," I said, hoping it would sound convincing. Most of the group nodded reassuringly.

But I also wanted to explore what appears to me to be one of the most central questions in the pedagogical power equation: What gets studied, and how? The notion of a 'negotiated syllabus' has been with us for many years now, but I had no real insight into students' attitudes towards what would be a very radical idea in Japanese education.

Me: So, how should we go about choosing what to study in class? Is that only the teacher's job, or should students help decide?

FP1: You always ask in the first class what we want to study, right?

Me: Yes, I have people in groups write down some topics they're interested in.

FP1: [general laughter]: But you don't let us study all the things we write down.

I had an idea of what was coming. "Sport, for example?" I asked. My guess was confirmed, and participants added a list of other areas I never seemed to cover in class, such as cuisine and fashion. My defence was that I simply wasn't interested in sport (wasn't it André Breton who coined my pedagogical motto: "Teacher, enjoy yourself! Otherwise you'll bore us."?) and that food and fashion seemed to me to be insufficiently 'serious' topics for a university-level course. This didn't go down well, and the students made it clear that if they were willing to work on topics of my choosing that didn't particularly interest them, I should also be willing to do the same. One participant noted that one course teacher made no attempt to find out what students might be interested in studying but claimed that they could live with that. If a teacher asked for suggestions and then didn't use them, however, students might feel "upset". Aoki (1999) also mentions a Japanese student's concern that a teacher "be true to her words."

I'd obviously stepped into something here, and although I might have pointed out that there wasn't enough class time to cover everything, and that social, environmental, and current affairs topics were consistently ranked in students' 'want lists' as more important than sports and so on, it seemed more appropriate in Japanese cultural terms just to admit that I could do better. As the discussion continued, I had to conclude that even the best-motivated and most able students participating in these discussions seemed, by and large, to feel that it's essentially the teacher's job to decide what gets covered in class. Why then were students at the start of each semester so eager to give me lists of preferred lesson topics? Informants agreed they needed more time to think about this apparent contradiction, and so this is a seam we'll continue to mine.

Returning the favour

Questions and outright complaints about other teachers also arose, and although they made me uncomfortable, I was of two minds about how to deal with them. One complaint was that a certain teacher was dealing at considerable length with a topic of, let's say, rather limited interest to the majority of the class. On the one hand, I felt uncomfortable about raising students' dissatisfaction with a colleague, but on the other hand, it seemed that students felt unable to express their views to him directly. It seemed like a dereliction of responsibility not to do something about the problem. A participant reminded me of what we'd discussed earlier: "Do you remember we were talking about the student who got up and left the classroom? I said we had tried to encourage him."

I could guess where this was leading, and I was right. There was a definite frustration on the group's part that teachers apparently didn't feel the need to, as it were, keep one another in line, as students tried to do with 'difficult' classmates. The fact that semester grade assignments tended to bunch up within the same few weeks showed, they thought, that teachers either weren't communicating enough or simply didn't care about the unreasonable workload they were placing on students. To my relief – I'd been looking for a chance to show that these discussions could bring practical benefits – this was an area I could do something about, and by taking students' complaints to the powers that be, it has been possible to require teachers to better coordinate due dates for assignments.

What I've learned

Things are changing rapidly in Japanese education. The ever-falling birthrate means less competition for college places, and colleges themselves are slowly waking up to the need to attract students. Yet even today many Japanese students do not perceive themselves as entitled to a say in their classroom experience. Teachers are still widely expected to define what should be studied, and how, and there are great barriers to direct or even indirect expression of dissatisfaction. Teachers and course supervisors need to actively elicit the opinions of their student population, and until Japanese students' 'hearts and minds' are better understood, simple questionnaire-style surveys may not be an adequate tool. The repeated meetings of a focus group discussion forum like the one I've described not only allow trust to grow in a natural, unforced way but also create a context in which participants can think at length and in depth about what they really want from a language course, and what they can bring to it. Aspirations and opinions can change – sometimes quite radically – from meeting to meeting, but this is appropriate to a process model of progress.

Honest instructor-student dialogue has the potential to create considerable discomfort on both sides, and perhaps to open up more questions than it answers. I have been confronted with one or two uncomfortable truths regarding my own classroom practice, just as student participants in the focus groups have come to question aspects of their attitudes towards learning and their classroom behaviour. Although I've learned things I wasn't conscious of before, for example, that 'negative' classroom behaviours may have a 'positive' underlying motivation, I've also been forced to question some of my political-pedagogical views, such as my enthusiasm for maximum student self-management and decision making. Student participants have had to think about how the pressure to conform in Japanese society can subtly influence student-student relationships within the classroom, and to think about their language education as a more dynamic process than traditional models have allowed.

It's hard for me to see how the insights I've gained through this experience of in-depth, open dialogue could have been acquired in some other way, even through the informal education I mentioned earlier. Rereading the journal I've been keeping throughout our discussions, I can see how my previous anxieties about becoming 'stale' or even 'deskilled' in a monocultural teaching context give way to questions and worries over how well I really understand my Japanese students, the needs they are trying to express, and the uncertainties they seem to be grappling with. Again and again I come up with new questions to think about, or new ways to think about older questions. I find more and more antidotes to staleness, and more openings for the reflection I'd sometimes felt was lacking from my teaching practice. Perhaps I just needed more to reflect about; I've certainly found a way to get it.

References

Aoki, N. (1999). Affect and the role of teachers in the development of learner autonomy. In J. Arnold (Ed.), *Affect in Language Teaching* (pp.142–154). New York: Cambridge University Press.

Holliday, A. (1994). *Appropriate methodology and social context*. Cambridge: Cambridge University Press.

Pennycook, A. (1989). The concept of method, interested knowledge, and the politics of language teaching, *TESOL Quarterly, 23*(4), 589–618.

Schön, D. (1983). *The reflective practitioner: How professionals think in action*. New York: Basic Books.

8 *My learning through journaling*

Forgiveness as a source of power and the communication of voice in the classroom

Jennifer L. Esbenshade

> Who we are as teachers and students in school is mediated by our culture of domination and by our social identities and lived experiences that have been forged within them. These cultures, our positions within them, and our experiences must be problematized and critically encountered. (Kreisburg, 1992, p. 198)

Forgiveness is a topic most teachers probably do not think much about. I too never considered what it meant in relation to teaching, especially not in my own teaching. As a student in an ESL teacher-learning program, I have reflected on each of the classes I taught in relation to my instructional strategies, students' responses, and overall student learning. But forgiveness never emerged as a critical consideration, until I conducted my own focused teacher reflection study.

Context

Throughout the course of a spring semester, I wrote a detailed journal entry after one of the two classes I taught. As a beginning teacher, I took on this project for my own professional development, rather than as any kind of requirement for a class. In developing this task, I decided to describe thoroughly the occurrences in only one of the classes I was teaching, since I wanted to explore the extent to which this journal actually helped me improve my interactions with and understanding of my class. So, the purpose of keeping the journal was twofold: to improve my ability to reflect critically as a teacher and to determine the extent to which the journal helped me to understand my students better.

The class I taught was a requirement for all undergraduate students at the university. All students must take a basic-level English writing class to improve their communication skills. Students who learn English as a second language have the option of taking the class with students who are native speakers of English, or they can take a more specialized class that is only for ESL students, in which American discourse forms and grammatical structures are emphasized.

The class I chose to journal about met at 8 a.m. every Tuesday and Thursday. It was composed of thirteen students (one of whom dropped the class in the final month) from around the world: Cambodia, Germany, Honduras, Iran, Korea, Puerto Rico, Russia, Sweden, Ukraine, and Vietnam. Each student brought a different perspective to the classroom, creating a unique environment in which to teach and to learn.

After each class, I spent anywhere from a half hour to two hours reflecting and commenting on the class. I noted the content that I covered in class that day and how the students reacted to it. I kept track of student interactions, with whom they chose to work, and how well they worked together. I also always commented on how I felt about the lesson: whether I felt my students were able to learn and to apply what I was teaching them.

At the conclusion of the semester, when I read through the entire journal, I realized that it contained numerous themes that I would not have been able to recognize had I not taken the time to journal about this class. With multiple readings, one theme in particular seemed to keep reoccurring in this class: forgiveness. Upon further reflection, I came to realize how acts that required forgiveness were closely tied into conceptions of power and self-empowerment, as well as to communication in the classroom.

Self-concept as a teacher

Various experiences and situations comprise teachers' notions of teaching. As Staton and Hunt (1992) state, agents, changes, context, and biography contribute to the formation of teachers' ideas of teaching. The first three components are more concrete in that they relate to a particular setting or occurrence. *Agents* are colleagues, students, and supervisors who directly affect a particular teaching situation (the *context*), and *changes* relate to dilemmas or other experiences that influence notions of teaching. On the other hand, *biography* is not so concrete. This term relates to our own ideas of and attitudes about teaching, most of which are developed from an apprenticeship of observation. First described by Lortie (1975), an *apprenticeship of observation* is the understanding of what teachers do that was learned from observing teacher behaviors from a student's perspective. This is a powerful component in determining conceptualizations of teaching because future teachers spend so many years as students watching a wide array of teachers. Yet, it is a component that many teachers do not consider in their own teaching because this learning was subtle and gradual and because it ties in closely with notions of self-concept as a teacher.

Self-concept, as defined by Cooper and Simonds (1999), is "how you perceive yourself intellectually, socially, and physically; how you would like to be; how you believe others perceive you; and how others actually perceive you" (p. 31). Self-concept is vital to how activities are carried out in the classroom, since it affects how we interact with students. Further, self-concept has a reciprocal relationship with communication in that self-concept affects how we communicate, and how we communicate affects our self-concept (Kinch, 1963). This points to the importance of teacher's self-concept and communication in the classroom. If teachers are not fully aware of their self-concept, miscommunication can occur, and, often, these miscommunications can require forgiveness on the part of students.

My journal recounted many occasions during the class when there was a need for my students, either individually or collectively, to forgive me for my mistakes. These incidents were the hardest to deal with both professionally and personally since they involved my self-concept as a teacher and my conception of power in the classroom. Fortunately, these incidents did lead to a deeper understanding of how I conceptualize teaching.

One of the areas of self-awareness pertained to grading. This area has always been extremely difficult for me, but I truly came to understand what grades meant to me as I reflected on an incident with one of my students. In this excerpt, I commented in my journal on how a student named Boris approached me to ask about his grade on an essay he had written:

I keep thinking back to the first essay when Boris questioned me about his grade of 95. Five points were taken off because he didn't do a required prewrite. He approached me. He sounded mad. I immediately said, 'You still got an A. What's the problem?' How stupid of me. I know I have always been so obsessed with grades I guess I just forgot that my students are too. One of the questions on the final college evaluations of the course, the SRTEs [Student Rating of Teaching Effectiveness] was whether the instructor promotes learning over grades. I was horrified at seeing this question and scared to see what my students thought. I wasn't rated too terribly, but I still felt dissatisfied with myself in that respect and that was last semester! Have I learned anything since then? Grades seem to be such an intrinsic part of me that I can't separate them from learning. I think I sometimes rank them as the same. Undoubtedly I tell my students this. Should I apologize to Boris or is it too late?

As shown in these reflections, I was surprised at how I as a teacher had conceptualized grades. This was one of the first incidences when I was able to understand fully that my reaction to a student was based on my own experience, my apprenticeship of observation. My schooling had taught me the power of grades, which I consequently had unconsciously imposed on my students without recognizing or valuing their own experiences related to grading. My ingrained notions were made all too apparent in my miscommunication with Boris. Even though I was fully aware of the pedagogical reasons for why grades are not indicative of learning, when I had an interaction with a student related to grades, my experience took over, demonstrating the power of these learned pedagogies.

Another area of self-awareness that I developed related to maintaining the balance between individualized and whole-class instruction time. Since my class was composed of students from various educational experiences and with different levels of English proficiency, determining how to best meet individualized learning needs without neglecting other students was a challenge I was aware of from the beginning of my teaching. I sometimes noticed that students seemed to fall through the cracks, as was the case with three students in my class. Early in the semester I approached two of these students to ask them to find particular grammar points to work on because their serious grammatical errors made their writing unclear. I asked them twice whether they had found any recurring errors. When they didn't offer any, I let the subject drop because I felt they weren't interested. I did not give them any further activities to practice, nor did I spend individualized time with them. In a sense, I let them slip by since I did not provide the instruction and encouragement they needed to improve their writing.

Similarly, regarding one student who was particularly shy in the class, Yi Sang, I noted several times in the journal how I needed to work at reaching him. At the end of the semester I reflected:

I really feel as if I have shortchanged Yi Sang all semester. He seems like such a wonderful person; it was just hard getting him to come out of his shell. I wonder what he is like outside of class. I often ask myself whether there was anything I could have done differently with him. Of course, I could probably ask myself that where every student is concerned, but for some reason he stands out the most – I guess because he stood out the least in class.

In many ways, I feel as though I let these students down, that my expectations were low. I had always wondered how it was possible for students to slide by or even "disappear" in school, like Yi Sang did. Even with such a small class I realize how easily this could happen. However, I also now recognize that the initiative cannot lie only in the teacher; it must also come from the students. The students' willingness to take extra steps in their learning springs from their understanding of the value of their education.

Teachers do play a part in enhancing this understanding, but much responsibility still lies with the students themselves since they must determine how hard they are willing to work to attain educational goals. When students and teachers are equally responsible in setting and achieving goals, student success is more likely to occur.

The last area of self-awareness I want to reflect on was how teachers' attitudes can either positively or negatively affect the environment for learning. I strove to maintain a positive atmosphere in class, but one day in particular that did not occur. I was in a bad mood when I came to class, and my mood was exacerbated when I found that students had not done their homework. I think that all the students could sense my anger, so they quickly set to work to avoid further irritating me. As the class wore on, I could not help but realize the futility of my bad mood, and I soon was laughing with my class. I just assumed that the first part of class was forgotten, but I realized two weeks later that it was not, as evidenced in some comments from their midsemester evaluations. In reflecting, I wrote:

Perhaps the most cutting comment was from Manuel. I know it was him from his writing style and vocabulary choice. He is generally happy with the class except he advised that I do not bring in personal frustrations to the class. He said I only did it once, and I know exactly what day he means. It was a needed reminder that my students need my encouragement, not my irritation.

I recognize from my own schooling experience how easy it is to tell when a teacher is in a bad mood and, thus, creates a negative environment for learning. In this case, my state of mind was obvious to my students as well. My own realization of my mood came too late in this instance, since I should have recognized and changed it before I even entered the classroom.

Recognition of power structures

For all three of these examples, a part of me still seeks the students' forgiveness, but there seems to be something inherent in the structure of school that does not allow teachers to cross that power line. Especially as a beginning teacher, I felt as if I had to maintain a power structure, and to apologize in such cases would have been a recognition of my failure, hence undermining my power.

My conceptualization of power, based on my apprenticeship of observation, is what Kreisberg (1992) describes as "power over" students in a classroom. In this classroom structure, the teacher is the ultimate authority and the arbiter of decisions and the students are passive observers. From my journaling and reflection with regard to grading, instruction time, and "moods," I realized that I wielded power over my students: I decided that a student should just be happy with his A, that some students didn't need any individualized instruction, and that I need not try to control the mood of a class.

This concept of power is in sharp contrast to another term used by Kreisberg (1992) – that classroom power structures should reflect an organizational framework of "power with" students. In this way, teachers and students share in the construction of power, with the goal being to empower the student both in and out of the classroom setting.

Student-student power structures and the development of voice

So if the goal is to share power with students and empower them, how is this goal manifested in the classroom? In a classroom setting teachers have an impact on students, students influence the teacher, and students affect one another. Students do need to play an active role in how the classroom is structurally organized, for they "attempt to share ownership of the [classroom] culture and become active agents in establishing, maintaining, and changing the conventions of the classroom culture" (Cooper & Simonds, 1999, p. 12). To become active agents, students need to be empowered in the classroom.

Kreisburg (1992) describes empowerment as "a personal transformation out of silence and submission that is characterized by the development of an authentic voice. . . . [It] is a process through which people and/or communities increase their control or mastery of their own lives and the decisions that affect their lives" (pp. 18–19). But as Rosenman (1980) warned, empowerment cannot be coupled with "the oppressive and unjust restraint of others" (p. 252). Student empowerment, then, is vital to creating just classroom structures where power is distributed and shared so that students can take an active role in their learning while teachers can still provide appropriate guidance. In this sense, empowerment needs commitment and trust. It needs support to foster a true expression of voice that seeks to validate the experience of both teachers and students.

This expression of voice is different from language itself. Ruiz (1991) describes language as general and abstract, something that has a life of its own. Voice, however, is particular and concrete, and when it is suppressed, it ceases to exist. That is, a student's voice is the particular language that he or she uses to express identity. If this voice is not nurtured, it will not serve to empower the student, and empowering students should be a goal in the classroom.

In the desire to express voice in my classroom, students sometimes encroached on others; this behavior undermines the notion of empowerment. Most of these incidents pertained to the actions of one student, Manuel. He was very bright and articulate, but his self-centeredness dominated his interactions, often to the point at which he offended others.

Students themselves then had to learn how to handle situations that not only required forgiveness of others in the class (usually Manuel) but also called for exploration of their own self and cultural identity in their expression of voice. For instance, in one entry I reflected on a discussion we had in class about war, particularly about the readiness of the United States to become involved in international situations. Since numerous nationalities were represented in the class, most students contributed deeply personal opinions on this matter.

A comment was made about the unwillingness of the United States to get involved in all situations, and I supplied the examples of Cambodia and Rwanda. I asked Hui (a Cambodian student) to comment on the Khmer Rouge, but he didn't say much. Manuel was quick to say, "No offense, but nobody cares about Cambodia." How I wished he could learn to say his thoughts without sounding so offensive. We had to step back and clarify what that meant in a nicer way. So much for getting the Asian students involved.

Manuel had been insensetive about my questions to Hui and also about Hui's personal involvement in the situation we were discussing. Manuel asserted his dominance in the class; he voiced sentiments most students would only think. (But through his brazenness he created an opportunity for other members of the class to exercise power, as I describe later.) A similar situation, in which students talked about their home culture, occurred later in the semester and makes this point.

Finally, Yi Sang briefly, very briefly described Korea. He didn't have much to say, as usual, and of course we didn't have much time left to talk. I felt as if I slighted him, as usual. He is just one of those quiet students who you don't really notice whether he's there or not. The one time he could share about his culture, he didn't say much and there was no time. To make matters worst, Jacob asked whether Korean people eat dogs. I felt my last drop of patience leave. Hui rolled his eyes at the ignorance. Yi Sang tried to talk, but Jacob pushed about the Olympics [how Korea experienced difficulty with the Seoul games because of this issue]. . . . I felt so bad for Yi Sang. I didn't feel good about how the class ended.

Throughout both of these situations, I observed the embarrassment of the students as they tried to respond to negative statements made about their own culture, which is intricately tied to voice. I wanted to apologize for the stupidity of both of these statements and step in to "fix" the problem. As the leader of the class, I had the power to create an opportunity to discuss how we need to think about our audience and our message as well as our responsibility to speak more carefully. Yet I felt it was essential at this point to share power with the students so that they could begin to learn how to handle these circumstances themselves.

Even though it was evident that they were angry and didn't know how to respond, many of these international students will continue to encounter such stereotypical notions. I felt that it was imperative for these students to learn how to become more self-empowered to develop their voice, especially with such blatant stereotyping, since as Ruiz (1991) states, "Teachers do not empower or disempower anyone. . . . They merely create the conditions under which people can empower themselves or not. It is certainly true that teachers impart skills – literacy, numeracy, and others: but these are not in themselves power" (p. 223). In the classroom, then, discussion and activities are needed that allow students to explore their conceptualization of self-empowerment and voice. In my classroom, students themselves slowly learned how to take control of such situations. At the beginning of the class, I was the source of control, especially for the comments from Manuel. I worked to develop techniques to funnel his energies into other activities and to start dialogue on some of his more controversial comments. As the semester wore on, students seemed to become more empowered and willing to take control of situations that occurred in the classroom. For instance, one of the shyer students, a student of few but wise words, reminded Manuel that he needed to learn to "hold his tongue": a reprimand much more effective than anything I could have offered. At another point in the class, two other students forthrightly told Manuel to "shut up" when he kept interrupting other people. I was taken aback by their use of power over him. Manuel must have realized his error, and his apology was evidenced by his silence and, then, his asking permission to comment.

Even though these first attempts at exercising their power in the classroom may not have been the most appropriate, students found their voices. They were willing to try to change the "conventions of the classroom culture" to ensure that power was more evenly distributed among them. It seemed as if they had become comfortable enough with one another that they were willing to take a more active role in the power structure of the class.

The final act of forgiveness

Despite some uncomfortable incidents that required realignment of power between students, the members of my class seemed to be developing a deeper level of understanding of and concern for one another, even though I was not always aware of these developments. This all became evident when, on the last day of class as I said my good-byes to the class, no one moved. The class was over, and no one got up to leave. Finally, they stood up and started to shake hands with one another. I heard things like,"It was great getting to know you," "I'll miss seeing you in this class," and "No hard feelings." I was stunned. The last moments of class were an incredible time of forgiveness and reconciliation.

Through this final event, I came to recognize in my journaling that a kind of "safe" environment had been created in the classroom. Students had been comfortable enough to explore their voices with one another. They had created their own power structures and were able to share in the responsibility of the class through the comments they made and the interactions they had. They had also seemed to have forgiven each other for those times when some of them tried to silence or discredit another's voice. It was a fitting end for an exceptional class.

Final thoughts

My personal learning from this experience grew from my decision to keep a teaching journal, one of many possible forms for introspection. No matter what form is used, I now recognize the need to participate in some kind of reflection so that issues that not are readily apparent in everyday experiences can be further considered and analyzed with respect to teaching practices. At the end of the semester, I acknowledged that I had a deeper understanding of some of the influences on and beliefs about my teaching and my interactions with this one class.

I came to understand numerous incidents that occurred in relation to my understanding of forgiveness as it pertained to power structures and student voice. However, at that point, my journal allowed me only to recognize these occurrences. When I began keeping the journal, I felt that my teaching practices would radically change in this class because of the amount of introspection I was doing. The more I continued the project, the more I realized that this wasn't true. Journaling is just a first step to becoming more aware of issues in the classroom and beliefs about teaching and students. Another step must be taken after this in order to change practices and to make practices align more with beliefs about teaching. As is evident in the reflections I have mentioned here, I am able to describe classroom incidents, even to categorize them, and to articulate my beliefs about and the influences on my teaching. I am now working on determining the methods to use to institute change in my teaching practices.

References

Cooper, P. J., & Simonds, C. (1999). *Communication for the classroom teacher* (6th ed.). Needham Heights, MA: Allyn and Bacon.

Kinch, J. (1963). A formalized theory in self-concept. *American Journal of Sociology, 68*, 481–486.

Kreisberg, S. (1992). *Transforming power: Domination, empowerment, and education*. Albany, NY: State University of New York Press.

Lortie, D. C. (1975). *Schoolteacher: A sociological study*. Chicago: University of Chicago Press.

Rosenman, M. (1980). Empowerment as a purpose of education. *Alternative Higher Education: The Journal of Non-Traditional Studies, 4*, 248–259.

Ruiz, R. (1991). The empowerment of language minority students. In C. Sleeter (Ed.). *Empowerment through multicultural education*. Albany, NY: State University of New York Press.

Staton, A., and Hunt, S. (1992). Teacher socialization: Review and conceptualization. *Communication Education, 41*, 110–137.

9 *Understanding our students' families*

The hidden community of international wives

Linda Winston and Laurie Soltman

Guo's story

Guo, an international graduate student from mainland China, was enrolled in Linda's spoken English course for international teaching assistants at Penn State University. By the middle of the semester Linda had identified Guo as one of two students whose pronunciation was particularly weak, and she was seriously concerned that he would not make enough progress to pass the final examination, which would also mean that he would not pass the course. During a midsemester meeting she expressed her concerns to Guo and discussed possible strategies for improving his English. Over the course of the next seven weeks his pronunciation steadily improved, and he passed his final examination without any difficulty.

Guo's speech displayed a remarkable amount of improvement, changing from nearly unintelligible to very clear and understandable. The unusually large leap in overall comprehensibility prompted Linda to ask Guo how he had managed to achieve such dramatic improvement in a relatively short period of time. Unlike other students, who often employ independent study strategies such as watching TV or reading into a tape recorder, Guo had involved his family in his program of study. After the midsemester meeting he had gone home and told his wife, Fenhong, all about the difficulties he was having, and the two of them sat down together to talk about how he could improve his English. It was Fenhong's idea for Guo to go to the public library every week and check out children's books to read aloud to his daughter, who would often correct her father's pronunciation. Guo enjoyed the nightly reading sessions with his daughter, and he also found that he learned about American culture through the stories. Involving his family made studying English more fun, which in turn encouraged Guo to work on improving his pronunciation.

Too often ESL teachers focus on the student without thinking about the context in which the student lives and studies, a context that frequently includes the student's family. By knowing about and involving the family,

118

we can help our students find English language study more fulfilling and, we hope, allow them to achieve greater proficiency as well.

The setting for our story

Guo's story illustrates how a connection between family and the ESL classroom can help our students. Every year students from all over the world relocate to the United States to attend graduate school. Many of them bring their families, and their spouses and children must also make the adjustment to life in the United States. This process includes many challenges for the entire family, especially for members with limited English skills. Although school provides a chance for international children to find friends and learn English, the spouses, generally the wives of male students, have fewer opportunities to improve their language skills. As a result, the wives of international graduate students often struggle to build a new life for themselves in an unfamiliar community.

Like their international classmates, American graduate students and their families also go through a period of adjustment when they move to a new town for graduate school. In fact, when we met one another in the master's program in Teaching English as a Second Language at Penn State, we had each recently experienced a difficult transition: moving to State College in Linda's case, and returning to graduate school in Laurie's. We chose to collaborate on a project for one of our graduate courses because we were both interested in how international residents, adjusted to life in State College. Our work as teaching assistants brought us into contact with international graduate students, so to broaden our understanding of the adjustment issues facing international residents, we wanted to speak with people who were not connected with the university. After determining that the most accessible (and largest) group of people who fit this description were the wives of international graduate students, we conducted interviews with eight women married to Penn State graduate students.

The women's stories taught us a great deal about the challenges faced by ESL speakers within the State College community. Most interesting to us were the role changes experienced by these women, many of whom had left their jobs to move to the United States, and the ways in which they dealt with their shifting identities. Some women relied upon other people from their home countries to provide support; others relied on their own strength to help them successfully make the transition to life in State College. Initially we viewed their stories as a portrait of a community outside

Penn State University without any relevance to the courses we taught or our students. Later we realized that the wives' adjustment to life in the United States, whether successful, stressful, or both, affects the ability of the international graduate students enrolled in university ESL courses to focus on their studies. Furthermore, knowledge of our students' wives can help us better understand our students, a realization we came to through an examination of our own transitions to life in State College.

Linda's story

In August 1995, my husband, Tor, and I moved to State College, Pennsylvania, from Changchun, People's Republic of China. We had spent the previous year teaching English as a Foreign Language to students at Jilin University in Manchuria, a job I found both challenging and extremely rewarding. We returned to the States so that Tor could begin a Ph.D. program in economics at Penn State University; I planned to find a job as a secondary school social studies teacher. Arriving in State College after most graduate student housing had already been rented, we finally found a small apartment in a neighborhood north of the campus inhabited primarily by retired people and young families. I spent the first six months in State College sitting in our cramped, dark apartment typing cover letters to send to thirty-five area school districts, none of which was hiring. Besides having career troubles, I felt isolated and longed to meet other women in similar situations. Most of Tor's American classmates were unmarried recent college graduates; his married colleagues were mostly international students who socialized primarily with one another and never brought their wives to department functions.

My frustration with life in State College affected Tor as much as it did me. Helping me cope took time and energy away from his studies, and more than once he offered to transfer to a university located in a larger city where I could find a teaching job. Because of my recent experience living abroad and the difficulties I was having adjusting to life in a new community, I wondered how the wives of Tor's male international classmates were coping with the strain of moving to a new country. I got my first glimpse into the lives of international graduate students and their families when I volunteered at the local literacy council to be an ESL tutor for the wife of a graduate student. Like myself, she also seemed to be struggling to adjust to her new role, and I became even more curious about the lives of international graduate students' wives.

Laurie's story

After having worked in the unique culture of professional baseball for ten years, I left the industry to enroll in graduate school at Penn State University. I was hoping to develop programs to better assist both international and American players as they made the transition to life in professional baseball in the United States. The need for such programs hit home as I experienced, somewhat painfully, my own shift in identity and comfort level as I moved from an environment in which I was wholly attuned to my role to one in which I was scarcely able to understand the first day's syllabus. The terms *Group work*, *Web searches*, and *on-line discussions* did not exist during my undergraduate years. When I asked at the university's library, "Where should I go to find the card catalogue?" the librarian aptly suggested, "Back about ten years." *Touché*.

In baseball, I had witnessed wives and girlfriends traveling with players and coaches, and often these women were identified during their travels solely by their role as wife or girlfriend. Regardless of their individual abilities and qualities, often their underutilized skills and abandoned careers resulted in identities based solely on their partners' role. When discussing their time in various cities with their husbands, several wives used phrases like, "When we were the pitching coach in Pocatello," highlighting their lack of a separate identity. Because I had long wondered how these wives or girlfriends felt and coped, once I began teaching at Penn State, I was equally curious about how the spouses of my international students handled such identity shifts while living in the United States.

Our story

As teaching assistants at Penn State, we both had the opportunity to teach language courses for international graduate students while pursuing our master's degree. We viewed language as a means by which a person's true personality can be released – a conduit to expression and self-actualization. Our teaching strategies stemmed from a fundamental belief that our students' individual voices remained unheard because of their limited English proficiency. We thought of lessons, activities, and time as the tools with which linguistic barriers that often inhibit the expression of an individual's personality could be removed.

As we found out more about our students, we discovered that many of them had brought their families to State College. Our students often mentioned their families in class and during office hours, and we continued to wonder about how the wives, in particular, dealt with the transition to life in the United States. Linda's struggle with the isolation of her first year in State College and Laurie's difficult departure from professional baseball fueled our desire to investigate the similarly dramatic changes experienced by these women.

An opportunity to pursue this interest came as a result of a course we took during our last semester in the MATESL program. The professor gave us a wide range of choices for our final assignment, including the development of a community-based research project. We were interested in interacting with a group connected with, but not part of, the community of Penn State students in which we studied and taught. We both thought of looking more closely at the lives of our graduate students' wives to find out how their lives had changed after they moved to State College and what type of interaction they had with the community at large.

Trying to find women to interview made us realize that their existence in the State College community was shadowy, if not invisible. Who were they? How would we make contact with them? Would they welcome us? With the help of our married international graduate students, we made the first contacts. Some of their wives were eager to help; others politely balked, and we did not push. Eventually, we made contact with and interviewed eight women, all of whom were living in the United States because of their husbands' graduate studies. None of these women was enrolled at Penn State. None held jobs outside the home. What were their lives like? What was State College like for them? We created a list of fifteen interview questions, and armed with a tape recorder and our curiosity, we set out to talk to them and to learn about their experiences.

The wives' stories

All the women we interviewed had experienced a change in identity upon moving to State College, although the nature of the change varied. Our interviewees fell into three main categories based on the women's identities before they became exclusively wives and homemakers in the United States: women who defined themselves as professionals in their home countries, women who acted as homemakers and mothers and also worked outside the home before moving to the United States, and women who were solely homemakers and mothers in their home countries and retained that role after moving to the United States. Lü (People's Republic of China), Zi (People's Republic of China), and Parang (Korea) fell into the first category. Lü was a customer service representative for Compaq in Shanghai, Zi worked as a translator and assistant for the vice-president of Panasonic in the company's Beijing headquarters, and Parang was a flight attendant with Asian Airlines. Three women fell into the second category: Haesak (Korea), Hong (People's Republic of China), and Fenhong (People's Republic of China). Haesak worked as a pharmacist and moved to the United States with her husband and infant daughter, who is currently in elementary school. Formerly an in-house accountant for a Beijing watch company, Hong gave birth to her son in the United States. Fenhong was a researcher in a government-run plant genetics and breeding laboratory; she and her husband have a preschool-aged daughter born in China and at the time of our interview were expecting a son. In the third category, Huang (Taiwan) and Galsak (Korea) were both homemakers with small children in their home countries; currently they hold the same roles.

Views of self: Identifying strengths and limitations

In talking with these women, we realized that their feelings about their current situations in State College were intimately linked to their perceptions of their own strengths and limitations. For example, when Galsak spoke of her current frustrations, her articulated lack of confidence seemed to stem directly from her self-perceived English inadequacies: "Sometimes, if I go to, yeah, when I go to my son's preschool, I want– I want to explain more for my son, but I couldn't, and I make mistake I didn't know that at the time but I turn around I thought this sentence is not right . . . Is very nervous. That is, I think that is very difficult for me to live in the United States . . . I'm . . . I'm not the person . . . I'm not. . . . " At this point, she waved her hands, and her eyes filled up with tears, punctuating her distress.

Fenhong saw her limitations largely as the result of circumstances beyond her control. Before arriving at State College, she expected that "U.S.A. have many . . . um, job– work– work opportunity to me. But, no!" She spoke about her desire to take the TOEFL and "get a larger degree" than the master's she currently holds. "I want to be a graduate student, some time. But it's difficult to me. Yeah, I will have a baby." Fenhong's dissatisfaction with her current situation was increased by her belief that work authorization restrictions make change impossible. "My feeling is not good. I think, um, in U.S.A. I don't have job. I, um . . . yeah, I can't earn money for family."

Huang, while acknowledging her language weaknesses, commented on her strengths as well, highlighting the orchestrated balance between her ability to physically manage the household and her husband's linguistic competency. "He [her husband] has the most language ability and he can do most communication with [her daughter's] teacher. . . . Yeah, we have a different gift, I think. [Her husband] is good in language and I give– I am better than him in performance. I can cook. I can use the tool. So we are match." Recognizing her limitations in English, however, eventually led Huang to acknowledge that she was not completely happy with her situation. When asked whether there was anything she cannot do because of her English, she noted "Yeah, a little bit . . . like teacher and parents meeting I will let [her husband] go. . . . Yeah [if I were in Taiwan], I think I can cover it. . . . So, I want to go back." She maintained her sense of humor throughout, describing her role here as to "push– push husband through the degree."

Haesak also displayed a sense of humor, laughing at her own linguistic frustrations and emphasizing the fact that they did not diminish her enthusiasm for being in the United States. "I like the volunteer of my daughter's class at both school. I love it, so, at– at– at school I talk . . . with my poor English with the teachers . . . it's uh, I think um uh my English is poor but I can do many things well . . . in here I got a rest time in my life . . . so I enjoy it."

Hong talked about both her strengths and her weaknesses, but contentment with her current role as a mother overshadowed her limitations. She thought it was "very bad" and "very hard" to live in State College without a job before the birth of her son; currently she finds that "it's OK" because she has a more clearly defined job taking care of her young son. Hong mentioned her limitations, but she always balanced those allusions with a description of her strengths and successes. Talking about buying stamps she said, "past– past time, I– I wait he [my husband] buy, he buy come home. Right now I think, "Maybe I can," so I try. Some time– sometimes I try, so I– Ica– . . . I can." She explained that when there are problems with their housing she "call my apartment office. . . . Sometimes easy, sometimes not easy. But, uh . . . um, offi– officer is very nice." However, she also admitted that "when we . . . telephone call, call telephone work I can't, I can't. Because, um . . . I can't speak clear– clearly."

Parang, like the other women, was keenly aware of her proficiency level in English. She was as eager to note her progress, though, as she was to bemoan her inadequate language skills. "In beginning times I can't– I can't call, I can't answer, I can't answer the– the phone. . . . If an American person called our– called me, I couldn't understand anything, so I just to said– say, said, I just said "I can't understand you. Your uh, your uh, your words. Please call later." I just say it and hang up, but nowadays I can– I can listen even though I'm not good at English here. I can answer 'yes' or 'no.'" She perceived her new-found free time as a plus: "You know, I don't have childr– child so I have a lot of time . . . uh, but I like uh these days."

Similar to many of the other women, Zi expressed frustration with her current situation. "In China I have a– a good job. . . . My salary is, uh . . . is, uh, higher than [my husband's]. . . . And I have a good position in my company. . . . I like to work, I like to, uh, that– that feeling, how to say? I know that time I, uh . . . I was– I have a worth– worthy, uh, in my life. So, but, when I come here I just do some, like, yeah housework and I think it's down . . . down a lot." She was sad about her inability to express herself completely to others and explain her thoughts and ideas. However, Zi also talked about an experience she had had living and studying in Japan as one of her strengths, and she drew upon this experience as a valuable resource that could help her understand life in the United States. "In Japan have, uh, same experience [as my current situation]. If I, if my English level is good, so, uh, the, uh, the American people can . . . can communication with me, but if I, if my English level is– is– is low they [Americans] can't– they didn't want to hear what I said, what I want to say. . . . It's very hard to me. But, uh, the same experience for me so I always, uh, I must, I have to study English very hard so I can . . . communication with . . . yes."

The woman who spoke the most about her strengths was Lü. A highly paid professional in China, Lü belongs to a privileged group of Shanghainese who can afford to purchase their own apartments and hire people to clean them. She used the word *famous* in reference to both of her previous employers as well as her former middle school, and she talked proudly about her work experience and her skills. Speaking of her tenure with Compaq she said, "I got a lot of honor when I were in the company," later explaining that "I have a good communication skill in China because our company– because I'm working in a customer service department." She also mentioned the work she did to set up a computer network at her university, saying that "I played Internet very early when I was in university. I'm the lead– the pioneers to play Internet in the university. Because when I'm in university we– we– out university construct– construct a campus Net. And I was one of the team who working for this campus Net. . . . It's only in 1995." The fact that she was such a highly skilled professional in China made the transition extremely difficult for Lü. "After I came here, I feel that I have to live off some persons. I– this feeling made me very un– uncomfortable. Because I'm– when I was born my father and mother told me that, 'You want to live depend on yourself. Because you are the person in the world. You are independence.'"

Connections to the community: Providing support or fostering independence

For those women who seemed to feel that their liabilities equaled or sur-passed their strengths, adjustment did not come without outside support. All the women we interviewed came from collectivist cultures, and each had her own way of linking into a community. Sadly, the Penn State community was not accessible to these women. Programs did not exist to address their adjustment issues, or to bring them into the university community, so they looked elsewhere for support. For some, it was available literally in their own backyard.

Graduate Circle is a housing community of international students with families, many of whom are from mainland China. The geographic prox-imity of neighbors who come from the same cultural background provides opportunities for social interaction, especially during the daytime, when the women and their children visit one another. Fenhong and Hong both lived in Graduate Circle, and they knew one another as well as many of the other Chinese families in the neighborhood. Fenhong explained that "Many Chinese friends live, uh, in Graduate Circle." Asked whether these friends helped her to adjust to life in the United States, she replied, "Ah, yeah. We always, uh, talk each other." The Eastview Community Center offers programs such as Mommy and Me and a weekly cooking class for residents of the university's married student housing, and both Fenhong and Hong took advantage of these opportunities to interact with other women in similar situations. Hong attended Mommy and Me twice a week, and Fenhong went to the cooking class, where she once led a demonstration of how to make Chinese dumplings. Hong explained that she and her friends usually visit "in my house, in my apartment, or . . . outside, or . . . Mommy and Me. . . . [We] talk. Yeah, talk about children, home, yeah."

The presence of so many other women from a similar cultural background in similar situations helped Fenhong and Hong to find friends and feel part of a community in State College. Haesak also commented that she social-izes frequently with other Koreans. "In– in this apartment there are many Korean couples, so I think that I talk to the . . . I meet many Korean wives in here." Even before arriving in State College, Galsak sought out the Korean community. "Before we came here, we contact the Korea Association and so they told my husband's department's friends, so they helped us." In fact, it was Galsak who reached out to Parang when she first moved to State Col-lege. "I, at the beginning, when I met Galsak, Galsak said to me, 'Let's go to English class with me,' so I at that time I go– I went to class with Galsak."

Along with geographical proximity and cultural background, churches provided a supportive community. Each woman we interviewed noted the role of churches in State College as a means to meet people and to learn English. For some, this accessibility was comforting. Galsak was one who embraced the church community. She studied not only English there but also American cooking. She credited the church with helping her and her family when they first arrived. "And when came here the church Korean church they heard we came here so they mmm visit my house they want to help us." Huang found similar comfort from the local Chinese church when she and her family first arrived from Taiwan. "It's easy to find the Chinese in church, and they will help us to know where we can go shopping, where we can get some entertainment, where we can go fishing." The church for her was not only a source of information but a place for friendship. "I think most– most close friends at church. We have the same religion, we have some, some, hmmm, we have some topic or some, some the same, we have the same topic we can discuss or talk about or sharing." For Parang, the church provided daily interaction and a slew of activities. "I– I go to church every Sunday and Wednesday and Friday. And I have three Bible studies in Korean." Although Haesak does not belong to the Korean church herself, she did note its presence. "My friends has a many social organization, yeah, through our church, yeah. Yeah, I don't, but most– most of my friend belong to the organization. In K– in here there is a two Korean churches."

In contrast to those women who relied upon community support, two women chose instead to deal with the difficulties of the role change independently. Lü and Zi did not speak much about community ties. Lü identified important differences between people in the Chinese community in State College and herself and her husband. "It's hard for us to make friends," said Lü. "Even with some Chinese people. Because you know that most international students, just like our Chinese persons, they came here, they have a heavy burden on their backs." Later on she explained that she felt different from these Chinese people because "we have working for a time then we go abroad. And have good position and quit our good position to come. Or sometime they– they don't think Chinese [China] is good enough for them to express their skills. So they go to abroad." Zi did not talk about differences between her and the Chinese community, but she expressed a desire to limit her social contacts to a small circle of friends. "I just want a few people to . . . to be like my friends. Because . . . no more– no more people I can, no more friends, but a good few. Just a little, because I have not such– such time to, yes."

The fact that neither Lü nor Zi identified themselves as part of a community within State College prompted both women to rely more upon their individual strengths to help them adjust to life in the United States, and it also seemed to encourage the two to think about changing their role once again to achieve greater personal satisfaction. "With my experience I always do something myself," said Zi, and Lü said that her familiarity with the Internet helped her to use it "as my– as my valuable source." The independent spirit Lü mentioned in her interview prompted her to spend time studying for the GRE exams, which she was planning to take in preparation for returning to State College as a student next fall semester. "I think at first I should got my degree. Then I can– I can do something else." Because of her dissatisfaction with her role change, Lü was actively involved in changing her situation. Zi also talked about continuing her studies and achieving her academic goals. "Recently I study English very hard," she said. "I want to enter the school to, uh, to get master degree." Because they did not receive as much support from communities as the other women, both Lü and Zi trusted in their own ability to change their current situation.

Linda reflects

This project affected me personally as well as professionally. Not only did I learn more about the challenges faced by my students' families and become more sensitive to my students' lives outside the classroom, but as the wife of a graduate student, I found that the interviewees' stories resonated with me and helped me make sense of my own early experience in State College. When we lived in "the horrible little apartment" (as I now fondly refer to our first home), I searched for a community of people to help me adjust to life in this new town. Unable to find such a community, I relied upon myself to find a new role, first as a substitute social studies teacher and then as a graduate student at Penn State.

I thought of these women and their experiences again after I gave birth to my daughter Lea in November 1999. For the second time since we moved to State College, I faced a difficult adjustment – this time from graduate student and ESL teacher to full-time mother and part-time ESL instructor. Things have changed, though, since my first year in State College. I rely upon the people I met during my time in the community to provide me with advice and support, and I draw upon the confidence I have in my ability to successfully negotiate my way through periods of adjustment. This latest role shift has been much less stressful than moving to State College, and Tor has been able to focus on completing his economics Ph.D. as a result.

My own experience demonstrates how the adjustment of international graduate students' families, and their wives in particular, to life in the United States affects the international graduate students themselves. The successful adjustment of their wives, whether facilitated by a supportive community or the strengthening of the women's independence, allows international graduate students to focus their energies on their studies, including the study of English. Wives who lack English skills must ask their husbands to perform duties such as buying stamps (Hong) and conducting business over the telephone (Parang), and the husbands must take time away from their studies to perform these tasks. Unfortunately, often the courses outside their field of study, such as English for international teaching assistants, are neglected when international graduate students have time constraints imposed by increased household responsibilities.

Laurie reflects

Upon returning to work in baseball, I have found myself more conscious of the ways in which we as a ball club can proactively address some of the identity issues facing wives and girlfriends as they travel with their partners. In one Canadian city, for example, wives are deprived of the outlet of even part-time employment because of work authorization constraints. As a result, we have begun a community action program through which wives and girlfriends can use their time to serve others, providing a sense of purpose and a meaningful role in addition to that of wife or girlfriend. I have also begun to plan for resource networks in each city, directing wives and girlfriends to local women who have similar interests and backgrounds. Often, local churches will actively welcome visiting church members, but some wives or girlfriends are away from home for the first time and don't yet know how to make that initial contact.

Perhaps most notably, with my sensitivities heightened by the interviews that we did, I have sought to change the way I think of the players' wives or girlfriends. Rather than perceiving them as yet another "project" I have to tackle, I have spent more time speaking with each of them, striving to demonstrate through both my time and my actions that I (and, tangentially, the ball club) recognize and respect their importance as individuals as well as their impact on our players. Part of this change in perspective has helped some wives identify tensions they had been experiencing. While visiting one club earlier this season, I noted that often player wives and girlfriends sit together or spend time together only because their husbands and boyfriends happen to play for the same team.

The commonality or sense of connectedness ends there. Assisting these women to find other outlets in the community not only helps them to foster a sense of purpose but also allows them to meet and be part of a community of people with whom they can sit and interact based upon their own interests and experiences rather than those of their husbands and boyfriends.

It struck me during our project how easily overlooked our interviewees were within our community. In both my personal and my professional life, I work to remember their stories and to reach out toward those in similar situations who lack voice and seek to fully express their personalities.

Our final thoughts

After visiting with these women and listening to, transcribing, and reflecting upon their thoughts and experiences, we would have liked them to have had the opportunity to hear how similar their tales were in many ways. We're not certain that any of them would have imagined the simultaneous universality and uniqueness of their stories, and we wish that they had more opportunities for meaningful interaction with one another and with the State College community at large.

As teachers, we have become more sensitive to the issue of access to ESL instruction. Most of the free ESL courses are conducted by religious groups in town, and our interviews made us aware of how that connection influences both the instruction and the students' responses to studying English. In addition, we discovered a lack of courses for intermediate-level speakers of English; the literacy council and community ESL classes offered by the school district provide instruction for people with very limited English language skills, and Penn State's courses are prohibitively expensive for a family living on a graduate student stipend.

Although instructors of international teaching assistants cannot provide language instruction for their students' wives, understanding the challenges faced by those wives can help instructors think of creative strategies that foster a connection between the English language study of our international students and their families. We hope that we can find meaningful ways to bridge the gap between our students' lives and their experience in the ESL classroom, because we realize that such connections are vital to helping our students become more effective English language learners. Involving students' families in the study of English can benefit everyone in the family, and might even make the process of adjustment to life in the United States a little smoother.

Part II   Discussion

1. What have these teachers done to develop a deeper understanding of their students? Which do you see as effective and practical, and why?
2. How have these teachers' perceptions of students changed the way they think about themselves as teachers and their daily classroom practices?
3. As these teachers uncovered differences between how they and their students experience their instruction, what changes did they make in their practices? What obstacles did these teachers need to overcome as a result?
4. What might be some of the rewards and challenges of using student focus groups to get at students' perceptions of their classroom language learning experiences?
5. How have these teachers managed to balance the personal and professional lives of their students?

Part II   Reflection

1. Reflect on a well-remembered event from your experiences as a student in a language classroom. Describe how this event encapsulates your conception of students; in other words, what does it mean to be a student? What are students' rights and responsibilities in the classroom? What is essential for teachers to know about their students in order to teach them better?
2. Create a list of questions that you would like to ask your students about how they are experiencing your instructional practices. Give the list to your students ahead of time, and then meet as a group to discuss them. Take notes of your students' perceptions. Consider how you might incorporate your students' perceptions of your teaching into your instructional practices.
3. Select one of the reflection questions from the beginning of Part II, "Inquiry into Language Learners." Write a short (two- or three-page) position paper on how you have or might have addressed the theoretical and pedagogical concerns embedded in these questions in your current or future instructional practices as a language teacher.

Part II   Action

1. Keep a reflective journal for at least four weeks in which you focus on a particular student in a class you are teaching. Describe how this student acts and interacts in your classroom. Then consider any of the following:

- Describe how you respond to and interact with this student over time
- Describe changes you witness in this student's participation patterns in your classroom activities
- Describe any interactions with this student or between this student and other students that you did not feel comfortable about
- Describe any insights you are learning about your students in general as you keep this journal about a specific student

Reread your journal and try to identify any themes or patterns that emerge. Reflect on and write about:

- How these themes or patterns embody your understanding of this particular student and/or of your students in general
- How these themes embody your principles of instructional practice
- How these themes embody any tensions that might exist between your practice and your beliefs about language learning and language teaching

2. Conduct interviews with your students or with your students' families to learn more about how their interests outside class can be used to develop their English proficiency.

Suggested readings

Cardoza, L. F. (1994). Getting a word in edgewise: Does "not talking" mean "not learning"? *TESOL Journal, 4*(1), 24–27.

Carroll, M. (1994). Journal writing as a learning and research tool in the adult classroom. *TESOL Journal, 4*(1), 19–22.

Cooper, P. J., & Simonds, C. (1999). *Communication for the classroom teacher* (6th ed.). Needham Heights, MA: Allyn and Bacon.

Delpit, L. D. (1988). The silenced dialogue: Power and pedagogy in educating other people's children. *Harvard Educational Review, 58*, 280–298.

Kreisberg, S. (1992). *Transforming power: Domination, empowerment, and education*. Albany, NY: State University of New York Press.

Ruiz, R. (1991). The empowerment of language minority students. In C. Sleeter (Ed.), *Empowerment through multicultural education*. Albany, NY: State University of New York Press.

PART III:
INQUIRY INTO LANGUAGE
TEACHERS

Teachers' inquiries into themselves and their own life stories represent yet another form of professional development. In Part III, "Inquiry into Language Teachers," the stories represent the evolving beliefs and practices of these teachers as they journey through various situations, crossing boundaries of different countries, cultures, and roles. In re-storying their past, these teachers integrate their conceptions of teaching, examples of their instructional practice, interactions with students and colleagues, and the ways they make sense of theory. Ling Shi writes about her experiences as a learner and then as a teacher of adults as she moves from China to Canada and then to Hong Kong. She discovers the power of names in the identity of her students, that is, how names can represent students' aspirations, students' objectives in learning a second language, the cultural values of students, and the triumphs and struggles of students. Kazuyoshi Sato describes his experiences as an ESL learner while an undergraduate in an American university, a novice teacher of ESL in a Japanese high school, a novice teacher of Japanese as a foreign language, a student in a MATESL program in Australia, and then as a more experienced teacher at Japanese universities. The sense of satisfaction he feels in each of these experiences lives on in and alters his later experiences. He learns that his desire for satisfaction has been the "driving force" in his growth and development as a teacher. Tobie Robison, using a different approach to self-introspection, draws together autobiography, a visual depiction of theory, and a theoretical analysis. She constructs a visual depiction of her understanding of pronunciation and, in doing so, articulates how she makes sense of the theory and research she has been reading in her MATESOL program. Such sense making enables her to tie these variety of sources together in unique ways to form critical theoretical knowledge that then enables her to understand herself better as a teacher and the choices she has made.

These teachers' stories reflect how the use of images and metaphor for teachers embodies experiences living on in other experiences. Images and metaphor, with powerful moral and aesthetic dimensions, allow these teachers to represent the complexity of their experiences. Their stories reflect the difficulty teachers have in implementing their beliefs about teaching because of their instructional context – issues of identity and loss of identity, use of English only in an EFL classroom, the polarization of theory and practice, and the elevated status of the native speaker teacher of English. As teachers restory their lives, they recount not only episodes of a particular place and time but also the conceptions, values, and goals that affect each new experience and contribute to their development.

Part III   Initial reflection

The teachers featured in Part III, "Inquiry into Language Teachers," explore the types of theoretical and pedagogical concerns reflected in the following questions. As you read their stories of narrative inquiry, reflect on the concerns embedded in these questions and how you have or might have addressed them in your own teaching.

1. How does restorying the past allow me to articulate my beliefs and values about language learning and teaching and align my instructional practices with those beliefs and values?
2. How does restorying the past allow me to recognize how my life is socially and historically situated and how my life experiences continue to influence me as a teacher?
3. How does restorying the past enable me to use specific experiences to articulate more general views about language learning and teaching?
4. How does the use of images and/or metaphors enable me to give meaning to seemingly unconnected experiences and ultimately describe my professional growth as a teacher?
5. How have my professional training and the theories of teaching, learning, and second language acquisition to which I have been exposed shaped me as a teacher?
6. How does restorying the past lead to personal and professional growth?

10 A tale of names

Ling Shi

I have been teaching ESL/EFL (English as a Second Language/English as a Foreign Language) for the past twenty-five years, moving between China, Canada, and Hong Kong. As a teacher, I am obsessed with names, memorizing and dealing with hundreds of them all the time. Sometimes there are so many that I can hardly distinguish which belongs to whom by the end of the school term. As a routine before classes start at the beginning of each term, I read lists of names, trying to imagine the faces that go with them. Very often, I come across a few familiar ones that remind me of my previous students. Otherwise, the names become alive only when I step into the classroom and check attendance. As the years have gone by, many names have slipped my memory. For example, I occasionally get a Christmas card from a former student whose name I can hardly recall. Once, I was approached in the street by a stranger who introduced himself as a former student. The smile on his face certainly caused an image of a hardworking student to flash in my mind, though I could not remember his name no matter how hard I tried. Among the endless lists of names, however, there are some that seem to have survived time. Each time I recall the past, my memories become mixed up with events associated with these names. These memories of names have haunted me and transformed my life. They give me new ways of seeing and thinking about my teaching life each time I tell stories about them.

An incident in junior high school

My obsession with names can be traced back to an incident that occurred when I was attending junior high school in China. It was in math class. The teacher was a middle-aged woman whom I can still picture and whose voice

I thank Lynne Earls, Shirley Marcel, and Carl Leggo for reading an earlier draft of this chapter. I would also like to acknowledge the insightful suggestions made by Paula Golombek and Karen E. Johnson.

I can still hear to this day. She seemed to have a permanent smile, for I can hardly recall her without a smile on her face. We heard that she had been transferred from a famous school and had won a medal for excellence in her work. With her, the boring equations and numbers came alive. Everyone was intrigued by the way she presented and explained the math problems. I, like all my classmates, liked her until one day something happened that changed my whole perception of teacher-student relationships: She mistook me for another student.

In one way, it seemed like such a small incident that could happen in any classroom. It was, however, significant to me. The teacher praised me for my progress in math by referring to me by another student's name. There was silence, awkward silence. Everybody was confused as looks quickly passed around the room, first to me, then to the student whose name was used, and then to the teacher. I knew that what was going through the others' minds was exactly what was going through my mind: "Who is making the progress, me or the other student?" As a twelve-year-old, I was very conscious of peers' opinions. I first got very embarrassed and then upset, though the confusion was soon cleared up as the teacher apologized. The excuse was that the two of us looked similar and also had very close student numbers. I did not believe her then, though I might give her more credence today. Nobody in the class thought we looked alike. I did not think that I even looked like anybody in my family, though some people thought there was some resemblance between my youngest sister and me. I could not forgive her for the mistake. I thought that I was an individual and different from everyone else.

I had a flash of insight that I was only a number to the math teacher. The teacher did not know me, not even my name. From that day on, my respect and love for her diminished. In fact, my relationship with all other teachers was affected by this incident. Why would a teacher's mistake over a name have such a great impact on me as a student? What was the discrepancy between the teachers' understanding and students' expectations in teacher-student relationships? The fact that I could just be a number and be mistaken for someone else was like a shadow. It implied hidden attitudes and beliefs, which bothered me and pushed me to search for answers when I myself became a teacher about ten years later.

Teaching EFL in China

I started to teach English majors in Chinese universities in the seventies in the late Mao years, when knowledge and intellectuals were considered shameful. Students addressed me as Teacher Shi in English. Although English speakers would not use this form, the alternative *Miss Shi* was considered bourgeois, so this was one of the many examples of how "Chinglish" (Chinese-English) terms were created.

I do not know how my colleagues and I survived those days. We had to teach English and, at the same time, criticize ourselves since English was equated with Western culture and capitalism. Teachers or students who worked hard or demonstrated a good command of English were considered "sick" with Western ideas. Everybody, therefore, needed to be monitored through constant self-criticism and criticism by their peers. Among those sad memories, one that stood out was about names. In English classes, students' names were translated into Pinying, the official alphabetic system of Chinese characters. They were then pronounced according to the English pronunciation, losing, therefore, the four tones in the original Chinese. As a result, the names sounded the way native English speakers would pronounce them. It never occurred to me that using English pronunciation for Chinese names would be a problem until one day, when the Party secretary (the political head of the department) summoned me to his office and told me that I needed to pronounce Chinese names in the Chinese way. "It's wrong to speak with a foreign tone or accent even when speaking a foreign language," he said with an authoritative voice. "It is worse and is a crime if you try to teach students to do the same."

The next day, I criticized myself in class and from then on used the tonal Chinese pronunciation for addressing students. As the class continued, I could sense a tension among the students as we all wondered where learning a foreign language would get us in China. My head swirled in confusion. So unbearable was the humiliation of self-criticism that I, like most of my colleagues, dreamed of quitting the English classroom. In those days, jobs in China were considered "iron bowls," meaning that we would never lose them. Once we were assigned to a post, we were expected to stay on, watching each other going gray. Changing jobs was, in a way, more difficult than going to jail in China at that time.

Moving to Canada

I moved to Canada in the late eighties and studied for a graduate degree. To follow the Western custom, I switched my names around and put my first name first and family name last, though I did believe, like most Chinese, that families were more important than individuals. I was known as Ling or Ms. Shi in Canada. My son joined me in Canada when he was ten years old. He soon adapted to the new culture and became a hockey and baseball fan.

One day he suddenly said, "Mom, I want to change my name."

"Why?" I asked, curious.

"I want to become a hockey player. But there is a problem. Every time I go out onto the ice and my Chinese name is announced through the loudspeaker, it sounds too short and strange compared with names like Wayne Gretzky or Felix Potvin." He stretched his voice to say his name aloud together with other famous names to illustrate the differences.

"Can I change my name?" he asked again, eyes glistening as if he was just a step away from his dream of becoming a hockey player.

I looked at my son. I could hardly imagine him using any of those names. "You can have an English first name, but I do not think you can change your family name."

I then paused, searching for ideas with which to convince him. I suddenly thought of my father-in-law, who was old-fashioned and also the absolute authority in the family. He should be able to explain everything to my son. "Why don't you write to your grandfather and ask for his permission first," I suggested, feeling relieved that I would not have to explain the details myself. My son knew who had the last say in the family, so he wrote a letter to his grandfather that evening using the limited number of Chinese characters he knew plus a few he invented on the spot.

His grandfather immediately responded with a long letter explaining that it was absolutely out of the question that anybody could change his or her family name. "The family name is handed down from our ancestors five hundred years ago," he wrote in the letter. For some reason, the Chinese think that five hundred years is the magic number needed to establish a family tradition. "One can never betray one's ancestors by changing one's family name. Wherever you go, you are my grandson and your name stands for our tradition." The old man was firm.

I read the letter to my son. I did not know whether a ten-year-old understood the relationship between names and tradition or the serious mistake he could make by changing his family name. There was, for sure, a sign of disappointment. My son looked sadder than if he had just missed a goal in one of his street hockey games.

I believe that this event affected our understanding (my son's and mine) of what names mean. Names in China represent a tradition, history, and the continuation of family but not new beginnings. As such, a name unifies and implies intimacy, collective memory, lineage, pride, and self-recognition. Therefore, we treasure our names as much as we treasure our individual selves.

Teaching ESL to Chinese immigrants in Canada

I learned more about names and naming from my immigrant students after I got a part-time job as an ESL instructor in an adult learning center. I taught two high-beginner classes, one a homogeneous class of Chinese immigrants, and the other a heterogeneous class of immigrants and refugees who spoke different L1s. My father-in-law's words drew my attention to the fact that very few of my elder Chinese students used English names. Among them was an old couple. Although they told me that they were in their late seventies, I figured that they were in their early seventies because Chinese people regard old age as a fortune and will add on a few years if anybody asks about their age. I used their Chinese first names in the class just as I did with other students. One day during the break, the husband came to me and said softly, "Please do not call my wife by her first name. It sounds so intimate. I am the only person who has been using it and is supposed to use it." I blushed and apologized. He reminded me of my father-in-law.

Another elder Chinese among those who did not adopt an English name was a retired army general from Taiwan. He would stand up and answer my questions in class like a soldier responding to a commander. Although I explained to him that he did not need to stand up, he insisted, "A teacher should be respected as one respects one's parents." One day when we had a few minutes to spare before the class, he showed me an old watch. "This is a medal given to me by our late president in Taiwan," he said as he pointed to the back of the watch. "Look, my name and his signature are engraved on it. It has been with me for forty years. The repairmen in Taiwan fixed it several times free of charge when they saw the signature." His voice was full of pride. It was clear why he would not choose to have an English name. Later I found out that he was a pilot and a war hero in the early fifties. He received the watch after his plane was shot down by the Chinese Communists.

Teaching ESL to immigrants from various countries

Compared with the Chinese students who attended class regularly, the heterogeneous class I had was unstable, with continuous intakes and dropouts. Whenever I had new students, I asked, as a routine, about their names and where they were from. Compared to the elder Chinese immigrants, students from other parts of the world seemed eager to adopt English names. I remember, soon after I started teaching the class, a Korean student came to me asking for suggestions of an English name. I tried to convince her that she could use her Korean name, but she insisted. So I suggested the name of one of my Canadian friends. She was so pleased with the name that she announced it in class on the same day. As time went by, more and more students asked me to give them English names. I quickly used up my friends' names and their children's names and started using my colleagues' names. As a result, I developed, over the years, a habit of collecting and recycling English names. To these students, having an English name was like having a new identity. The excitement on their faces when they received their English names reflected their eagerness, as new immigrants, to be accepted by Canadians. Contrasted with the Chinese, who took pride in guarding their names, the immigrants from other countries showed a more flexible identity as evidenced in the way they adopted English names. Peoples' attitudes toward their names are mirrors of different cultures or individuals in an ESL classroom.

A few students, however, got their English names in an unusual way. One student from India had a long name that everybody in the class had problems pronouncing and remembering. Also, I soon found that he had problems distinguishing the *s* and *sh* sound.

"S," I modeled.

"Sh," he tried very hard.

"S," everybody in the class tried to help.

"Sh," he imitated.

"See me," I tried again, pointing to myself.

"She me," he repeated.

"No, see me." I was desperate.

"She me," he repeated somewhat hesitantly.

I did not know how to overcome my inability to correct his pronunciation when one student saved me. He suggested that we call him Sam. "We do not have to remember his long Indian name, and he can practice the *s* sound every time he uses his name," he explained. Everybody thought it was a good idea. I welcomed the suggestion, too, for I saw it as a chance for me to move on to something else. So, the Indian had an English name. I heard him repeating "Sham Sham" in the hallway after the class.

I went home that day feeling bad that the student was named because of his problem with an English phoneme. I also felt ashamed that I had problems with pronouncing his Indian name. The next day, I asked him to teach the whole class how to pronounce his name. He was so pleased. It was his turn to correct everybody else in the class, including me, the teacher. His English name, *Sam*, was quickly forgotten as everybody learned how to pronounce his Indian name, and he learned how to pronounce the *s* and *sh* sounds. Before long, I started to understand how his Indian name took on many colors and shades of meaning. He told me how he was addressed differently by his mother and other wives of his father. (His father had four wives in India.) He also showed me a picture of a girl and told me that he had just married the girl on the telephone so that he could sponsor her to be a landed immigrant in Canada. "I was very excited to hear her calling my name," he said. I had heard about people getting married under the sea or up in the air but had never heard of anybody getting married on the phone.

Soon after this student left to work in a factory doing general labor, Anna joined the class. Anna was a refugee from Yugoslavia. She used to own a building in which she ran a bed-and-breakfast. Her former husband, who had run off with another woman, had given her the building. "I had a lot of money, but they bombed the building and now I have nothing," she said sadly. She was very well dressed, and her perfume was expensive. Maybe I showed too much interest every time she told her story. One day she invited me for coffee in a café near the school. "I need to talk to you," she said. Perhaps there was nobody she could turn to except me, I thought, so I went with her and then listened, correcting her mistakes occasionally as she struggled along in halting English.

She told me that she had another English name, Christine. "I use my real name only in the English class," she told me. "Why?" I asked. She explained that she lived and slept with men in return for free accommodation. She felt it was easier using another name in this role. I could not believe my ears, and I asked her why she did not rent an apartment for herself. "It is too expensive," she said. "The allowance from the government is not enough for a decent apartment." She received over $600 from the government every month, so I suggested that she rent an apartment and share it with somebody. "I can't live like that. I have never lived like that. It's too hard for me," she said. I do not know how she did it, but she said she went from door to door and asked whether she could stay for free. "Some men allow me to stay for a few days. I sleep with them. But I use another English name," she repeated, as if the other English name was a mask concealing her real self. At that moment, she was staying with a man from her home country. "He came twenty years ago and has a beautiful house," she said with a voice full of hope. "He says he loves me." We both hoped that the man would marry her some day. For a few days, Anna did not come to class. Then, she appeared at the door one day after class looking miserable. We went for coffee.

"He wanted me to move out," Anna managed to explain between her sobs. "I begged him not to kick me out. I thought he loved me but now he does not want me anymore." She pulled up her sleeves and showed me the bruises. "He hit me last night." Her eyes overflowed with tears.

"Do you want some legal assistance?" I asked, not wanting to hear the heartbreaking details. There was a brief silence as Anna considered my suggestion, "No, I don't want him to know my real name."

I felt a sudden burst of sorrow for her. To her, the name was her last hope against the loss of innocence. I encouraged her to move out and make a living on her own. "Why don't you work as a live-in nanny? You could make more money than the government gives you," I said thinking about her skills in managing a bed-and-breakfast business. I then helped her circle some ads from the newspaper and told her how to make phone calls. "Tell them your real name," I advised. After a month or so, Anna came to the class during the break with candy and cookies. "Eat and celebrate," she said, "I have a good job. I take care of two little girls. The parents loved my cooking." From the big smile on her face, I knew she was happy. "I am going to sponsor my daughter to come to Canada," she said to me, her eyes shining with dignity and self-respect. Her expression has returned to me again and again. I feel that I experienced something I never dreamed of when I first got into teaching. Teaching ESL, as the story of Anna has suggested, is a career of commitment and the evolving of trust, caregiving, and guidance.

Some time passed, and soon students who studied with Anna had all left for either higher-level classes or jobs. One day a man dressed in a tie and three-piece suit came to class and introduced himself. Most of the students in my class were refugees, new immigrants, or unemployed people. We had never had a student who dressed in such a formal and elegant suit. We all looked up to him as he told us that he was an engineer and manager of a big firm in Russia. Instead of using his first name, the whole class used his family name and called him *Mr.* I also addressed him formally, sensing that he probably had always been and probably would still like to be addressed as such.

The next day, he did not wear his suit and tie but was still in a crease-free shirt. We were talking about how to look for jobs and prepare for interviews. "I know all about these. I interviewed many people for my firm in Russia." There was a look of depression in his eyes. I never had the courage to ask him how and why he became a refugee. All I knew was that he was married and had five children. It is hard for most refugees to leave home, rich or poor.

A few weeks later, he started to miss more and more classes. One day he came wearing an old T-shirt. His hair, wet from a summer drizzle, hung over his forehead. I greeted him, trying not to think about how he had looked the first time. He turned around, and I saw a few words on the back of the T-shirt: *Jack, son of a bitch.* People write all kinds of things on their T-shirts, but it was the first time that I had seen something like this.

"What does it mean?" he asked me. I felt that he should know the meaning and might want to change his shirt after I explained. He listened carefully, his eyebrows arched at the word *bitch*.

"The Canadians are funny," he said. There was a kind of indifference in his voice as if he was not taking in all that I said. He did not seem embarrassed at all.

"Where did you get this?" I asked.

"From the Goodwill store. It was free," he said, and his voice still sounded indifferent. "I like this name *Jack*. I will use it as my English name. Everybody has an English name here. Why shouldn't I?"

In the days that followed, students started calling him *Jack*. However, Jack soon stopped coming to class completely. I got the feeling that something had happened. One day a student told me that he had run into Jack in the street and learned that Jack's wife and children had left him. He had become an alcoholic and spent all his money drinking. My heart sank. For nights I could not sleep, thinking of the trials that Jack had to face. Refugees like Jack went to Canada to escape poverty, war, or other problems, only to find themselves depressed and homesick. I felt that something was missing, something that I should have been doing but hadn't done. I felt helpless and hoped that Jack would come back to class when he was sober and needed some respect and dignity between drinks.

Apart from depressed refugees, my classes occasionally included young pretty girls from China, Thailand, and Korea who came to marry Canadians. These girls were gambling for a better life by marrying somebody they hardly knew. Their husbands were usually middle-aged or older. One day a girl from Thailand came and introduced herself as Mrs. Beckett. She blushed at the English name she had taken from her husband saying, "I was legally married to my husband when I was seventeen and waited for three years for immigration papers."

"Are you happy?" I asked and heard the doubt in my voice.

"Yes," she said with some hesitation, "he told me he did not want to marry a white woman because he would need to make an appointment to sleep with her."

"But I don't think my husband is as rich as he told my mother." She then showed me some paper and asked, "Can you help me read this?"

I looked at it and saw that it was a bank statement for Mr. Beckett. "This is your husband's bank statement. Didn't you ask him?"

"No," she said, "I saw this letter today and guessed it was about his money. So I took it without telling him." She paused and then continued, "So I am right, he doesn't have much money. I am going to write a letter to my mother tomorrow. She wanted to know how much money he had." She was disappointed when she said this.

"You are very young, and one day you can find a job and make money on your own," I tried to cheer her up.

"Yes," she said as the clouds on her face cleared, "I learned how to style hair." She moved her hands in the air as if she was cutting somebody's hair. "I did my hair myself," she said proudly.

I looked at her hair. It was waved and styled nicely. "Sure, you can have your own store one day."

At this, she laughed like a child. Mrs. Beckett never missed a class for two months. Then she went to a school for hairdressers. Though I never saw her again, I always looked inside whenever I passed a beauty salon. I hoped someday that I would meet her and let her cut my hair. I guess students like Mrs. Beckett were important reasons why I had always enjoyed teaching ESL. I felt so proud of them as well as of myself when they left the class and moved on to greater achievements.

Teaching EFL in Hong Kong

After I finished my graduate study, I went to teach in a university in Hong Kong. The first problem I had was my name. In a city where the West meets East, I did not know whether I should call myself *Ling Shi* in the Western way or *Shi Ling* in the Chinese way. My first bank check was returned because the bank said I was Shi Ling, not Ling Shi. Most Chinese people in Hong Kong had an English first name. I guessed it was because they would like Westerners to recognize and use their first names and, at the same time, observe the Chinese custom of putting their family names first. Since I did not have an English name, the Westerners in Hong Kong had no idea of how to address me. Some called me *Ling*, others *Shi*. When they wanted to address me formally, they called me either Dr. Shi or Dr. Ling. I soon got used to all these names. To avoid embarrassing anybody by telling them they were wrong, I accepted all versions of my names.

One difference between my job in Hong Kong and that in Canada was that I needed to give grades to these university students, and, every now and then I wrote reference letters for those who applied for overseas exchange programs. So names were important, and there was no excuse for mixing them up. About 95 percent of the students had English first names. What caught my attention was that many names were not actually proper English names. These unusual names were popular topics for teachers at the lunch table.

"I had a student called Cabinet," said one teacher.

"I had one called Pajamas," said another.

Everybody choked on their food as they laughed. I laughed too, though I had grown too hardened over the years to be surprised or shocked by names.

Why on earth would people choose such names? To find out the answer, I asked, as an introductory activity, all the students to talk about their English names – whether they knew the meaning of the names, and how and why they decided to choose that particular name. It turned out to be a very successful communicative activity. Students enjoyed getting to know one another through stories of names and naming.

I soon learned that most Hong Kong students had an English name because they were required to have one for their English classes, regardless of whether the teacher was a local Chinese teacher or a native English speaker. They found it convenient to use English names in schools and later at work, though most of them chose not to register their English names legally. In selecting an English name, many students actually picked one randomly from dictionaries or from books or movies in which a favorite character appeared. The less creative students would use suggestions from their parents, siblings, or friends. Sometimes the person who named them made a spelling mistake, for example, *Jerffrey* for *Jeffrey*, *Pheobe* for *Phoebe*, *Paymund* for *Raymund*, *Vevien* for *Vivian*, *Kennis* for *Kenneth*, *Heidy* for *Heidi*, or *Steeve* for *Steve*.

Some students chose their names to express dreams, their own or those of their parents. Chinese have always believed that names and naming will bring fortune to them. One student was called *Winnie* because her parents wished to win at the mah-jongg table. Another student was called *Pattie* because her parents liked to get paid quickly every time they won at the horse races. One student called herself *Wing* because she wanted to have wings so that she could fly high in her career. Another student chose the name *Carmen* because he wanted to be a man with a car.

Many students chose uncommon or original names because they wanted to be special or different from others. I had an Iris, a Chester, and a Kit in my class. Some students named themselves after their favorite food such as *Candy* and *Almond*. One student called herself *Fanny* because it sounded like *thank-you* to her. Another student was called *William* because he had a wide body. A few students were named after the month in which they were born such as *June*, *July*, and *April*.

The openness and assertiveness my Hong Kong students showed in their names and naming was in contrast to their passive manner and silence in class. Hong Kong students were known for their reluctance to speak in class. As I called out these unique names, I felt as if a great supply of energy and creativity was waiting just behind a closed door, if only I could find the key. I believed that the key would be found in classroom tasks. So I tried to design activities inviting students to share their experiences and interests. For example, to help the nursing students learn to do research required in their studies, I organized the English classes around a small-group project – a health-related survey on a topic of their choosing. Most students did surveys on topics such as diet and nutrition, fitness and exercise, teenagers' attitudes toward premarital sex, or child abuse. The group discussions on how to design questionnaires and analyze the data were well attended. Everybody was so involved in talking that I had to stop them several times when time was up. The final group presentation in the class was also impressive. Students asked one another questions and discussed the findings and the intervention that might follow. Showing the same creativity and practicality they demonstrated with their English names, Hong Kong students participated eagerly in class if the learning was intrinsically motivating and related to their goal of learning English, which was obtaining a good job.

Conclusion

Threaded together by a bunch of names, the stories in this chapter illustrate that personal constructs of names and naming are a social process of establishing one's existence. Different people attach different values to their names. Some, such as the students in Hong Kong, believe that names exercise power and command, so they chose English names to guide them to success. Others, such as the retired Chinese army general and the old man who claimed ownership of his wife's first name, believe that names are personal because they are shaped and painted until they look just like the people they identify. Since names and identities are an integral part of a sociocultural and historical context, my memories of teaching are partly a collection of names that have amused, worried, and embarrassed me as a teacher at various stages of my career. Stated another way, teaching is a journey from which I extract episodes or stories to negotiate between language and identity, to develop my professional identity as a teacher, and to transform student teachers and inspire them to be better teachers.

Arising from second language classrooms, my stories of names suggest an intimate connection between language and identity. I came to understand that learning a new language is like acquiring an additional identity while experiencing the uncertainty of my own identity in Hong Kong as a person speaking two languages. As a language teacher, I saw many of my ESL students adopt English names to signify their second identity. Others, however, struggle and negotiate between old and new identities. For example, many old immigrants from China, where family tradition is highly valued, would treasure and keep their Chinese names as a reminder of who they are and where they are from. Some of them, like the Chinese retired general, would choose not to have an English name, as if adopting another identity would signal the loss of a memorable past. A few people, like the Party secretary in Mao's China, would regard the pronunciation of students' names in an English class as the basis of a political battle to defend Chinese culture. Over the years, I witnessed many students who had gone through trauma, slipping in and out of identities associated with their first and second language. For example, Anna felt inferior as a refugee, Jack was depressed from feeling unwanted in a new culture, and Mrs. Beckett found herself a deceived stranger in a new land. My experiences suggest that a second language teacher should make students' voices heard and their feelings attended to. Teaching a second language implies providing spiritual and moral support to help students negotiate between old and new identities.

The narratives of names are also revelations of my identity as a language teacher. They give a voice to my fear, joy, worry, and concerns in day-to-day teaching. As the years go by and I tell these stories again and again, the names or stories, at first not connected, start to form patterns. They are, as Bruner (1986) suggests, no longer a simple chronicle of events but a way of perceiving and organizing experiences. It is through this narrative process that I have become not only a more thoughtful teacher but also a better human being, caring and respectful of individuals. The transformation process is woven with personal, cultural, and professional histories. First of all, the story of the math teacher in high school uncovered some of the sources of my views on teaching. I then learned how the large sociopolitical system influenced and constrained language classes when I was criticized in China for how I pronounced students' names in English. Moving from one country to another, I experienced various language curricula that were closely related to the lives and needs of students. My experiences show that a second language teacher needs to play multiple roles simultaneously: a guide who leads the way into the new land and culture, a person who understands and provides moral support for the troubled, an intellectual who respects the depressed, a friend who listens to the miserable, a knower who provides advice for the lost, and an explorer who searches for the potential. My journey of teaching is full of twists and turns with no shortcuts. As stories are reheard and rearranged, each time the reflection and theorizing become "increasingly probing and systematic" (Weber, 1993, p. 76). Narrative, as Connelly and Clandinin (1988) put it, "is the study of how humans make meaning of experience by endlessly telling and retelling stories about themselves that both reconfigure the past and create purpose in the future" (p. 24).

I am now teaching in a language teacher training program. As I continue to live out my values, beliefs, and emotions in my classes, I sometimes tell stories, placing my students in my ESL classrooms, with all the vivid and concrete details, and inviting them to relive my experiences. As I tell these stories, I hope that they will blossom into other stories years later. Following Jalongo and Isenberg (1995), I believe that stories not only illuminate one's own life but also elicit stories from others. To encourage my preservice student teachers to tell their stories and analyze and reflect on them, I ask them, as one of the course assignments, to select an experience from their practicum as the basis for a case study narrative. As teachers and as learners, we become story collectors and storytellers, believing that the essence of teacher training lies in the sharing and accumulation of narratives based on the choices, challenges, and concerns that we make out of everyday teaching.

Narrative, as Preskill (1998) suggests, "is both idiosyncratic and universal, particularistic yet familiar" (p. 345). As I collect my thoughts for each of my teacher-training classes, I wonder how many other teachers have stories or reflective experiences like mine. Just as we need to understand how people associate themselves with their names, we must learn, through continuous inquiry, to live, respect, and recognize our lives as language teachers. I close my eyes and see a sea of faces, faces that once made me happy or worried. In retrospect, it is the students who have taught me about teaching in a second language classroom through their stories. As I continue to tell old stories and collect new ones, I am fueled with desire to be a better teacher.

References

Bruner, J. (1986). *Actual minds, possible world.* Cambridge, MA: Harvard University Press.

Connelly, F. M., & Clandinin, D. J. (1988). *Teachers as curriculum planners: Narratives of experience.* New York: Teachers College Press.

Jalongo, M. R., & Isenberg, J. P. (1995). *Teachers' stories: From personal narrative to professional insight.* San Francisco: Jossey-Bass.

Preskill, S. (1998). Narratives of teaching and the quest for the second self. *Journal of Teacher Education, 49,* 344–358.

Weber, S. (1993). The narrative anecdote in teacher education. *Journal of Education for Teaching, 19,* 71–82.

11 Seeking satisfaction

Kazuyoshi Sato

When one finds a school climate that makes it possible to take pride in one's craft, when one has the permission to pursue what one's educational imagination adumbrates, when one receives from students the kind of glow that says you have touched my life, satisfactions flow. . . . The aesthetic in teaching is the experience secured from being able to put your own signature on your own work – to look at it and say it was good. It comes from the contagion of excited students discovering the power of a new idea, the satisfaction of a new skill. . . . It means being swept up in the task of making something beautiful. (Eisner, 1983, p. 12)

The notion of satisfaction means to me experiencing positive emotional moments in classrooms. I know it when I see students' eyes filled with interest, share excitement with students, feel good rapport with students, and am impressed with students' creativity. In contrast, I do not feel satisfied when I get through a lesson without having received any response from students, when I see students confused and not involved in an activity, or when I notice that something is wrong but I must continue to teach for a discrete-point test. I think that I am addicted to this feeling of satisfaction.

I first experienced satisfaction as a second language learner of English. Since then, it has been a driving force in my professional development because, I presume, I would like my students to have the same sort of satisfaction that I have had. Therefore, I spend time developing materials so that I can create satisfaction for others in my classrooms.

For more than a decade, I have been developing my teaching approaches through trial and error. The more moments of satisfaction I experience, the more I am encouraged to take risks to create more of them. I can recall four episodes from which I derived different kinds of satisfaction in different contexts that seem to have influenced how I teach a foreign language: first, my L2 learning experience in the United States – my personal satisfaction as a second language learner, second, my teaching experience (at a high school) in Japan – struggling with the constraints of teaching English in Japan, third, my teaching (Japanese) and learning (master's degree) experiences in Australia – the satisfaction I felt from meeting students' needs, and finally, my teaching experience (at universities) back in Japan – knowing students' perspectives and building a learning environment. In particular, as a nonnative English-speaking teacher, I think that my beliefs about language teaching and learning are based on my L2 learning experience in the United States.

Episode 1: Enlightenment

The first type of satisfaction was what I felt as a second language learner in the United States. It was completely different from what I had thought about English language learning in Japan. My image of a good English learner was one who knew many words, could understand grammar and translate difficult essays with complex structures into Japanese, had good marks on tests, and passed the entrance examination of a prestigious university. This is a fair description of the grammar-translation (*yakudoku*) method, which has been dominant in Japan. I began to question these beliefs when I was a student in an English conversation class at university. I could not make myself understood in English. I realized that the way I had studied English was useless for communicating in English.

However, when I was a senior at a university in Japan, I decided that I wanted to be a high school teacher of English. I was ashamed of becoming an English teacher without having some command of spoken English. I took a leave of absence and went to Santa Monica City College to major in speech, because I wanted to improve my communication skills.

On the first day of class for Speech 1, I was shocked. I was the only overseas student. I could not follow what the teacher said. I talked to him after class. I said to him, "I want to improve my speaking skills, because I want to be an English teacher in Japan in the future. But I could not understand today's class. I wonder if I should drop this class." He said to me, "Why don't you try if you have such a goal?"

The first assignment was to make a ten-minute demonstration speech in front of the class. I decided to introduce sumo, a national sport in Japan. I borrowed a book about the history of sumo from the library, wrote a speech, memorized it, and prepared for my presentation. Before I began my speech, I left the classroom to disguise myself as a sumo wrestler. I took off my trousers and put on shorts, put several pieces of newspaper under my T-shirt to make a big stomach, tied my hair in the samurai fashion, and returned to the classroom. I started my speech by demonstrating a ring ceremony. I could tell that the audience was attracted to my speech, and this surprised me. I said, "This is sumo, a national sport of Japan. I will demonstrate sumo to you." Then, my words got in the way. I thought that I had memorized them, but they did not come out naturally. I was desperate to continue my speech. I knew that ten minutes had passed, but the teacher let me continue my presentation. At the end, I asked for two volunteers for a match. I became a referee. The audience really enjoyed the match, and I received lots of applause. However, it took me about thirty minutes to finish my speech. Then, I went to the teacher to receive my evaluation. I expected that I would get an F (failure). I was apprehensive. However, I received an A. I could not believe my eyes. The evaluation card included eight criteria: (1) posture and movement: A; (2) facial expression: A+; (3) eye contact: A; (4) voice, volume, pitch: A; (5) speaking rate and fluency: B; (6) gestures: A; (7) enthusiasm: A; (8) speech composition: A; and total speech grade: A. His comments were: "Good use of nonverbal display, voice projection is good, speaking rate is very good, posture and movement are good. Good sense of humor. Watch your clutch words – [in Japanese] 'Ah.'" I was astonished at the way my evaluation was done. It was like a Copernican revolution to me, because I had been accustomed to discrete-point tests as in Japan or with the TOEFL. At the same time, I was encouraged by the teacher's comments. I became aware that a good speech would entail more than good pronunciation and fluency. I gradually improved my confidence in communication skills through my classes. After a one-and-a-half-year stay in the United States, I went back to my university in Japan. Then, I became an English teacher in a private high school. I had a burning desire to make a change in English language teaching in Japan. In particular, I wanted my students to have the same experience I had had. I was enthusiastic about implementing *my* ideals in classrooms.

Episode 2: Hope and despair

The second episode highlights my struggle with the constraints of teaching English in a high school in Japan. Although there were moments of satisfaction, I had difficulty most of the time putting my ideals into practice. Few teachers understood what I wanted to do in this school. Fortunately, outside the school, I met a small number of teachers who belonged to a study group. They recognized what I did and supported the way I taught English. I admit that I had to compromise with some aspects of teaching in this school context, but I did not or could not abandon my desire to change things.

I cannot forget my first lesson. At the beginning of my class, I introduced myself to the students in English. I told them to take notes. I intended to surprise them by using only English in the classroom. After I introduced myself, I showed the video "We Are the World: USA for Africa." The song was popular at that time, and everyone knew it. I explained to the class that each student should play the role of one singer and we would sing this song in harmony. They volunteered for their favorite singers, and we started to practice. A week later, they performed the song in beautiful harmony, and I videotaped their performance. Everyone enjoyed singing the song. I was satisfied that the students had had the same kind of learning experience I had had in the United States. I realized that it was possible to motivate students with interesting materials even in Japan.

However, soon after I started to teach at this high school, a rumor began that all I taught was singing. In fact, I remember the day the principal passed my classroom to check up on how I was teaching.

I knew, however, that I had to teach from the textbook for the common test, so I rushed to cover some pages before the midterm test. After the midterm examinations, the average score of each class was reported in an English department meeting. My class was the worst of ten classes. One experienced teacher said to me, "You did nothing but sing songs. No wonder, your average score was the worst." I could not say anything. I had expected that my students would do much better on the test. But they did not. I faced a dilemma. Should I quit using English songs, movies, and so on, and focus on the textbook so that my students could do better on the test? I could not find the answer. I asked my students what we should do.

I explained my desire about teaching English. I said to them, "English is a means of communication. Being able to communicate in English will enrich your life. We can learn English from songs, movies, newspapers, magazines, news, and so on. The textbook is not the only source. But, I wonder whether we should quit singing songs in this class." All the students wrote their comments on papers and gave them to me. They were all in favor of singing songs in class. One student said, "Don't stop singing songs. I enjoy singing songs and watching movies. We can do both. We will study harder for the next test in order to increase our average score." I was encouraged by their comments. I didn't stop singing for the seven years I taught English in this high school.

Nonetheless, I began to pay more attention to the average scores of my classes. In other words, I had to compromise and accept the workplace reality that teachers had to drill students for discrete-point tests and university entrance examinations, which had nothing to do with English as a means of communication. I quickly developed some techniques to help my students memorize grammatical points and new words. It was easy for me to rely on the traditional approaches through which I had learned English as a high school student. I gave my students more vocabulary quizzes and checked homework as other teachers did. Gradually, the average scores of my classes started to increase, and the experienced teachers stopped complaining. However, my dissatisfaction grew while I was teaching. I did not enjoy teaching according to the textbook, and I knew that my students did not enjoy being taught according to the textbook. But we had to cover certain pages of the textbook for the test. I taught grammatical points deductively, and then did mechanical exercises. I often told my students, particularly before the test, that a certain grammatical point was important or that they should be able to translate a certain English sentence into Japanese.

My struggle continued. I kept on singing with students, while doing what other teachers did. As I became accustomed to the traditional way of teaching, paying more attention to classroom control, I took fewer risks, and tried out fewer new ideas in regular English classes.

Few of my colleagues understood my ideas about teaching. However, I met a group of teachers outside the school during my second year there. These teachers had formed an informal study group. I had an opportunity to present what I taught in a workshop. I learned that a minority of teachers supported what I did and had an interest in innovative ways of teaching, but confronted difficulties in the classroom. I attended the study group periodically and began to expand the network through which I could encounter new ideas. I found out that it was possible to implement my new ideas even in my school. I started some elective classes such as Improving Listening Skills, Speech, and Newspaper Reading. I had opportunities to use authentic materials in these special classes, and I enjoyed teaching the classes. However, I continued to teach according to the textbook in regular classes. Then, in 1993, the ministry of education (*Mombusho*) announced that it would introduce new guidelines for communication-oriented English the following year. We were surprised to hear that English conversation class would be mandatory in high schools. We started to discuss the matter in department meetings. There were two native English-speaking teachers, but it was evident that we, Japanese teachers, had to cover some English conversation classes. We were at a loss as how to teach this new subject. Many teachers demanded that we have more native English-speaking teachers and have them teach these new classes. A couple of experienced teachers quit teaching before their retirement age. I decided to go to Australia to start my master's degree. I could not endure teaching without satisfaction. I wanted to study new teaching approaches.

Episode 3: Trial and error

The third episode focuses on the satisfaction I felt from meeting my students' needs. Soon after I started studying for my master's degree in applied linguistics (language teaching), at the University of Queensland in Australia,

I began to teach Japanese at two universities. Looking back on my teaching experiences in Australia, I am appreciative of having had workplace conditions in which there was freedom to develop materials to meet students' needs.

Although I had finished a correspondance course to obtain a certificate to teach Japanese, I was apprehensive at first. I remember the first day of my class for beginners. I intended to begin my lesson by introducing a famous Japanese song called "*Sukiyaki*." But I could not find the main switch that played the tape recorder. Students seemed to be uneasy, too. Several minutes later, one of them spoke up. "Teacher, are you OK?" I had to decide what to do. I made up my mind to sing the song by myself without the music. After I finished singing, there was applause. My students were all smiling. It was a good start. I introduced myself to the class in simple Japanese with gestures. Then, I told the class to open the textbook. We were supposed to finish one lesson, which usually consisted of one new grammatical point for a sixty-minute class. After I explained the grammatical point according to the textbook, we finished two exercises. The class was over. I thought that I had managed to finish the first class. Then, one female student, apparently older than I, came to me and said, "Teacher, please give us more time to speak Japanese in class. We want to be able to communicate in Japanese." I said "Yes" but was a bit disappointed. What she meant was, "I don't like your teaching style." I had to find ways to increase students' opportunities to use Japanese and to teach a grammatical point at the same time.

I observed other teachers' classes and read many other textbooks and materials. Also, I referred to the books I had used in my master's degree courses. Two books used in Second Language Teaching Methodology were Brown (1994a, 1994b). I began to be interested in communicative language teaching and how to teach grammar inductively by using various communicative activities. Interestingly, I found out that many textbooks and activity books I had brought from Japan were useless, because they used only mechanical exercises to teach grammar. However, I happened to find a couple of new books that offered collections of communicative activities to use for introducing points of grammar. I decided to use some of the activities and adapt them to suit my students.

My trial-and-error teaching has continued in my Japanese classes since that time. Sometimes, I have taken four hours to develop an activity for one lesson. I remember one lesson for beginners in which I was supposed to teach them how to tell time. After the students learned basic expressions to use for telling time, I changed the exercise in the textbook. The exercise, asking students to describe a daily routine of a Japanese office worker, seemed to be boring for my students. Instead, I devised a task. I said to them, "This is pair work. You will be tour guides for a group of Japanese tourists who visit the Gold Coast. You have to plan a one-day bus tour to show the group around the Gold Coast. I will give you fifteen minutes for this activity. Then, I would like you to present your plan to the class." I gave them an example to show how to say what to do at a certain time to the group. They worked in pairs enthusiastically. The presentations went well. Each pair described its special information about the Gold Coast, such as good little-known spots and special foods. There were moments filled with surprise, laughter, and applause. I was impressed by their creativity and enthusiasm.

Gradually, I gained confidence in developing activities and using some authentic materials. To introduce Japanese culture in advanced classes, I used news, cartoons, movies, and TV programs, which I videotaped whenever I returned to Japan. We discussed social problems, simulated job interviews, and even performed a sequence from a cartoon. I also used many articles from newspapers and magazines that were related to the discussion topics. I came to acquire the techniques needed to develop authentic materials into communicative activities so that students would have more opportunities to use the target language in classrooms. When I was a high school teacher, I tried to incorporate authentic materials, but I did not know how to develop materials. As a result, my classes were teacher-centered, and neither the students nor I had a chance to communicate in English. I did not understand how students would learn best at that time. In contrast, as I succeeded in developing activities and enjoyed teaching, I began to believe that students learn best when they are engaged in communicative activities for meaningful purposes. My teaching style started to change from teacher-centered to teacher-as-facilitator.

Episode 4: Challenge

The last episode deals with the satisfaction I received from getting to know students' perspectives and building a learning environment. I had not felt this kind of satisfaction thus far. The use of action logs in the classroom helped me develop good rapport with students, and helped students to develop rapport with one another, which created a learning environment.

I returned to Japan in the late nineties and started data collection in a high school for my Ph.D. research. I was interested in examining how teachers of English understood English language teaching, how they actually taught in classrooms, and how they learned to teach in a particular school context. Although the government introduced new guidelines on communication-oriented English in high schools in 1994, little was known about English teachers' understandings and practices in Japan. While doing research, I resumed teaching English as a part-time teacher at three universities. I wanted the challenge of using only English in the classroom, and this was possible at the university level.

I was fortunate to be offered a workshop class in one university in which I could introduce Australian English and culture in English. It was a content-based language teaching module. Before the workshop started, the four teachers (I was the only nonnative English speaker) who would be in charge of the class gathered for a meeting. The coordinator explained the goals of the course, schedule, assessment, and some students' comments from the previous year. The first-year students (about 160 students) were divided into four groups, and the four teachers would rotate to a new group every six weeks. After each class, students were expected to write action logs. These records included the date, their English target (in percent) and English used (also in percent), today's partner, an evaluation of each activity ranked on a scale of "interesting" and "useful," and comments about what they learned and liked (see Murphey, 1997; Woo & Murphey, 1999).

My first class started. As mentioned previously, I wanted to challenge myself to use only English as the language of instruction. I carefully prepared for the lesson, but I admit that I was apprehensive. After I introduced myself briefly, I asked students several questions in English. This is the same activity I had used when I was a high school teacher. I explained the course outline and moved to group work. I made groups of four and asked each group to choose a captain and a secretary. I delivered a handout including ten items (mainly true or false questions) about Australia to each member of the class. First, they worked on the questions individually for a few minutes. Then, I told each captain to lead the discussion so that each group would come to an agreement on each item. Examples of the statements or questions were: "Australia had been colonized by England," "Identify the Australian flag," "The population of Australia is smaller than that of Tokyo," and "Koala is an aboriginal word that means 'It does not drink water.' " After several minutes' discussion, we checked the answers. Every group got 1 point for a correct answer. Then, I showed TV commercials I had videotaped in Australia and gave several more questions. They seemed to enjoy watching the commercials. Finally, each secretary counted the total points, and we congratulated the winning team. After the first two classes, I collected some students' comments from their action logs. They included the following comments (quotes uncorrected):

Before the class begins, I had a little tense because I didn't know what kind of class the teacher would make. However, there was no need to worry about it. Yoshi [the teacher] was a very interesting teacher and the class was so funny. At the moment, uneasiness suddenly disappeared from my heart.

I like Quiz very much because I can learn a lot of new things about Australia. The most surprising question is that Australians spend more money in gambling than Americans.

Students seemed to enjoy quizzes in group work. I enjoyed teaching, too. However, I was aware that a minority of students often used Japanese during activities. I did not want to force them to use English, because I wished to sustain a pleasant atmosphere in class. I was at a loss as to what to do. About that time my coordinator suggested that the action logs be made into a newsletter. The newsletter worked well. As soon as I delivered the printed copies to the class, they seemed to be absorbed in reading other classmates' comments. Some students were happy to find their own comments; others started to write comments in their next action logs. Students started to share the experiences they had had in foreign countries.

When I was in England, I heard people saying "Ta" when I bought something. So this was the same as you taught us today and it's true that word was used in U.K. as well!!! Also, my host mother taught me that "Ta Ta" means "bye-bye" and also, "You're welcome"!? To know those words was very interesting and when I use those words to the native people, they become more friendly with us! And I think that's fantastic!

Before I went to Australia, I had been taught that Japanese killed many Australian soldiers and they remember. So, host mom's father had thought that I had been one of very very bad Japanese. But by talking with me, he changed his mind.

Stimulated by getting such information from fellow students in newsletters and group work, students began to learn not only from the instructor but from their classmates. In particular, they seemed to appreciate the opportunities to use English in pair and group work.

We had group work today. It went very well, because you told us to choose a leader first. We used only English while we were discussing. I enjoyed discussing with classmates.

To my regret, I often use Japanese when I can't understand how to say in English. But today, I could talk only in English. When I calm down and think, I can talk only in English, I think that I should try it this way from now.

I worked with my friend at pair work. We talked about our news at first. I enjoyed it so much! We didn't use Japanese at all. I want to say "Well done!" to me and [friend's name]. I think the most important point about English is to enjoy it. I enjoyed this lesson so much!

Nevertheless, I noticed that some students were still worried about making mistakes in class. At the beginning of the fourth class, I decided to share my English learning experiences with students. I wanted to tell the class that I learned English by making a lot of mistakes. To tell the truth, until the last minute, I wondered whether they would listen to my story. Also, I had to fit this into my tight schedule. But I could not ignore what a few students confessed to me, because their anxiety was the same as mine had been. I took a chance, and it worked well. Here are some comments from the second newsletter (several students requested another newsletter).

I learned that I don't have to be worried about making mistakes. I can't improve my English without making mistakes. I've been abroad twice. The first time, I was too shy to speak English. The second time, I spoke a little bit English. But I didn't speak enough as I was very afraid of using wrong English. Now I regret it very much. I think I won't be afraid of making mistakes the next time I go abroad or in the class from now on.

I also enjoyed your mistake story. I envy you because you had courage to ask some English speakers when you began studying English. Now, there are many overseas students in [name of university] and I want to talk with them, but I can't do it. On the [name of school] School Festival day, I was selling curry and rice and at last I managed to talk to an overseas student in English! It needed me a lot of energy, but I think it made me improve a little!

One student shared her mistake story with us:

When I went to one junior high school in Melbourne and studied in English classes, I was asked what I hate. I wanted to answer "What I hate is frogs," but I answered "What I hate is flags." The teacher wondered and made a strange face. I wondered why he did so, and I asked my friend. I understand the mistake. So I know the words "frogs" and "flags" very well.

As we shared our comments and experiences with one another in this class, the percentage of students' use of English started to increase. Furthermore, students became more interested in Australia and began to share new information about Australia. At the end of six weeks, students were expected to write an essay (600 to 1,000 words) by doing miniresearch about their favorite topics.

I read a book about Australia. So, I fond an interesting phrase. That is "She is apples." I couldn't understand first. Then, I read well. This phrase means, "She is all right." I don't know whey they say "apples." But I think it is very interesting. I'm gong to look for more.

I get information about Aborigines from my partner. They have a music instrument. They call it didgeridoo. I don't know about it in detail. I want to investigate it.

Six weeks is too short to introduce Australian English and Australian culture to a class. However, the students seemed to enjoy sharing their new information, experiences, and opinions with one another in these classes. I learned many things from the students and received a kind of satisfaction from getting to know students' perspectives and responding to them that I had never felt before. In particular, I learned that sharing students' comments through newsletters helped create a collaborative learning environment. I struggled to find a way to increase the quantity of students' English in class until I realized that creating a learning environment works much better than simply repeating: "Speak only English in this class!"

Conclusion

My four episodes represent my language learning and teaching history. Reflecting on those episodes, I realize that my beliefs about language teaching and learning have been evolving (see Sato & Kleinsasser, 1999). Each episode is an example of the "multilayeredness" of the notion of satisfaction. I could not forget my L2 learning experience in the United States and wished my high school students to have the same kind of personal satisfaction I had had as a second language learner. I felt satisfied when I succeeded in implementing *my* ideals in teaching English in special classes. But, in regular classes, I was dissatisfied with my routine practices, just as other teachers were. In contrast, I enjoyed teaching Japanese through trial and error in Australia. I received satisfaction from meeting students' needs by developing materials. Discovering students' perspectives through action logs and responding to them help one build a collaborative learning community in which students are free to express their perceptions and experiences without being afraid of making mistakes in the target language. Although I received different kinds of satisfaction from many places, events, and experiences, I believe that my need for satisfaction has been the driving force that has led me to grow and develop as a teacher. It has affected me as a person, as a learner of teaching, and in my daily practices. From this point of view, I agree with what Huberman (1992) concluded in his life-cycle research on 160 teachers: "The strongest sources of career satisfaction may lie potentially under our noses, in the classroom, provided that some minimal conditions – some slack, variety, challenge and tolerable work assignment – are met" (p. 132).

Moreover, I came to understand the importance of a teaching environment in which teachers can experiment with new ideas. It was not until I taught Japanese in Australia that I began to recognize this. I was fortunate to have opportunities to develop materials to suit my students in Australia, and colleagues there who gave me the space to do it. If I had stayed and continued to teach with dissatisfaction in Japan, I might have given up my career as a foreign language teacher. To be honest, it was torture for me to endure the routine practices of examination-oriented English without satisfaction in Japan. Thus, now, when I make a plan and have to decide what to do, I try to take a little risk. Maybe that is because I do not want to regret not trying new things and not continuing to learn and develop as a teacher. I also recognize the significance of the study groups in Japan and my master's studies in Australia in the encouragement and support for my risk taking. I was desperate to find better ways to teach a foreign language. What I have learned through my trial-and-error teaching experiences is the importance of a teaching culture that fosters risk taking for professional development.

As I had discovered satisfaction from the first risk I took – giving a demonstration speech on sumo – I also discovered satisfaction from creating materials and collaborative environments that encouraged risk taking on the part of my students. Thus, these two things – risk taking and supporting environments – are essential to both language learning and teacher development. Without them, teachers can continue to teach according to standardized curricula for second language learners; however, with them, students and teachers will be learning for life, with satisfaction.

References

Brown, H. D. (1994a). *Principles of language learning and teaching* (3rd ed.). Englewood Cliffs, NJ: Prentice Hall Regents.

Brown, H. D. (1994b). *Teaching by principles: An interactive approach to language pedagogy.* Englewood Cliffs, NJ: Prentice Hall Regents.

Eisner, E. (1983). The art and craft of teaching. *Educational Leadership, 40*(4), 4–13.

Huberman, A. M. (1992). Teacher development and instructional mastery. In A. Hargreaves & M. G. Fullan (Eds.), *Understanding teacher development* (pp. 122–142). New York: Teachers College Press.

Murphey, T. (1997). Content-based instruction in an EFL setting: Issues and strategies. In M. A. Snow & D. M. Brinton (Eds.), *The content-based classroom: Perspectives on integrating language and content* (pp. 117–131). New York: Addison Wesley Longman.

Sato, K., & Kleinsasser, R. C. (1999). Communicative language teaching (CLT): Practical understandings. *The Modern Language Journal, 83*(4), 494–517.

Woo, L., & Murphey, T. (1999). Activating metacognition with action logs. *The Language Teacher, 23*(5), 15–18.

12 *The art of drawing theory*

A teacher's personal and professional sense making

Tobie Robison

Introduction

Anyone glancing at my day planner would never suspect the intensity with which the entries were made. Twenty-four pages, scribbled on and rather ragged at the edges, remind me of the ups and downs, the moments of elation and worry, the assignments, the appointments, and the requirements of my first experience with teaching solo in a public high school. Having just completed a master's degree under the guidance of the editors of this book, I entered the teaching profession with the firm conviction that I am a bona fide teacher-theorist. The theoretical underpinnings of my classroom are grounded not only in the published work of tenured scholars but in my personality. My life experiences, in and out of the classroom, my personal beliefs, my knowledge of theory, and my concern for sincere communication all contribute to my performance as a teacher. Thankfully, my first five months in a high school classroom have only confirmed this. In fact, I believe that it is this knowledge, this conviction that I too have an intellectual say in the daily choices that affect my teaching, that made these months so enjoyable.

This chapter describes events that sparked, influenced, and upheld – and are continuing to uphold – my desire to teach. It evidences the force of previous learning experiences upon the daily decisions that I make in the classroom. One section – in fact the impetus for the article's title – describes a graduate-level assignment that helped me articulate an idea that has significantly affected my teaching philosophy – that I am both a theorist and a practitioner within the classroom. Education is a lifelong process. The fact that I have much to learn is exciting. Good teaching, after all, begins with learning. Herein lies the focus of this chapter.

Background

New Year's Day, 1989; Memphis, Tennessee: My sister and I dragged our Huffy 10-speeds out of the box-filled garage and began our first trek around our new neighborhood. Another year, another city. Growing up with a father who worked as an Air Force pilot and for various airlines and with a mother who adjusted readily to the transitions his work entailed, I had become accustomed to change. New friends, new teachers, new towns, and new conditions were and are simply a part of life. To live contentedly, I learned that I must adapt to my circumstances and embrace change as a challenge, not a curse.

My love of language and teaching springs directly from my transient childhood. Moving frequently (eleven times during the first two years of my life) and constantly having to initiate friendships as a result have taught me the importance of sincere communication. People, especially young people, can spot a counterfeit immediately. Once this detection has been made, all discourse plunges to frivolity: the listener eyeing the speaker with distrust, the speaker totally oblivious to the listener's reaction.

Relationally, insincerity is destructive, and so honest communication should be cultivated. The most disturbing effect of distrust, however, is the breakdown of genuine exchange it causes within the classroom and in the workplace, the missing rapport between students and teachers, employers and employees. The individuals from whose example I have most benefited have the capacity to communicate effectively and the willingness to adapt to diversity, two vital components in the teaching profession and in interpersonal relations. These life-affecting men and women love their work and make every effort to share their knowledge and exuberance within their various settings. Accomplishment of such achievements requires flexibility, for every human being is different, approaching life with an individual learning style, specific needs, and a unique cultural and family background.

Decision

I did not realize my predilection for the classroom until I was in college. Yes, like many children I arranged my dolls (including my younger sister) in rows and fervently taught them the ABCs. For many years, however, I thought that medicine would be my field, my high school transcripts reflecting this goal with a multitude of math, science, and even Latin classes. People often told me I would make a good doctor because of my "bedside manner" and my love for others; therefore, I continued merrily on in my studies. Then, one day it hit me: I really did not like what I was doing! My forte is language; my love is literature. Why then was I spending hours in the chemistry lab?

Being rather flexible and well acquainted with change, I switched my major to English and eventually added French. Yet, what is love for anything, including a particular subject, if it is not shared? Teaching gives me the opportunity to share my literary and relational enthusiasm with my students, you might say, transforming my bedside manner into a deskside manner.

I enrolled in my undergraduate university's school of education expecting to learn how I might better share my enthusiasm. With each new education class, I waited for a grand revelation. It never came. Instead, I learned how to write a solid lesson plan (complete with behavioral objectives). I memorized Bloom's taxonomy and Maslow's Hierarchy of Needs. I read countless case studies, and then wrote papers describing how these theories might apply in a classroom. I practiced teaching, pretending that my college peers were middle and secondary school students. After I completed the necessary requirements, my professors patted me on the back, congratulated me on my "natural teaching ability," and sent me headlong into student teaching.

Training

I had completed numerous practicums before – short-term experiences under the constant supervision of a cooperating teacher. Nothing, however, could have fully prepared me for the day when I introduced myself as student teacher. Something in that title invites testing. My first students could sense my fear, and they did nothing to alleviate it. These ninth-graders had their own faces to save, their own images to uphold. Trying to accommodate the new teacher was definitely not a high priority, especially since I was so different. The majority of my students were African-American, many of whom lived in the city's housing projects. With my blond hair, my Anglo-suburban accent, my pressed clothes, and my naïveté about life's hardships, I was definitely not an object of affection. This would be the true training ground.

For ten weeks, I worked in a high school, and then I spent five weeks in a middle school that had similar student demographics. What I learned during that trying semester almost caused me to renounce the idea of teacher training. While in front of the class, I rarely relied on the information I had been taught in education classes. Rather, I constantly referred to episodic memories of former teachers and past student experiences. I remembered Mrs. Jones, who set up our advanced placement (AP) English class in a circle, making herself a participant in, rather than the leader of, discussion. Mrs. Birge also came to mind. She had taught me Latin for two of the three years of my study, and it was through her that my thirst for language emerged. I pictured her, festooned with a laurel wreath, confidently singing out the Latin subjunctive of "Let It Be." Whoever thought a "dead" language could be so alive? I wanted to emulate these teachers in my own pedagogical style, drawing from them the qualities I most admired and leaving their not so admirable traits to memory.

My classroom recollections were not always pleasant. The embarrassment I felt when my AP chemistry teacher publicly ridiculed my long, overly poetic exam answers stuck with me. Therefore, I vowed never to make fun of my students. Confidence should be theirs, and I wanted to help instill it. Another experience I would have liked to forget occurred in lecture-based classes. I have heard this approach called the "drinking from a fire hose" style, and I attest to the metaphor. A year's worth of nonstop note taking never did anything for me, except to leave me with wrinkles on my forehead and a huge knot on the third finger of my right hand. My students would not be subject to this type of instruction. I would encourage them to be responsible for their own learning, and I would be a facilitator, rather than a dictator.

Further training

In addition to my practicum and student teaching experiences, I served as an English tutor at my university's undergraduate learning center. Each day I was greeted by students, some of whom were nonnative speakers of English, who presented me their written "masterpieces" and then waited expectantly for my analysis of their work. Together we discussed the necessities of clear, concise content, the complexities of grammatical structure, and the subtleties of lingual rhythm. My experience as a second language learner throughout college and during a five-week study program in French-speaking Quebec had taught me the importance of patience and diligence with the spoken or written word. Hence, I took my job very seriously. These one-on-one meetings with students reemphasized my love of teaching, for they occurred in a context that I could creatively control. Although employment by the university necessitated some restriction, tutors were allowed freedom in trying new ways of helping students. The challenge and adventure bound up in this freedom compelled me to continue with the profession. However, such liberty carried with it huge responsibility, one which required that I constantly reflect upon and revise my teaching.

To encourage and guide me during this period of self-evaluation, Dr. Louise Bentley, professor emeritus and previously chair of the English Department, met with me once a week. Dr. Bentley had a reputation for being one of the toughest professors you might encounter but one who offered the most intriguing, organized classes and seminars. Though I never attended one of her courses, I had heard testimonies from former students, some of whom were now professors. The verdict was always the same: Dr. Bentley could not contain her passion for literature, for her students, and for the sharing of knowledge. Her willingness to pass on what she had learned through experience evidenced itself further in her mentorship of me. We would spend hours together, munching on brownies she had made and sipping hot tea, discussing various approaches to use in the classroom. How might I make the myth of Phaëthon pertinent to the seventh-grader? Could Shakespeare's love sonnets possibly interest Caholis, my six-foot-two friend from third period? These were the types of questions I asked. These were the issues we laughed about, fleshed out, and dreamed up solutions to. I will not forget her influence and inspiration. Dr. Bentley took the abstractions of my classes in education and made them real: She gave personality to theory.

Revelation

I did not entirely scrap the knowledge I gleaned from my educational training in my actual teaching – though I had initially thought that this would be the case. As the weeks passed, I realized that I was drawing upon theory in my decision making. However, I was filtering all theory through my personal judgment, through my idea of what good teaching is, through my intuitive screen. Such practice was illustrated to me through the advice of a college professor of language methodology. After our class had spent a few weeks studying various methodological approaches, Professor King looked at us directly, scanning faces that no doubt revealed dependence upon textual facts. Then she told us to close our books. "Now that you know what others have said," she stated quietly, "find out what *really* works in your classroom." She was not demanding that we dismiss theory but that we combine and expand upon various theories in order to personalize them to our specific situations. This is what I had been doing when I relied upon memories to guide my teaching. My personal experience had become embedded into my theoretical understanding; the two were inextricably related.

Theory versus practice

My conviction that teachers could truly possess autonomy within the classroom encouraged me to attend graduate school to pursue further educational research. When I received the registration materials from the TESL master's program I was to attend, I found that I would begin my studies with three courses and serve as a teaching assistant for two classes in ESL composition. I formulated a general hypothesis of what each subject would entail. Surely the TESL and applied linguistics courses would be steeped in practice, with the former being directly related to my assistantship. The third course for which I registered, Theory of Second Language (L2) Acquisition, would provide a theoretical backbone for pedagogy. As is often the case, my assumptions were wrong, and each course began, ironically, with the theory versus practice debate. Thus for the first few weeks of graduate school, my professors reinforced the idea that a teacher should be viewed and should act as a genuine theorist. I favor this idea because I am also a teacher, and I have found through conversations with fellow teachers and the writings of teacher-theorists and theorist-teachers that I am not alone in this view. Moreover, by articulating mainstream theory in light of actual classroom experience and by recognizing personal beliefs and practices as a part of this theory, teachers can begin to eradicate the "research versus practice" divide.

The assignment

The graduate-level course, if successful, opens the door for discussion on the theory versus practice debate. It encourages the voicing of ideas and the articulation of these ideas in writing and dialogue. Graduate classrooms also tend to encourage an understanding of the modes of expression within higher education learning. Usually, this translates to extensive reading, countless reaction papers, and three-hour seminars dominated by theoretical discussion. Although these are beneficial, it comes as a relief when the professor introduces some alternative form of expression. The relief may initially be tinged with incredulity – "How can I, a master's candidate, get out the crayons and draw a picture to represent this complex phenomenon?" Yet, the disbelief creates intrigue and the challenge of attempting the unfamiliar. This is precisely what the visual representation exercise I discuss in this chapter did for me. In a course on North American English phonetics, the professor gave this assignment: Visually represent pronunciation, both its segmental features and its suprasegmental features. To complete the assignment, I had first to articulate the concepts and then think about how my pictorial articulation might be questioned and understood by others. I had to consider the piece's purpose and audience; I had to draw theory.

Articulating the theory embedded in my drawing

With my own teaching philosophy falling in line with the current trend toward more global emphases, I decided that my drawing must begin with the suprasegmental. *Segmental features* are discrete aspects of language such as individual consonants and vowels, whereas the term *suprasegmental* refers to more global aspects such as stress, rhythm, prominence, and intonation. My decision to begin with suprasegmentals may also have sprung from pieces that I had been reading for another class during the very week that this pronunciation assignment was given. For a seminar on communicative language teaching, I had been reviewing the works of Dell Hymes (1967, 1971) and M. A. K. Halliday (1978), specifically the import they place upon the socially interactive nature of language.

The research of Hymes and Halliday differs significantly from the prominent linguistic theory of the mid-twentieth century, primarily the work of Chomsky (1965), in the emphasis given by Hymes and Halliday to culture and context. Hymes rejects Chomsky's view of the "ideal speaker-listener" (1965, p. 3) in favor of a linguistic understanding that asserts communication's appropriateness (1971, p. 5). Halliday furthers this idea, concentrating upon language's function, "the use to which language is put, the purpose of an utterance rather than the particular grammatical form an utterance takes" (Savignon, 1997, p. 19).

This trend toward function and meaning over linguistic form led me to choose *language function* and *context of situation* as the "overarching" elements in my visual representation (hence the arches above these terms; see the accompanying figure). I cannot claim that this choice in representation is based entirely on theory, however. The two "golden arches" that meet in the center may also be seen in relationship to a less academic but definitely important symbol. After all, graduate students do have to eat.

From these suprasegmental features flows yet another global issue, that of prosody. I have labeled this section of the drawing the "Amorphous Pool of Prosody," based on my experience in learning the meaning of the word. During a fall semester class in discourse analysis, the class was introduced to this novel term, or at least it was new to me. As we learned the principles of Conversation Analysis (CA) set out by Atkinson and Heritage (1984), it became clear that prosody is responsible for an enormous portion of communicative import. However, it was not until the end of the semester that I could confidently explain what *prosody*, in its broadest sense, means or consists of.

According to my dictionary, *prosody* deals with the "scientific study of speech rhythms." Yet, I knew from my class in discourse analysis that we were categorizing a great number of phenomena in addition to rhythm under the rubric *prosodic form*. For me, the term therefore had an amorphous quality, remaining elusive of definition. Fortunately, a definition is provided in *Teaching Pronunciation: A Reference for Teachers of English to Speakers of Other Languages*, one of the texts used in the course for which

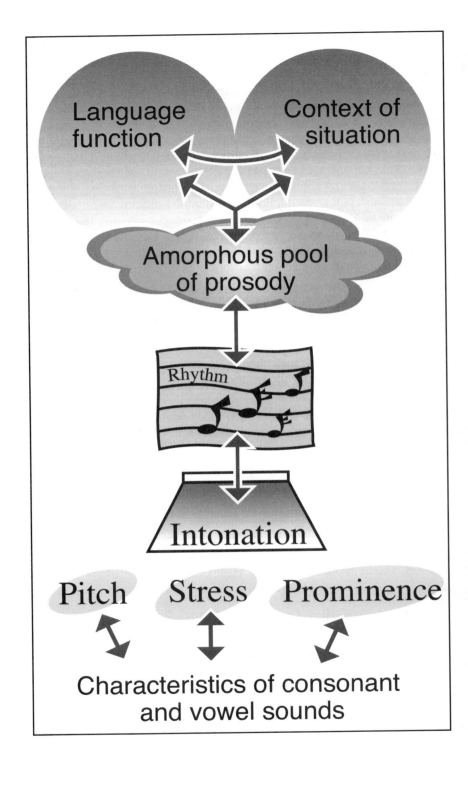

this assignment was completed. Celce-Murcia, Brinton, and Goodwin, the authors of this text, add to my dictionary's definition of the term, listing intonation, volume, tempo, and rhythm all as prosodic elements (1996, p. 200).

Though rhythm and intonation are both aspects of prosody, I chose to represent them in my drawing as separate and specific categories. Yet, although I separated them, I wished to recognize their necessary interrelationship, a characteristic that applies to every grouping within the visual depiction. To highlight this connection, I joined each element to the next with a double-ended arrow, indicating that the relationship works in both directions. Each element influences what follows it and what comes before, and all elements are dependent upon one another.

To signify rhythm within the visual depiction, I chose an easily recognizable symbol – that of a staff of music. The stress-timed nature of English, composed of both individual words and whole sentences, refers to "the regular, patterned beat of stressed and unstressed syllables and pauses" (Celce-Murcia, Brinton, and Goodwin, 1996, p. 152). Spoken language has a definite musical quality about it. An aspect of such linguistic musicality may be traced to intonation, the "melodic line" within spoken discourse, its rising and falling in pitch (p. 184). Thus, although rhythm and intonation are unquestionably related, separating them in the figure allows each to be more clearly defined. By dividing them, I hoped to show in a somewhat ironic fashion how inextricable they truly are.

I chose a megaphone to symbolize intonation. The megaphone in the drawing is announcing other segmental features that comprise intonation, such as pitch, stress, and prominence. Although these three concepts are integrally related, as are rhythm and intonation, I wanted to separate them as well to underscore the way each term is used within the teaching of pronunciation. According to Celce-Murcia, Brinton, and Goodwin, *pitch* may be most easily distinguished by its reference to the "relative highness or lowness of the voice" (p. 184). However, differentiating between *stress* and *prominence* seems to me to be a more difficult task. *Stress* may refer to either the individual word, "the pattern of stressed and unstressed syllables within a word" (p. 132), or the stress pattern of the entire sentence, a concept mirroring intonation. *Prominence*, or "which word the speaker *wishes* to highlight" (p. 176, emphasis added), also includes stress. As its definition suggests, however, prominence takes the speaker's intent into account as well.

Having defined *pitch, stress,* and *prominence*, I return to the visual depiction. Proceeding from the three latter features are the most segmental features in the study of pronunciation – the discrete characteristics of the individual consonant and vowel sounds. Although these sounds appear at the foot of the visual depiction, this does not imply that they are the foundation. If a foundation had to be chosen, it would be found in language function and the context of situation, the overarching elements discussed earlier.

This top-down approach does not imply linearity of progression, however. In fact, in creating this depiction, I struggled most with how to balance relationships and distinctions, the connections between the components and their differences. A great help in this struggle came in the pronunciation class following the one in which this assignment was given. The members of the class sat in a circle, as was the general custom in this course, and the professor asked those who wished to do so to describe their visual representations. Two students had made their drawings in the form of concentric circles, with the various concepts forming the rings around the common center.

Viewing the conceptual interpretations of my peers helped me explain my own drawing more clearly. Even though I had arranged the depiction in a flowchart fashion, my conceptualization had placed *context* at the core of the drawing. Seeing the work of others and sharing my work with them helped me to refine my own understanding of the theory in question, namely, a personal philosophy of pronunciation. The theory became personal as I took ownership of my visual depiction through a verbal explanation to the class.

Recognizing myself as a theorizer in this process

My desire to articulate theoretical concepts in images and words springs from an incident that occurred during my application process to different master's programs. My undergraduate degree is in English and French, and I have a minor in history. However, when I chose to complete my graduate work in a more linguistically oriented area, one university denied me acceptance to its department. When I questioned this decision, I was told that it was neither my Graduate Record Examination scores nor my transcripts that had led to the decision. I was denied admission because of my personal statement – one that emphasized a love of teaching. Surely, someone so interested in the application of linguistics could never be interested in the study and development of theory – sarcasm intended. Fortunately, this denial allowed me to enter a TESL program that integrates theory and practice.

Completing the pictorial activity for the pronunciation class helped me to bridge the perceived and often very real gap between theory and practice.

My visual depiction is based in linguistic and pedagogical research. Yet it also represents my own theory of spoken language, of teaching, and of myself. The drawing, whether intentionally or not, reveals personal philosophies, a view of language as being inseparably situational and syntactical, for example. It also helps me to clarify these ideas for myself.

I have chosen to become a teacher because I love the classroom setting. I love to learn and to watch learning take place. I approach the scientific art of teaching from this philosophical foundation. The manner in which I think of myself as a teacher stems from personal educational experiences, from a modeling of those who kindled curiosity and a protest against those who squelched it, and from a desire to be continually taught. These aspects of my personality and my personal history largely determine the decisions that I make in the classroom. They help diminish the theory-practice divide by revealing a filter through which published theory is discerned and personal theory is created. Such clarification seems to me to be the most important element in teaching and in my growth as a teacher, for it is in understanding the many influences and interrelationships supporting my own theory that I am able to illustrate them, via words or images, for others.

References

Atkinson, J. M., & Heritage, J. (Eds.). (1984). *Structures of social action: Studies in conversation analysis.* Cambridge: Cambridge University Press.

Celce-Murcia, M., Brinton, D. M., & Goodwin, J. M. (1996). *Teaching pronunciation: A reference for teachers of English to speakers of other languages.* New York: Cambridge University Press.

Chomsky, N. (1965). *Aspects of the theory of syntax.* Cambridge, MA: MIT Press.

Corder, S. P. (1973). *Introducing applied linguistics.* Harmondsworth, Middlesex: Penguin.

Halliday, M. A. K. (1978). *Language as a social semiotic: The social interpretation of language and meaning.* Baltimore: University Park Press.

Hymes, D. (1967). Why linguistics needs the sociologist. *Social Research, 34,* 632–647.

Hymes, D. (1971). Competence and performance in linguistic theory. In R. Huxley and E. Ingram (Eds.), *Language acquisition: Models and methods.* London: Academic Press.

Savignon, S. (1997). *Communicative competence: Theory and classroom practice* (2nd ed.). New York: McGraw-Hill.

Part III   Discussion

1. How has restorying past experiences influenced these teachers' current instructional practices and conceptions of themselves as teachers?
2. What are the limitations of restorying the past? Can these limitations be mitigated?
3. How can images and/or metaphors be used to capture teachers' understandings of themselves, theory, their practice, and their students?
4. How might teachers continue to use restorying of experiences to sustain their professional development?

Part III   Reflection

1. Describe a metaphor or create an image that embodies your conception of yourself as a teacher. Trace your experiences as a student, a language learner, and a language teacher in terms of this metaphor or image. Then use this metaphor or image to identify the threads that bind your experiences together and capture your professional growth as a teacher.
2. Select one of the reflection questions from the beginning of Part III, "Inquiry into Language Teachers." Write a short (two- or three-page) position paper on how you have or might have addressed the theoretical and pedagogical concerns embedded in these questions in your current or future instructional practices as a language teacher.

Part III   Action

1. Write an autobiography in which you capture the richness of your experiences and beliefs as a student, language learner, and language teacher. Identify important people or critical incidents that significantly influenced your understandings of your professional development as a language teacher. Then, critically analyze those experiences and beliefs in terms of how they have shaped you as a teacher and a learner of teaching. Finally, apply the resulting insights you gained to your current or future teaching practices.
2. Create a visual depiction of a concept or idea that is relevant to your teaching. Reflect on this visual depiction in terms of your own personal experiences as a language learner and/or a language teacher. Then reflect on this visual depiction from a theoretical perspective, that is, the role that theory and/or research play in this concept or idea.

Suggested readings

Bailey, K. M. et al. (1996). The language learner's autobiography: Examining the "apprenticeship of observation." In D. Freeman & J. C. Richards (Eds.), *Teacher Learning in Language Teaching* (pp. 11–29). New York: Cambridge University Press.

Jalongo, M. R., & Isenberg, J. P. (1995). *Teachers' stories: From personal narrative to professional insight*. San Francisco: Jossey-Bass.

Johnson, K. E. (1999). *Understanding language teaching: Reasoning in action*. Boston: Heinle & Heinle.

Preskill, S. (1998). Narratives of teaching and the quest for the second self. *Journal of Teacher Education, 49*, 344–358.

Weber, S. (1993). The narrative anecdote in teacher education. *Journal of Education for Teaching, 19*, 71–82.

Woo, L., & Murphey, T. (1999). Activating metacognition with action logs. *The Language Teacher, 23*(5), 15–18.

PART IV:
INQUIRY THROUGH PROFESSIONAL
COLLABORATIONS

Professional collaborations, defying the notion of the solitary classroom teacher, represent another critical form of professional development for teachers. In Part IV, "Inquiry through Professional Collaborations," teachers' stories of inquiry stem from participation in collaborative professional communities, one at the same institution, another with teachers located at different institutions. Collaboration can occur through teachers observing one another, videotaping one another and then watching the tape, talking in nonevaluative ways, and analyzing the talk between collaborators. Although the immediate objective is to examine some aspect of their practice, these teachers learn much about their conceptions of teaching, their students, the institutions in which they teach, and the value of a community of teachers. Michael Boshell writes of his struggle to understand the "quiet" students in his fifth-grade bilingual science class in Spain and discovers that nonevaluative dialogue with colleagues outside his own institution enables him to find "his own answers to his own problems." Steve Mann reflects on how the "talk" among supportive colleagues in a British university language program creates a nonjudgmental approach to individual self-development within a group context.

These teachers examine their instructional practices through professional collaborations and learn about themselves, their beliefs about teaching, their students, the pedagogical reasoning behind their practice, and the tensions they face in their practice. At the same time, they come to value the group identity, support, and communication that professional collaborations generate. These teachers' stories of talk with professional colleagues, in which evaluative comments are stripped away, create space for alternative ways of talking about teachers, students, and teaching. Such space enables teachers to reclaim their own professional development.

Part IV   Initial reflection

The teachers featured in Part IV, "Inquiry through Professional Collaborations," explore the types of theoretical and pedagogical concerns reflected
in the following questions. As you read their stories of narrative inquiry,
reflect on the concerns embedded in these questions and how you have or
might have addressed them in your own teaching.

1. How can I see my instructional practices and myself as a teacher differently?
2. How can I reframe my own classroom dilemmas?
3. How can I nourish and sustain my professional development throughout
   my career?

13 What I learnt from giving quiet children space

Michael Boshell

From 1989 to 1996 I worked as a teacher in a bilingual English-Spanish primary school in Zaragoza, Spain. The children at this school received a bilingual education in every major subject from the age of three until the age of sixteen. In the area of natural and environmental science, the topics to be taught were divided equally between the Spanish and the English teachers. I was the fifth-grade English teacher, and in my class there were twenty-four children. I was responsible for teaching natural and environmental science topics in English to these ten- and eleven-year-old children. The children themselves were generally motivated and actively encouraged and supported by their predominantly white-collar middle-class parents. Thus the children came to school with a positive attitude towards the subjects they were learning.

In the classroom itself, a typical natural or environmental science lesson would proceed in the following way: I would enter the classroom with a variety of visual aids based on the topic that we were about to study. Having pinned up the visual aids, I would then lecture on the topic, referring to the visual aids as I proceeded. For example, if we were studying food chains in the desert, I would first show the children pictures of relevant food chains and then move on to explain how each animal depended on another animal in order to survive. I referred back to the pictures as I went through the explanation.

Once I had presented the topic in this way, I would proceed by encouraging the children to become more actively involved in the class by answering questions on the topic or summarizing what they had heard. However, despite this encouragement, a number of quiet children did not respond at any length. Their participation tended to be limited to very short answers to direct questions. Sometimes they started off explaining something about a particular topic but did not complete the explanation. Because of this, I felt that I had no way of knowing whether they had understood what we were learning.

I felt that if I asked these quiet children, they might be able to tell me why they were not contributing fully. I decided to take them aside after

180

a lesson as a way of ensuring that they did not feel 'singled out' in front of the whole class. I asked the students, individually, why they were not participating fully in class. When they did not answer promptly, I suggested that perhaps they had not understood the lesson. However, they indicated that they had understood, but they still seemed incapable or unwilling to explain why their participation tended to be limited in class.

Unable to obtain an answer from the quiet children themselves, I turned inward. I felt that maybe I was the reason why the quiet children participated only in a limited way. Indeed, this is the possibility I investigate in this chapter: Maybe it was the way I acted in class that affected the quiet children. In order to find out whether this was the case, I decided to talk to my study colleagues in Madrid, Spain.

At the time, I was studying for a master's degree in teaching English. This was a distance learning programme set up by Aston University (Birmingham, England). The course was designed for TEFL teachers living outside Britain who were unable to study full time in Britain because of family and/or work commitments abroad. To study for this degree, teachers were required to have at least five years of TEFL teaching experience. I had been teaching for six years when I enrolled in the course in January 1993. From 1987 to 1989, I worked in two language schools in Bilbao, Spain, where I taught EFL to young learners (seven to eighteen years of age). From 1989 until I began my master's distance programme, I taught EFL and natural and environmental science in Zaragoza. Three other teachers had also decided to take this course. We formed a study group that met fortnightly in Madrid. The idea was for us to help and support one another in our studies. We thought we'd take turns presenting course-related topics, or we might simply read through one another's assignments.

The group had been up and running for nine months when we began an assignment for a teacher development option. The assignment involved each of us looking at a 'problem' or issue in our own teaching and coming together to talk in order to gain a fuller understanding of it. I felt that my colleagues within the group might be able to help me understand what was taking place between me and the quiet children. As Edge (1992a, p. 4) argues, "By cooperating with others, we can come to understand better our own experiences." It was through talking with my colleagues that I gradually came to realise that the problem did lie in me, and that it was I who had to change, if my quiet children were to participate in my class. How my colleagues aided me in this realisation, and how I changed will be the focus of this chapter. However, prior to discussing this topic, I need to describe the social and educational context that the children and I were part of. It is perhaps only then that the reader will appreciate the magnitude of the problem that I faced.

Situation

The school in which I was teaching was a parents' cooperative. It had been set up and was owned by a group of parents who wanted to be fully involved in their children's education. As a consequence, the parents had direct input into how the school should be run and the educational principles upon which it should be based. They had been educated in a system in which the teacher dominated and controlled the classroom and teachers' authority was absolute. The parents felt that they had been denied the opportunity to take an active part in their own learning and had merely been expected to listen and accept the knowledge and authority of the teacher. This was not what the parents wanted for their own children. Whilst they were able to accept 'authority' in terms of what Stevick (1980, p. 286) argues as "a relationship in which both parties believe that one of the parties is competent to direct, guide, or instruct the other," they felt that the children should also take an active part in their own learning. In other words, although the parents saw the need for a teacher to introduce and explain a scientific topic to the children, they also believed that the children should then be encouraged to express and use what they had learnt. Indeed, this belief comes across in the school's annual pamphlet, *Nuestro collegio* (1994, p. 2), in which the school's beliefs and principles are outlined:

Se anima la participation de los niños en clase. Deberian poder expresarse y manipular lo que aprenden en la aula. [Children are encouraged to participate in class. They should be able to express and use what they learn in the classroom.]

This belief was reaffirmed on many occasions when I met children's parents, who praised any kind of activity that involved maximum participation from the children, whether this was through acting out a role-play on stage or presenting a project in class.

In light of this, I went to Madrid to speak to my study colleagues. I was aware of the school's beliefs and felt that I did try to encourage children to participate, and yet I was faced with a group of children who would not or could not participate fully in class.

Focus

Cooperative group work 1: Becoming aware of my dominance

In attempting to understand what was happening in our classes, we decided to draw on Edge's (1992b; in press) notion of Cooperative Development, which he defines as "a way of working with someone in order to become a better teacher in your own way: Two people cooperate for an agreed period in order to allow one person to work on his or her (self-) development" (p. 62).

Over the years we had all been observed and taken other people's ideas and suggestions for how to become better teachers. Cooperative Development seemed to be a fresh approach. Although we would be working with other people, they would be helping us to see ourselves clearly and helping us to develop as teachers in our own way. Implicit to this process is the role of what Edge (1992a) calls the Speaker and the Understander. The *Speaker* is the person who wishes to speak about a problem or an issue that he or she faces in his or her teaching. The *Understander* helps the speaker by listening carefully and helping the speaker to develop himself or herself.

Henny – one of my study colleagues – volunteered to be my Understander. Henny helped me to develop my own understanding of what was taking place between the quiet children and myself. In these initial weeks I came to understand that I did indeed have a problem with my quiet children. Henny helped me to see this for myself and helped me to focus on this problem by employing some interactive techniques that Edge (1992a) puts forward.

Two of these techniques seemed important in terms of my own development at this initial stage: Reflecting and Focusing (Edge, 1992a, pp. 28–44). *Reflecting* describes the process whereby the Understander helps the speaker to see his or her ideas clearly. This is done when the Understander acts as a mirror in order to reflect the speaker's own ideas. Henny, as the Understander, attempted to do this by paraphrasing what I was saying. At first, though, she seemed unable to accurately capture how I felt about my effect on my quiet children. This was because I was not very sure myself. In any case, her inaccurate reflections of what I was trying to say forced me to think again and express myself further. Indeed, as I became clearer, the reflections became more accurate. Here is an extract from our conversation:

Mike: Yeah, I'm serious in the classroom, and that's why they might participate in a limited way. I never smile, and I reckon that could make them a bit wary of me.

Henny: Let me see. You're saying that it's because you're serious that they don't participate in any great detail.

Mike: Hang on, perhaps it's not because I'm serious. After all, you can be serious, but still organise them into pairs whereby they are more likely to participate in greater depth, just that you do this in a serious way! No, I think it's because I'm a dominant type of teacher.

Henny: So you're saying, that despite being a serious teacher, that's not important. You could provide them with pair work, just that you would go about organising this in a serious way. It's you being serious that puts them off.

Mike: Yeah, that's right. Being in pairs would probably make them feel more comfortable, and more likely to participate. No, it's definitely me being dominant that puts them off. I try to control absolutely everything in class, and what's more I rarely allow them to do pair work.

Henny: So it's your dominance that puts them off from contributing more.

Mike: Yeah I think it must be.

Thus it was through interacting with my colleague that I gradually came to see my problem more clearly. Toward the end of the interaction, she was successfully reflecting how I felt, to the extent that I now firmly recognised that it could be my dominance that discouraged my quiet children from participating as much as they could.

However, I was still unsure about what aspect of my dominant behaviour affected the quiet learners the most. At this stage, there was a need for *Focusing*, in which both the Speaker and the Understander concentrate on one aspect of the Speaker's chosen topic. In my case, I needed to focus on what was the most significant aspect of my dominant behaviour. I would then be in a position to examine why I acted as I did in the classroom. As Myers (1993, p. 15) suggests, "if we are not aware of what it is that is driving our behaviour, then it is difficult to change what we do (or the way we do it) at anything other than a cosmetic level." Indeed, my colleague in her role as the Understander invited me to do exactly that: to concentrate on what I felt to be the most crucial aspect of my dominant behaviour. In order to focus more deeply, I drew upon Edge's (1992a, p. 37) idea of a 'focusing circle.' This consisted of drawing a small circle and writing what I considered to be the general problem inside it: too dominant. I then drew a bigger circle around the small one and divided the space between the two circles into four equal segments, in which I wrote certain features of my dominant behaviour in class. Even as I was writing, I became aware of certain aspects of my behaviour that I had never realised before.

As Freeman (1989, p. 34) argues, "[A]wareness may be immediate or it may be delayed, occurring sometime later when something or someone triggers it." I was fully aware of the fact that I shout, stare, and demand a great deal of the quiet children. However, I had not been aware that I might deny them 'space'. By *space*, I mean what Stevick (1980, p. 20) calls 'the learning space of the student', in which quiet children have control over their language and themselves. However, I still needed to be sure that this was indeed the case. I decided to check this by monitoring myself. This would involve observing myself in the class to see whether I did, in fact, deny them enough space, and how I did this. As Richards (1990, p. 119) suggests: "Self-monitoring can help narrow the gap between teachers' imagined views of their own teaching, and reality." Although I felt that I tended to deny the quiet children space, this needed to be observed in practice. I wanted to see whether this focus, which I had arrived at with the help of my colleagues, accurately reflected my classroom teaching.

Self-monitoring: Denying the quiet children space

I arranged for a colleague to videotape one of my lessons. Unlike other forms of self-monitoring, the video camera seemed to be a way in which I would make myself more 'visible' because I would be capturing what Richards (1990, p. 124) calls "the moment-to-moment process of teaching." This would, I hoped, enable me to learn a lot from how I acted in the classroom. The lesson was on the topic of the solar system. The children were required to listen to a taped conversation about the planets. They would listen once, and I would ask them what they had understood. They would listen again and, consulting with a partner, note specific information about each of the planets in table format. I would then ask them questions related to the information.

Once the lesson was over, I watched the video and came to the conclusion that I did indeed deny the quiet children 'space' when they attempted to participate. I did this in two ways and in two senses: I limited their discourse space, by using my language to control them and what they were saying. And I limited their physical space by constantly approaching them wherever they were sitting. Regarding the first point, Stubbs (1983, p. 48) refers to teacher's language of control as *metacommunication*, defining it as 'communication about communication'. He lists eight types of communication, which according to van Lier (1988, p. 218), can be considered 'strategies of control'. However, from watching the video, I felt that in denying the children space, I had employed three of Stubbs' (p. 51) strategies: controlling the amount of speech, summarizing, and checking or confirming understanding.

Controlling the amount of speech

In the first part of the listening task, in which the children had to comment on what they had understood, the more active children participated. However, when the quiet children did attempt to contribute, I seemed to interrupt them and finish off what I thought they were saying. For example:

Teacher (myself):   So, children, tell me about Mars then. How about you, Camino? Can you tell me something?
Quiet child (Camino): It's a small planet and its . . . [interrupted by me]
Teacher: That's right and it's quite far from the Earth as well. That's what you wanted to say, wasn't it Camino?
Quiet child (Camino): [No response]
Teacher: Okay, children, have you got that? Let's move on then.

I was indicating to the quiet children how much they should say and also drawing my own, unfounded conclusions about what they might have gone on to say.

Summarizing

There were occasions when I did not interrupt the quiet children. However, even when they were allowed to finish their contributions, it seemed as though I attempted to summarise what they had said to the whole class. For example, after Paula, one of the quiet children, gave a brief description of Venus:

Teacher (myself): So what Paula is really trying to say is that Venus would be a very difficult planet to live on because of the very hot temperature on its surface. Did you get that, children? Shall I repeat that?
Other children: No.

After this, Paula stared at the teacher (myself) and did not say anything. Thus, I was assuming that the other children in the class had not understood what the quiet children had tried to say without actually knowing whether this was indeed the case. Furthermore, by summarizing what they had said, I was indirectly indicating to them that their contributions were not good or clear enough for the rest of the class to understand.

Checking or confirming understanding

I also noticed that after finishing off or summarizing what the quiet children had attempted to say, I would then turn to them again. I would check each one to see whether he or she had been following me. I might ask one, "Do you understand me?" to which the quiet child would normally reply, "Yes." I would then immediately follow this with, "Are you sure you've understood?" and would then finally ask a question such as "So you do understand me then?" to which the answer would again be "Yes." I had repeated the question over and over again – using different wording – because I wanted a longer reply from the quiet children.

Regarding physical space, I observed that I seemed to be constantly approaching the quiet children in the second part of the listening task to see how they were coping. I might lean over them, point out something on the table they were filling out, intervene in what they were saying, or even pick up the sheet to see how they were doing. Thus, I was always 'around them', trying to ensure that they were completing the task properly.

It seemed at this point that all the strategies that I had employed had in fact restricted the quiet children's space. The strategies I had used to control their oral contributions had effectively denied them space within which to speak freely and without interference, or I would be constantly 'around' the quiet children, limiting their space to work individually or in pairs.

However, at this stage one might argue that the fact that I watched the video with a firm idea of what I expected to see might have influenced my interpretation of what was going on. Indeed, Nunan (1989, p. 76) points this out when he argues: "[O]ur preconceptions about what goes on in the classroom will determine what we see." Thus one could argue that because my focus or preconception had been to see whether I did deny my quiet learners space, I tended to look for examples of behaviour that confirmed this focus.

In order to see whether my observation had been unduly influenced by my original focus, I asked several colleagues to watch the video. I did not hand them any kind of observational scheme based on preselected categories, and although they probably watched the video with what Nunan (p. 89) terms their 'own interior observation schedule', they were at least unaware of what I was looking for. I deliberately chose three work colleagues whom I trust, and after they watched the video, we met in a small private room. I valued their opinions and was confident that the comments they were about to make about my teaching would not go beyond the walls of the room. They offered comments such as:

You didn't let Camino finish what she was saying on a number of occasions. (Lynne)

You repeated what Alberto was trying to say. (Melanie)

Parece que estas nervioso Mike, no les dejes en paz. [You seem nervous, Mike, you don't leave them alone.] (Mari)

My colleagues then, were merely reaffirming my own perceptions that I did deny the quiet children space. The question now was how I would respond to this realisation. I decided that maybe my colleagues in Madrid could help me find my own answers to this problem.

Response

Cooperative group work 2: The reasons behind denying the children space

Part of my response to this problem lay in working out why I denied these children enough space in which to contribute and work. I again sought the help of my study companions in Madrid. Henny was keen to take on the role of the Understander again.

At this point, I was not sure why I felt the need to control the quiet children's language and the quiet children themselves. I explained to my colleague, however, that I did know that I was under immense pressure at school to ensure that the children understood the content I taught. This comment led Henny to use another Cooperative Development technique, Thematising. Edge (1992a, p. 46) defines *Thematising* as suggesting that there could be a connection or a 'thematic relationship' between two statements that the speaker has made. My colleague asked me whether there was any connection between denying the quiet children space and feeling pressure from parents. This made me realise that perhaps there was a connection between the two. I explained to my colleague that, because I was responsible for ensuring that the children did understand the content, I felt I needed to control the language and the activities within the classroom. My colleague then reflected this back to me: "Am I right in saying that you think that, because you'll be held responsible if the children don't understand, that is why you attempt to control the language and activities?"

This helped me see that if they did not understand a particular topic, I would be blamed. Out of this came the idea of fear. My colleague asked me whether I wanted to focus on fear in more depth. This I did, commenting that I was afraid to give the quiet children control over their topic-related language and tasks. I felt that if I did, they might not understand the content. This explained why I tended to either interrupt and finish off what they were saying or summarise what they had said. Through using both strategies, I felt that I could make the quiet children's contributions clearer, so that they themselves – on hearing my explanation – would better understand the content.

However, as I pointed out to my colleague, this did not reduce my fear. When I asked them whether they had followed my explanation, they merely responded, "Yes." This increased my fear, because I couldn't judge whether they had understood me or not. I would have liked the quiet children to give a longer reply, such as "Yes, I have. You said that Pluto is the farthest away." This sort of response, though, was not forthcoming. I felt that I had no way of knowing whether they had indeed followed and understood my explanation.

On hearing this, my colleague used another Cooperative Development technique, *Challenging*. Edge (1992a, p. 53) suggests that when the Understander hears different statements from the Speaker that seem contradictory, the Understander can present them back to the Speaker, so that the speaker can 'reconcile them.' It is through reconciling the two statements that the Speaker can make his or her ideas more coherent. My colleague presented me with two such statements: "I hear you saying that your quiet learners answer "Yes" only when you check to see whether they've followed you and understood your explanation. You would like them to give a longer response than "Yes." How does that link up to what you were saying before, about controlling the quiet learners' language?

Having these two statements presented to me made me reexamine the problem. Perhaps there was a link between how I intervened and took over from the children – either whilst they were speaking or had just finished contributing – and them merely responding "Yes" after being asked whether they had understood.

What this showed me was that I lacked faith in the quiet children. I thought that if I gave them space to contribute and work with the topic, there would be no guarantee that they would learn the content. I felt that the only guarantee I had of the quiet children coming to understand the content would be if I had control over their language, and over them. Yet because of the minimal responses they gave, I had no evidence that this was the case.

My intention now was to come up with a course of action that I could employ in the classroom. I felt that my goal was clear. Through self-reflection (aided by my colleagues), I had come to realise that because of my lack of faith in the quiet children, I now controlled them and the language they used in unhelpful ways. I felt that the most obvious goal now would be to see how I would react to, and what I would learn from, giving the quiet children far more space.

Activity 1: Giving the children space

Drawing on the previous lesson, in which the quiet children had listened to and worked on a taped conversation about space, I thought up an activity that would involve the quiet children and would show what they had learnt from the lesson. They had heard about the size, colour, and distance from the sun of the various planets. I gave them some wire, cardboard, needles, cotton, and paint. I then asked them to make a space mobile (of the sun and the planets) using the information I hoped they already knew and the materials I had just given out.

I had decided that I was not going to intervene. They were to have what Stevick (1980, p. 19) calls the *initiative*; that is, they would be able to make "decisions about who says what to whom and when." The quiet children, then, were in control of making the space mobile. Whereas before I had always decided who should speak, what they should speak about, when they should speak, and for how long, I had now handed over control to the quiet children themselves.

In this sense, I was also giving the quiet children 'control' in the way Stevick (1980, p. 17) suggests: "the structuring of classroom activity." The quiet children were the ones who would have to decide what to do with the material. In groups, they would first have to discuss how they were going to make the space mobile, decide on the size, position, and colour of the planets, and then finally construct the mobile. I was interested to see how they would cope with the space I had given them. And in terms of my own development, I wanted to see how I would react and what I could learn from this experience of taking a back seat while the quiet children dealt with their new-found space.

Giving the children space: Success or failure?

The activity did not work; in fact, it did not get beyond the initial stage. The children merely sat at the table and stared blankly at the materials before them. My immediate reaction was one of frustration, for two reasons: First, I had given the quiet children 'space', that is, both initiative and control, and yet they had not known how to use it. Second, I felt that I could not intervene, despite the quiet children not knowing how to proceed, for intervention would have spoiled the goal of the activity itself. Nevertheless, I wanted to intervene and found it frustrating that I could not.

Cooperative group work 3: Evaluation of Activity 1

At this stage I felt I needed to consult my study colleagues once more. I commented on how my original goal had been to see how I would react to and what I would learn from giving the quiet children space. I explained how they had not responded and how, as a consequence, I had felt quite frustrated.

On hearing this, Henny – taking on the role of Understander – asked me whether I would like to focus on this feeling of frustration. I explained that I had always denied the quiet children space, but now that I had provided them with an activity for which they were solely responsible, they had not known how to use their space. Henny drew on Thematising to help me see for myself how my concerns were connected: "So you're saying that you're frustrated as you've always denied your quiet children space, and yet when you give it to them, they can't do anything with it. Could there be a link or a connection in here somewhere?"

Hearing this made me realise that the reason the quiet children had not been able to use this space may have been exactly because they had never had it before. They had been taken from a situation in which they had hardly any space to one in which they were expected to plan and contribute orally as much as they wished. The fact that they had not been able to take advantage of this situation seems to support what Stevick (1980, p. 20) suggests about space: "If there is too little, the student will feel stifled. If there is too much, the student will feel that the teacher has abandoned him."

My quiet children probably did feel abandoned. It made me realise that maybe I did need to be involved. I suggested to my colleague that since the quiet children were used to a strong teacher presence, the situation I had placed them in was too unfamiliar. I felt that they needed a situation that would not be too unfamiliar, that is, one in which I would give some kind of guidance. This guidance would come in the form of explaining to the quiet children what a space mobile is and how they could use the different materials to make one. After this initial guidance there would be no more control from the teacher. They would be able to make the space mobile, using whatever language they wished and speaking to whomever they liked.

By operating in a more familiar world, they would be more likely to take advantage of the space available and participate more fully. This would be in line with Stevick's (p. 20) observation: "In exercising 'control,'... the teacher is giving some kind of order, or structure to the learning space of the student. In encouraging him to take 'initiative', she is allowing him to work and grow within that space."

I now had to rethink my goal. I would exercise some control, or give the activity some shape. After the initial stage, however, I would stand back and let the children complete the activity by themselves. My goal now was to see how I would respond to and what I would learn from this reconfiguration of my teaching. It is this experience to which I now turn.

Activity 2: Giving the children manageable space

One of my colleagues videotaped the lesson, and even in the initial stages, I was probably controlling too much. Having shown them how to make the space mobile, I also suggested the language they could use in their groups. Indeed, even in the later stage, there were times when I would approach them or, equally important, they would approach me, asking for advice. However, for the most part in the later stage, I was detached from the quiet children and they seemed to be content working in groups. I noticed that they were participating and were also using most of the topic-related language without any great difficulty.

Furthermore, I did not feel frustrated. The quiet children were now showing that they could use space when it was given to them in an appropriate way. And I felt that I had been involved, that I had an important role to play in helping them use this space. By explaining how to make the space mobile, I had provided a not-too-unfamiliar world in which they would want to participate.

Evaluation of Activity 2: What did I learn?

At the beginning of the activity, I didn't want to be too involved; however, after a while, I realised that I had nothing to fear by relinquishing some control. I noticed that the quiet children did know the topic and were more likely to participate if they had some space in which to do so. Furthermore, I realised that I had a role to play in creating this space, by providing the structure for, or giving some shape to, the activity itself.

Outcomes

The experience of having seen the quiet learners working and communicating successfully had wider implications for me both as an individual and as a teacher. Perhaps more than anything else, I needed to have more faith in myself. I needed to believe that my ideas could work in practice and that I had a positive role to play. I also needed to have more faith in the quiet children themselves. They showed me what they were capable of, once they had been given space in which to work.

Furthermore, I now felt that I was starting to give the quiet children an opportunity to be involved in their own learning. Now I was at least providing a classroom situation in which all children had the opportunity to participate and use what they had learnt. I was able to arrive at this resolution with the help of my colleagues in Madrid. The interactive techniques they used were crucial to my professional development. The techniques of Reflecting and Focusing were essential in helping me to develop a focus for the problem. The techniques of Challenging and Thematising were of equal importance in enabling me to work out why I had this problem. More than anything else, the techniques allowed me to develop my own focus and then enabled me to find my own answers to why I had denied the quiet children space. The fact that I had worked with other colleagues did not mean that I, as a teacher, had been changed and developed by them. Rather, they had cooperated with me in order to work on my own self-development. They had helped me to see what was taking place in the classroom, why it was taking place, and how I might change it. As Edge (1992a, p. 4) argues: "I need someone to work with, but I don't need someone who wants to change me and make me more like the way they think I ought to be. I need someone who will help me see myself clearly." I knew the context I was working in, I knew the children both as people and as learners, and I knew what the school expected of me. Therefore, I was ready to take responsibility for my children's development and my own. It was *I* who had to find my own answers.

Conclusion

From the very beginning, I had a vague idea that it was perhaps the way I acted in class that discouraged the quiet children from participating. However, it was only through working with my colleagues and observing myself that I came to see what the problem was. I discovered that I denied the children space: first, by controlling how much they said and when they should say it, and second, by being constantly 'over' them and not allowing them any physical space in which to communicate with one another. By talking to my study colleagues in Madrid, I came to understand *why* I did this. I denied them this space simply because I lacked faith in them. I did not feel that they could handle the responsibility of learning and using the information I had presented in class. Yet, when I gave them manageable space in which they could grow, they participated more fully and showed me that they did know the content. From my own point of view, I helped create this space for them, but I came to realise that, despite giving up some of my control, I too had a role to play in helping the quiet children take advantage of their new-found space.

In a general sense, I learned that quiet children need to develop in their own space. They need a certain amount of distance from the teacher so that they can work out what they want to say and how they want to say it. This does not mean that the teacher should abandon them, leaving them in an unfamiliar world in which they don't know how to function; rather, it means that the teacher should provide a structure so that children know where they are meant to go.

Whilst I could have relied on my own initial feelings that I was the reason why my quiet children were not participating, I would never have been able to come to realise exactly *how* and *why* I was thwarting their participation in class. I needed to draw in other experienced teaching colleagues who could help me see myself more clearly without imposing on me their own ideas of what makes good teaching. This, for me, is the power of collaboration.

References

Edge, J. (1992a). *Cooperative development: Professional self-development through cooperation with colleagues*. Harlow: Longman. This text is now available at http://www-users.aston.ac.uk/~edgej/cd/titles.htm

Edge, J. (1992b). Cooperative development. *ELT Journal 46*(1), 62–70.

Edge J. (in press). *Continuing cooperative development*. Ann Arbor: University of Michigan Press.

Freeman, D. (1989). Teacher training, development and decision making: A model of teaching and related strategies for language teacher education. *TESOL Quarterly 23*(1), 27–45.

Juan de Lanuza. (1994). Nuestro collegio [Our school]. Zaragoza: Institucion Hispano-Britanico.

Myers, M. (1993). To boldly go.... In J. Edge & K. Richards (Eds.), *Teachers develop Teachers Research* (pp. 10–26). Oxford: Heinemann International.

Nunan, D. (1989). *Understanding language classrooms: A guide for teacher-initiated action*. Prentice Hall International.

Richards, J. (1990). *The language teaching matrix*. Cambridge: Cambridge University Press.

Stevick, E. (1980). *Teaching languages: A way and ways*. Rowley, MA: Newbury House.

Stubbs, M. (1983). *Discourse analysis: The sociolinguistic analysis of natural language*. Oxford: Blackwell.

van Lier, L. (1988). *The classroom and the language learner*. Harlow: Longman.

14 Talking ourselves into understanding

Steve Mann

Introduction

I am one of a group of teachers and teacher educators who decided several years ago that we needed a space in which to articulate our current thinking on personal teaching and research issues. We already had regular teacher meetings, but they were agenda-driven; they were geared to producing outcomes at a group level. We needed a different sort of talk in which, as teachers, we could work with something that was perhaps tentative, troubling, incomplete, partial, or emergent. This would be a way of allowing the individual a chance of constructing a view of experience and knowledge within the support of a group. This chapter is a personal account of a process of professional exploration and development. It is an account of a process that has helped me to better understand my dialogic and reflexive relationship with my teaching context.

Meeting expectations

It is my experience that when a group of teachers get together, there are expectations that, in talking about their work, they will demonstrate that they 'know what they are doing'. This expectation is so strong that it actually takes some effort to deconstruct its implications. In other words, we might get dragged into a simple oppositional stance at this point. Let me give you a fabricated example:

I should like to thank my Aston University LSU colleagues for their valuable and detailed responses in interviews and discussions and for giving me permission to record what are often very personal and frank statements of current thinking. With regard to the personal nature of this interaction, I have used pseudonyms except for my own contributions. I would particularly like to thank Julian Edge for pointing out the Taylor quotation, as well as several other contributions. Julian Edge is writing a book (forthcoming) that presents his continuing cooperative development work.

A: I think when a group of teachers get together there's tremendous pressure to demonstrate that you know what you are doing.
B: Well, of course, teachers ought to know what they're doing! Who wants to be taught by someone who doesn't know what he's doing?

If anyone makes a statement that is open to question, it will be questioned, and usually before the statement is in fact fully formed. We often end up with half-articulated ideas that are half understood.

I want to demonstrate, in this chapter, how a process of group development has given me the space to articulate my ideas in a way that I think has had a number of outcomes in both my thinking and my practice. All the sessions have been recorded, and extracts from these sessions are included here to highlight specific personal outcomes and processes.

Back in time, then . . .

At the beginning of 1998, there was a collective sense that, as a group of teachers and teacher educators, we needed time for exploration through talk of key teaching and research issues. We all worked in the Language Studies Unit (LSU) at Aston University. However, we did not all go to Aston University on the same days, for we worked in and around Birmingham, Lichfield, Warwick, and Stratford. We have particularly close ties with The Brasshouse Language Centre in Birmingham, which teaches adults from countries all over the world. A number of the staff work at both Aston University and The Brasshouse.

The language development programmes in Aston University include, in the main, international English language teaching preparation courses and English for Academic Purposes (EAP) courses for students already in degree programmes. The LSU at Aston University provides tailored EAP courses for students studying a wide variety of undergraduate and postgraduate science and business programmes. Over the years, the LSU has developed a reputation for English for Specific Purposes (ESP) course design and delivery. We sometimes get learners from outside the 'academic community' who have unique target needs. For example, one of my students was a member of the Aston Villa football team; at least initially, he was having a great deal of difficulty with 'soccer speak'!

In addition to language development programmes, a variety of teacher training and teacher education programmes are offered, among them Introduction to TESOL Certificate courses, Advanced Certificate, Diploma, and MScTESOL programmes. In 1998 our group had six members. The growth in both language development and teacher education programmes meant that we were able to increase the number of staff in 2000. Indeed, during the first part of 2001, we took on several new staff on a part-time basis, and we are now offering them the chance to join the development group I feature in this chapter.

All full-time and part-time staff working in the LSU are required to attend a unit staff meeting. The agenda at this Tuesday lunchtime meeting is usually so full that we do not have sufficient time to fully explore ideas and issues. In 1998 we made the decision to ring-fence Tuesday afternoons (there is no teaching on Tuesday afternoons) so that we could create extra space for professional talk, distinct from the talk in our existing meetings.

We wanted the group to focus on one individual at a time and give each person the benefit of undivided attention. So, the individuals within the group take turns to be the Speaker for a meeting. It is an opportunity to talk through an idea, an issue, or a personal concern. The choice of topic is determined solely by the individual, and the topic may or may not have immediate relevance to the group.

The ethos of this meeting owes much to Cooperative Development (Edge, 1992), in which ideas for group development are presented for colleagues

- Who already share and wish to enhance a positive working relationship
- Who want to explore the potential of a nonjudgemental approach to individual self-development in a group context

Especially during the early sessions, the group consciously used some of the moves practised in Cooperative Development, particularly those termed *Reflecting, Focusing*, and *Thematising*.

What do we do in the sessions?

During the first year of these sessions, the meetings took place in pairs. In the first meeting (the Speaking session) a participant acted as Speaker. The others in the group acted as Understanders. In the second meeting (the Follow-up session) the group, using critical extracts recorded from the first meeting, discussed the nature and value of the moves made during the first meeting, drawing on the experience of both the Speaker and the Understanders. This retrospective analysis of critical incidents confirmed that stripping out evaluative comment, suggestions, and comments was helping the Speaker to work in a different way. The Follow-up session helped us sharpen and refine our procedure and practice.

Typically, in the first meeting of the pair, the Speaker speaks for 25 to 35 minutes, with the others acting as Understanders. During the remainder of this meeting, the Understanders become Speakers and take turns articulating a response (what we have come to call a *Resonance*). The orientation of Resonances is more "what Ellie has helped me to see is . . ." than "I think I see this differently from Ellie. . . ." In other words, Resonances are meant to be nonjudgemental and nonevaluative.

Some examples

I will concentrate on two sessions in which I have been a Speaker. I hope that the examples will be indicative of the process involved and will also demonstrate how the sessions have been useful to me in terms of specific outcomes.

During the first session I explore a feeling I have that the more I plan (for lessons or sessions), the less well I communicate. I strongly felt this, but I had never articulated it. During the second session I talk about pastoral care. I have special responsibility for the pastoral care of students, and I had already talked about this subject in other kinds of meetings. In the second session, I review progress and experience and also try to formulate my current understanding of what pastoral care might mean.

In both sessions I am 'talking my way into understanding'. Looking back and listening to the tapes a year later, it is obvious to me that these sessions provided space and time for articulation. It is also apparent that the other individuals in the group helped me articulate my experience in ways that would not be available in other kinds of meeting and teacher talk.

What was different? What do I mean by *articulation*?

In a sense the Speaker is allowed to work in a space that is similar to the Vygotskian idea of ZPD (Zone of *Proximal Development*): striving to articulate what is confused or partially formed, working at the cutting edge of current understanding. Taylor (1985) provides an insightful definition:

Articulations are not simply descriptions. . . . [A]rticulations are attempts to formulate what is initially inchoate, or confused, or badly formulated. But this kind of formulation, or reformulation, does not leave its object unchanged. To give a certain articulation is to shape our sense of what we desire or what we hold important in a certain way. (p. 36)

As teachers, we are on the receiving end of a potentially confusing amount of knowledge, facts, and opinions. We hold on to some of this received knowledge amongst a whole jumble of things we believe, think we know, and value. However, we do not fully own something if we have not articulated it for ourselves. The kind of session I am detailing here allowed me to integrate some of these disparate or confusing elements. For me, the process of articulation forms the shape of my experiential knowledge (Wallace, 1991).

The first session: Planning and communication

The first session features an issue that had become important to me in my teaching. Here is how I introduced the topic:

    1 Steve: As soon as I enter into a planning world (.) in terms of talking
             (0.4) it seems to cause some kind of stress,
      Nick: Mmm
      Steve: which I– which I feel imposing on me. and this imposition, (.)
    5   this structure that I've preplanned, (0.4) I find is– is a saddle (.) a
             chain (.) something which inhibits me.
      Nick: So can we just clarify where we are now? you're now into (.) what
             may not be a continuing topic but the first area of topic focus is
             what you're working on now and that is this preference of yours
   10   for off-the-cuff talk as opposed to planned talk. (.) you're saying
             (.) that if you plan something then when you start to talk you feel
             that that plan is an imposition on you and constrains you and ties
             you down and you feel you're not being as productive as you
             could be.

I am supported in these introductory comments by Nick, who picks out the key elements and gives me a chance to 'hear back' a version of where I am in my emerging focus. From my current 'writerly' perspective, the images related to stress and constraint seem exaggerated, but Nick doesn't question the representation, he just reflects back a version of what he has heard. In fact, it would be easy for me (and probably Nick), in another talk situation to ridicule this representation (saddle and chain) as 'over the top', self-indulgent, even a little ridiculous. It strikes me that although these group development sessions are by no means humorless, the humor, sarcasm, parody, and banter that attend our other meetings are here pushed to the edge. There is therefore less need for self-conscious self-censorship.

I went on from this early exchange to more fully explore my ideas and preferences for ways of working with a group that are not planned but prepared. I got to this realisation by working through a number of related issues and stages:

1. I opened by articulating a feeling that when I am very planned, I feel stress (see preceding dialogue).
2. I related my experience as an actor and my preference for improvised theater over scripted plays. I established that this may be a strong influence on communicative events in my classroom.
3. I realized that my preference for improvisation may be connected to my teaching because I feel that the students are more involved (that is, they help to direct the process).

The following is an extract in which the Understanders (Ellie and Helen) help me to articulate an understanding of how planning can make me less responsive as a teacher. It builds on the ideas of involvement, noticing, and responding to signals from the students:

15 Ellie: You feel that– do you feel that you've had some sort of signals and been unable to change your response to it?
  Steve: I think it's partly that and partly the fact that I don't feel open to any signals =
  Ellie: = So you don't feel you see them
20 Steve: .hhh (0.6) I see the two things in opposition >you know< this driving force to get through this plan (0.4) does mean that perhaps I don't even see the signals
  Helen: So it's as if you're looking back into your head all the time rather than looking out and communicating with

I move through this dialogue to the next two stages in my thinking:

4. I think that this 'connection' with the students helps facilitate a more 'of-the-moment' communicative event.
5. I make a distinction between planning time *for students* (in order to help facilitate on-task communication) and planning done *by the teacher* before the session.

In the next dialogue you can see how stage 5 leads me to consider the relationship between planning and communicative events. Here, I make a clear distinction between the way my preferred classroom methodology has evolved and the role within a task-based methodology of planning time for students:

25 Steve: I think it's obviously a personal thing because you look around and you see people do plan to a greater or lesser extent (.) and it– methodologically is interesting with that article in Jane Willis' collection (.) the planning time for tasks (.) is it Martin Bygate?
  Mary: Mmm

30 Steve: Do we want students to plan things and what sort of effect does that have on the language (.) it's perceived as being a good thing (.) a benefit to allow students to– to plan (1.4)

6. I remember a distinction I have heard between (task) tension that can help and tenseness that does not. There is a helpful amount of 'tension' for me in not overplanning a session. There is 'tenseness' if I plan to a high degree.
7. There is an outcome for me in that I clarify a distinction between *being prepared* (that is, having things I could do) and *being planned* (which directs and often inhibits a communicative event).

Through similar stages, the Speaker shapes experiential knowledge by making distinctions, connections, extensions, and clarifications. The preceding dialogues provide examples of how Understanders support the Speaker's articulation. The motivation for this kind of Understander move is twofold:

- It is a chance for the Understander to confirm that she is on the same wavelength. The motivation is to *enable the Speaker* to hear a version of what has been said.
- The Understander may not be sure that she is on the same wavelength. Here the motivation is to *enable the Understander* to carry on properly understanding.

In the early sessions, it was very difficult not to offer an opinion or a suggestion or to evaluate (either positively or negatively). We have been successful in stripping these elements out of the moves that the Understanders make in the sessions. However, this does not mean that all Understander moves are successful for the Speaker. Sometimes the Understander *is* on a different or slightly different wavelength, and therefore, the understood version or elements are not close enough. In the following exchange it is clear that Robert's emphasis is not a fully acceptable version or element of what I have been saying:

Robert: Is it the case that you don't know where to go until someone has made a contribution?
35 Steve: I think there are plenty of places I <u>could</u> <u>go</u>, (.) I'm not talking about knowing nothing about the area you've allotted to talk about. I'm not talking about no prepar<u>ati</u>on, (.) no <u>read</u>ing no <u>think</u>ing around the area . . .

Clearly, although it is not an acceptable understanding move, it does help clarify what I am *not* talking about. In retrospect, I think that "you don't know" in line 33 is too strong. It touches the same nerve that I referred to earlier when I said that there is pressure to "know what you are doing." However, it does help me to further my emerging distinction between prepared and planned. Indeed, a few moments later Nick is able to 'understand' this distinction:

> Nick: And that's the big distinction I hear now in what you're saying,
> 40 (.) between being pre<u>par</u>ed to enter the arena (.) and the idea of having a <u>plan</u> which you think will ride roughshod over the various possibilities that could have occurred in that arena
> Steve: Yes <u>yes</u> (.) and another thought hits me from that, (.) from the preparation planning distinction, . . .

This gets an enthusiastic endorsement in line 43, and once this distinction is resolved, it leads immediately to another related idea, a movement explicitly signalled by "another thought hits me."

In summarising this session, I would say that this process helped me to articulate something that I think has been an important part of my teaching since the mid-eighties. However, I had not been able to fully form or 'justify' this position. The session helped to me to do that, and at one point I say:

> 45 Steve: I do feel in a lucky position to be able to come in and <u>ram</u>ble <u>on</u> like this (.) I think there <u>is</u> an element of trust there which is important
> Sam: Yeah

The trust between the group has been built up through the process. This is an important outcome in its own right. The nonjudgemental and nonevaluative atmosphere creates the space for Speakers to talk themselves into different understandings.

A second session: Pastoral care

The second session I have chosen as being indicative of the process of group development for me is related to a specific role I play within the LSU: I am responsible for the pastoral care of students. To some extent the title came before the job description, and I am still trying to formulate the nature of the role. A working definition for *pastoral care* is that it is looking after the whole person as well as his or her 'academic progress'. We are concerned with personal, financial, and social well-being, particularly when those aspects of students' lives affect their progress in courses and programmes.

In the first dialogue I am struggling to start, and I feel that somehow interaction is the key for tutors:

Sam: Okay errrm so pastoral care but specifically interaction is the sort
50   of thing you want to bring together (.) that's what you want to
        [explore?
Steve: [Yeah errm
        and when you say that I wonder if there is actually anything else
        (.) is there anything else in the field of pastoral care which isn't
55   interaction in some way.

Sam's reflection foregrounds these two terms (*pastoral care* and *interaction*) and helps me to consider their relationship. As we can see from "when you say that," I am explicitly signalling the power of 'hearing' a version of my words coming back. This enables me to move to a position where I question whether, for me, pastoral care and interaction are in fact synonymous. All the time the Understanders are trying to help in this process. A few moves later, Sam wonders whether I have altered what I mean by *interaction*. However, my focus is still working from 'pastoral care', and although I am not happy with his version of what has changed, it does help to pin down just how *interaction* is integral to pastoral care in a way that a *system* is not:

Sam: So it's not (2.2) is that a <u>change</u>? Have you just <u>changed</u> what you
        mean by interaction?
Steve: No I think what I've done is I've realised that when I talk about
        pastoral care (.) I've thought about pastoral care (.) it's one of
60   those words which (.) which I've been living with for a long time
        errrm I did a PGCE at Warwick and my option was on pastoral
        care
Sam: Mmm
Steve: That was in a state school setting and it was very much a new
65   subject then (.) it was very– almost trendy new thing pastoral care
        (.) and I've always lived with that word and I think I've always
        thought of it as a system and now I'm thinking of it more as
        interaction and I think it's a difference in emphasis

The lexical items used (*pastoral care, interaction, system*) are placeholders in the sense that they are initially fuzzy. When they are placed in the same frame, they start to resolve themselves in relation to each other. This is a good example of Taylor's (1985, p. 36) process of 'formulation, or reformulation' not leaving 'its object unchanged'. The articulation itself has a reflexive relationship with our sense of what we 'hold to be important'.

There is an interesting comparison to make between this session and the earlier one. In the sense that the first session was about the development in my thinking about my personal methodology, it really had no direct repercussions for the rest of the group. To put it crudely, my planning or not planning sessions is unlikely to affect the others' decision making in the degree to which they plan. However, in this session, any thinking I do on pastoral care may affect the others in the group; if I proposed a new procedure for conducting tutorials, it would have specific outcomes for the individuals in the group. In the following dialogue Nick tries to reflect back a feeling he has picked up on of frustration. He also reflects back two possible causes of the frustration:

> Nick: When you were talking about that earlier (.) was there a frustration
> 70   that– either that we're not doing these things or <u>it</u> isn't happening
>   (.) you were talking about >you know< I can't tell you what to
>   do but on the other hand if they don't do it we can't talk about it
>   and–
>
> Steve: I think there's a frustration (.) but errm it's not with the group (.) I
> 75   mean it honestly isn't with the group (.) it's with the nature of our
>   jobs of what we have to do (.) that we don't we have that time (.)
>   I mean it's that dilemma that I've tried to talk about before that
>   (1.2) in some ways (.) maybe (.) and this is a thought that's just
>   come into my head (.) maybe I need to take more responsibility
> 80   of trying to (.) carve out time (.)

Whilst I accept and work with the frustration, I reject the idea that the frustration is a factor of the groups' inaction. It leads to thinking about ways in which I can 'carve out' time for this priority. Some of the most useful understanding moves are the ones that attempt to capture the affect, the mood, or the feeling behind what is said.

On the receiving end of 'understanding'

I want to finish with two dialogues in which Robert is acting as Understander. I want to include these examples of 'being understood' because they offer an interesting comparison. In the first example, the Understander imports his or her own agenda into the 'understanding'. In the second, the focus is wholly on the Speaker's agenda (that is, imported from previous discourse).

For me, then, in the first example, I do not think that the move is a successful one. It may well be an honest attempt to understand, but two features of my response or lack of response in lines 89 and 91 suggest that there is too much interpretation. Robert has not so much helped me to make a distinction as supplied me with one of his own. Both pauses (lines 89 and 92) are long. My orientation to the distinction is ambivalent, and I think that it is because it is more Robert's than mine.

> Robert: I'm now getting a dual picture of pastoral care (.) one is some-
> thing initiative taking (.) you have to care to do certain things.
> Right? (.) another is the more passive participative where pas-
> toral care is the care that I feel more than the care that I do (.)
> 85   right you talk about– I have understood you talk about the neg-
> ative thing (.) the thing that I do. Should I do, should I say these
> things? (.) in other words a plan of campaign or a strategy for
> how you go about it (0.6) and the other is that it is happening
> while you're doing it. Is it both of these together? (4.2)
> 90 Robert: Or is neither of them? Have I got it wrong
>   Steve: I think it's an interesting distinction (.) the distinction between
> the pastoral you feel and the pastoral you do (5.2) errm my gut
> feeling is that you– we in the pressure we're under (.) cannot
> sustain the pastoral caring element always

This reflection does not help me move on. I think the key is in the objecti-fication in line 91. It does not feel like my distinction. However, Robert's next Understander moves *do* help me to work through another distinction that enables me to draw out threads of my articulation and shape a very useful distinction for me:

> 95 Robert: Have you moved over the last half an hour? (.) a little bit (.) from
> the purely interactive to the more proactive (3.6)
>   Steve: Yes I think so (.) I think that's true

A few moves later, this distinction cements itself and, reflecting the 'dual relationship', enables me to think (notice the long pause in line 98) so that I can extend my emerging perspective on pastoral care into three categories:

> Robert: Does that mean a dual relationship of the pro and inter? (5.2)
>   Steve: Yeah (.) I like that distinction (.) we have reactive, proactive,
> 100   and interactive =
> Robert: = Reactive being the fire-fighting? =
>   Steve: = Yeah

This distinction has proved to be very useful for me in the way I now conceptualise the role I have and the work I do with other tutors in the promotion and enhancement of pastoral care.

Group communication, cooperation, and collaboration

It is important to me that these meetings are voluntary. Wallace, in speaking about teachers working collaboratively, says: "Collaboration has to be voluntary, it should not be imposed. Cooperatives have had a pretty good track record: collectives have not been so successful" (1998, p. 254).

Some teachers within our department do not feel that they would benefit from this use of time. Those of us in the group find that being the Speaker is an enjoyable experience. It is rare to feel so listened to. We have recently started to invite other teachers and teacher educators to try this 'development discourse'. Invited newcomers speak of initial nervousness at the prospect of speaking for such a large portion of a meeting. This feeling quickly dissipates because the Speaker senses the trust and empathy built up through the first few nonjudgemental understanding moves.

The role of the Understander

This kind of articulation allows the Speaker to work at the cutting edge of understanding and also to formulate and shape experiential knowledge. This happens because the Understander gives up some of the interactional space for the benefit of the Speaker. In our first few sessions it was difficult for the Understanders, for there was a feeling of frustration because the balance was tipped much more to listening than speaking. This 'limiting' of contributions to those which are for the benefit of the Speaker takes time to become routine. However, it was also apparent, a few sessions into the 'experiment', that there were also outcomes for the Understander. Once you got used to it, it was liberating to really listen to and follow someone else's opinions, positions, and perspectives that do not normally have the space for such full articulation. It was also positive to see specific outcomes for those involved in their practice and their own understandings of their practice. The development of this sensitivity, displayed through appropriate Understander contributions and shaped around the emerging articulation of the Speaker, is the key. Understanders become sensitized to the way in which they can work to create space for the Speaker and offer opportunities for the Speaker to hear versions and elements of what has been articulated.

Metadiscussion

Earlier I described how in the first group meeting a participant acts as Speaker, and in the second, the group, using critical extracts recorded from the first meeting, discusses the nature and value of the moves. Here, there is particular emphasis on the Understanders' moves and their effect on and perceived contribution to the Speaker. Retrospective group discourse analysis has increased our group understanding of the complexity of group interaction. An example of this understanding is the realisation that retrospective discussions make evident occasions when what is said, what is meant, and what is understood as meant do not necessarily agree. Participants believe that even more 'misunderstanding' may be happening in unit staff meetings but that the rapid-fire, turn-taking, and agenda orientation may mean that misunderstandings are hidden.

Evaluation and argument

In concluding this account, I want to return to the importance of stripping out evaluation and argument in the alternative professional talk described here. Clearly, we need to distinguish two senses of evaluation. On the one hand, we have evaluation as a sustained search for judging the effectiveness and appropriateness of our professional practice. On the other hand, we have evaluative orientation in professional talk. This second sense of evaluation is precisely what we are seeking to limit. In other words, the recognition of the pervasive and intrusive evaluative element of professional discussion was a primary motivation for experimenting with the discourse rules of our new types of meetings. Constant evaluative orientation causes argument. However, there are two different sorts of argument. Jacobs and Jackson (1981, p. 120) report a distinction made by O'Keefe (1977), who drew attention to:

two importantly different senses of the term "argument" that have not been carefully distinguished by argumentation theorists: argument 1 refers to a kind of speech act – something a person makes; argument 2 refers to a kind of interaction – something people have. This difference in the sense of "making" and "having" arguments is marked in everyday language use in the difference between "arguing 1 that something" and "arguing 2 about something".

Our other meetings certainly provide more routine grounds for argument 2 in the sense outlined by Jacobs and Jackson. Participants expect there to be occasional disagreements even if agreement is the preferred and expected outcome. In group meetings we eliminate argument *about* to make maximum space for argument *that*.

Conclusion

One outcome of this experience has been to seriously evaluate the talk we create in our professional lives. Cooperative development helps colleagues understand one another and respect differences where they exist. The Rogerian ideals of respect, empathy, and honesty sustain and are renewed by the practice. You cannot understand colleagues' ideas, views, and beliefs easily. It is tempting to believe that you do, and this belief short-circuits full understanding. By using cooperative development and putting aside our normal evaluative discourse, we open up *different* possibilities, not necessarily better ones. It is a different kind of space with a different kind of discourse that adds to our existing ways of talking rather than replacing them.

About six months after we started this work, Deborah Tannen's book *The Argument Culture* appeared, in which she says:

We need to use our imaginations and ingenuity to find different ways to seek truth and gain knowledge, and add them to our arsenal – or, should I say, the ingredients for our stew. (1998, p. 298)

We believe that this project is a step forward in meeting this kind of challenge. The benefits in shaping group identity, support, and communication are already tangible, and there is a unanimous feeling that this experimentation with our way of speaking to one another is a valuable addition to existing professional talk. In the meetings in which I have been the Speaker, I am sure that I have made significant movements forwards in the development of my experiential knowledge through this process of articulation.

References

Edge, J. (1992). *Cooperative development: Professional self-development through cooperation with colleagues*. Harlow: Longman. This text is now available at: http://www-users.aston.ac.uk/~edgej/cd/titles.htm

Edge, J. (forthcoming). *Continuing cooperative development*. Ann Arbor: University of Michigan Press.

Jacobs, S., & Jackson, S. (1981). Argument as a natural category: The routine grounds for arguing in conversation. *The Western Journal of Speech Communication*, 45, 118–132.

O'Keefe, D. J. (1977). Two concepts of argument. *Journal of American Forensic Association* 13, 121–128.

Tannen, D. (1998). *The argument culture*. London: Virago.

Taylor, C. (1985). *Human agency and language*. Cambridge: Cambridge University Press.

Wallace, M. (1991). *Training foreign language teachers: A reflective approach*. Cambridge: Cambridge University Press.

Wallace, M. (1998). *Action research for language teachers*. Cambridge: Cambridge University Press.

Part IV   Discussion

1. How did these teachers' involvement in sustained professional collaboration enable them to view classroom events in a new way?
2. How did these teachers' involvement in sustained professional collaborations influence their understandings of themselves, their students, and their instructional practices?
3. What are the limitations of establishing and sustaining professional collaborations? How can these limitations be mitigated?
4. What are teachers' responsibilities to one another when they engage in professional collaboration?
5. How can participation in professional collaborations enable teachers to nourish and sustain their professional development?

Part IV   Reflection

1. After writing an autobiography (see Discussion Questions for Part III), exchange your autobiography with those of other teachers. Discuss similarities and differences among your autobiographies. Reflect on what you have learned as a result of reading other language teachers' autobiographies.
2. Select one of the reflection questions from the beginning of Part IV, "Inquiry through Professional Collaborations." Write a short (two- or three-page) position paper on how you have or might have addressed the theoretical and pedagogical concerns embedded in these questions in your current or future instructional practices as a language teacher.

Part IV   Action

1. After videotaping a class and identifying a critical teaching incident (see Narrative Inquiry for Action for Part I), watch the video with a group of teachers. Discuss alternative interpretations of the event, as well as alternative approaches to dealing with the issues involved.
2. Reflect on a dilemma that you face in your teaching (for example, getting quiet students to participate). Write a one-page description of the dilemma, including how you are currently dealing with it. Share your description with a colleague. Then generate a list of alternative ways that you might manage this dilemma. Analyze each point on your list,

and try to determine the consequences of managing the dilemma in this particular way.

Suggested readings

Brock, M. N., Bartholomew, Y., & Wong, M. (1992). "Journaling" together: Collaborative diary keeping and teacher development. In J. Flowerdew, M. Brock, & S. Hsia, (Eds.), *Perspectives on second language teacher education* (pp. 295–307), Hong Kong: City Polytechnic of Hong Kong.

Edge, J. (1992a). *Cooperative Development: Professional self-development through cooperation with colleagues.* Harlow: Longman.

Edge, J. (1992b). Cooperative Development. *ELT Journal, 46*(1), 62–70.

Edge, J., and Richards, K. (Eds.). (1993). *Teachers develop teachers' research.* Oxford: Heinemann International.

Freeman, D. (1998). *Doing teacher research: From inquiry to understanding.* Boston: Heinle and Heinle.

Kemmis, S., & McTaggart, R. (1988). *The action research planner.* Geelong, Australia: Deakin University Press.

Wallace, M. (1998). *Action research for language teachers.* Cambridge: Cambridge University Press.